FIND IT FAST

an
(Sept. 23 - Oct. 23).
fficult relatives; delay the final agreement
matter until next week. Shifting emotional moods of older

ZIGGY

FIND IT FAST

THIRD EDITION

*How to Uncover
Expert Information
on Any Subject*

Robert I. Berkman

 HarperPerennial
A Division of HarperCollinsPublishers

FIND IT FAST (*Third edition*). Copyright © 1994 by Robert I. Berkman. All rights reserved. Printed in the United States of America. No part of this book may be used or reproduced in any manner whatsoever without written permission except in the case of brief quotations embodied in critical articles and reviews. For information address HarperCollins Publishers, Inc., 10 East 53rd Street, New York, NY 10022.

HarperCollins books may be purchased for educational, business, or sales promotional use. For information, please write: Special Markets Department, HarperCollins Publishers, Inc., 10 East 53rd Street, New York, NY 10022.

FIRST EDITION

Library of Congress Cataloging-in-Publication Data
Berkman, Robert I.
    Find it fast: how to uncover expert information on any subject / Robert I. Berkman.
    —3rd ed.
        p. cm.
    Includes index.
    ISBN 0-06-273294-3
    1. Handbooks, vade-mecums, etc. 2. Information services. 3. Library
resources. 4. Reference books. 5. Report writing. II. Title
    AG105.B553 1994
    031.02—dc20   93-50922

94 95 96 97 98 DT/CW 10 9 8 7 6 5 4 3 2 1

To Sol, Pat,
Budd, and Don

Contents

PART I: UNLOCKING THE INFORMATION VAULT

How to select the right library . . . getting the most out of any library . . . the best library resources: newspapers, special periodical indexes, magazines, and newsletters . . . people information . . . business and industry information . . . "insider" directories

Contents

Contents

PART II: EXPERTS ARE EVERYWHERE

Contents

order . . . writing tips: determining what information is worth including, being complete, making conclusions, being fair, quoting sources

PART III: TWO SAMPLE SEARCHES

Acknowledgments

I'd like to express my gratitude to the people who in one way or another had a big part in making this book come to pass.

Mary Walsh gave me encouragement at the most critical moments—without it, this book would not have been written. George Finnegan has been a true mentor. I'll always be thankful for the chance to work for him and receive a once-in-a-lifetime learning opportunity. Janet Goldstein, my editor at HarperCollins, believed enough in the book to give it a chance, and always gave me her support and great ideas.

I'm grateful to Nancy Brandwein, Ken Coughlin, and Lilli Warren, all of whom provided critical insights, suggestions, and critiques of the final manuscript.

I also want to thank Sandy Gollop for her assistance, knowledge, and kindness; my colleagues at PIN for their encouragement and interest in the book; Debbie Cohen for her hard work and sharp eye for detail; Ginny Fisher; and Pam and Jeff Goodman for so generously helping me out in the final stages. Trisha Karsay put in a lot of hours and top-notch work—her enthusiasm for the book meant a lot to me and is genuinely appreciated.

A special thank-you goes to everyone in the Norris family up in Cape Cod for providing me with such a beautiful and relaxing spot to think and write.

And finally, thanks to my parents and brothers for their love, support, and invaluable ideas.

Preface to the Third Edition of *Find It Fast*

Welcome to the third edition of *Find it Fast*. This book, last published in 1990, has been thoroughly revised for this most recent version. To do this, I've gone through and checked every source, eliminated any no longer available, updated others where necessary, and added the best new resources I've come across during the last three years. There's also a much expanded discussion of online computer searching, a full examination of the latest electronic database technology: CD-ROMs, and a discussion of the Internet.

Stepping back a bit, what's been happening in the information world since 1990? As you might expect in this fast-moving and changing arena—a lot.

First, there's been no slowdown in production of new information: the explosion of both print and electronic sources continues unabated. This includes a continuation of the trend towards coverage of international information; now, many information producers are increasing attention to previously ignored regions such as Eastern Europe and China. On the downside, this mushrooming of resources has caused an "information glut."

This "infoglut" is causing many people to experience a kind of "information-paralysis"—the panicky feeling that there's just too much "out there." Some vendors, as we'll discuss below, are helping persons stricken with this malady by introducing software products that are designed to create better **access** to all of this data.

As you might expect, the number of electronic databases—as well as their usage—has been increasing particularly fast. This edition offers a much expanded coverage of database searching, and compares and evaluates leading online providers. But the biggest growth in the electronic information world has not been so much in online services, but in CD-ROMs—laser discs that store about 250,000 pages of information. Sales of these products began to take off in the early 1990s, and there are no signs of a slowdown. We'll also discuss how you can search some of the best CD-ROMs absolutely free at your local library.

Two areas that have been getting a huge amount of hype in the popular press are the Information Superhighway and the interactive "revolution." Let's look at the "Information Superhighway" first. In a nutshell, it's a concept where the federal government, in partnership with private vendors, would enable the construction of a giant national electronic computer network. This network would link together diverse organizations and users, ranging from schools and libraries to businesses and governmental research centers. The network would allow users to share information, obtain data, and exchange ideas. The analogy to a highway is a good one—during the mid-1950s the U.S. government needed to lay concrete so people could use their cars to travel to communities around the country. For the 1990s and beyond, the raw material for transportation is fiber optic cable and the "vehicle" traveling the route is digital data.

Then there's the interactive "revolution" we've all been reading about so much. That's the buzzword used by the popular press to describe the latest proposed electronic technologies that will allow two-way communication between persons in their home and electronic information providers. While most of the attention has been on future entertainment-type applications such as videos-on-demand, there should also be opportunities for access to reference and research data in the home as well. This could include things like encyclopedias, news headlines, stock and financial data, library catalogs, and so on. Of course, most of this can already be obtained through established online services, but there will likely be some useful new research applications not yet available.

Both of these developments are still in the planning stages, and do not truly impact today's researcher yet. However, while much is still speculation, there's a strong indication that both the information superhighway, and home interactive applications will merge and expand, creating new opportunities for researchers. There's intense interest among global giants in the media, telecommunication, and software industry. Firms like Microsoft, AT&T, Apple, TCI, Paramount, and many more are working feverishly to quickly move in on the emerging electronic information world. And you can bet that if firms like these are devoting a good chunk of their marketing budget to increasing awareness, you are going to hear about it—and hear about it—and hear about it. . . .

Possibly the most intriguing of the proposed new digital services are experiments and research into customized electronic news services. According to this scenario, readers would determine precisely what kind of news items and stories would be "sent" to them daily. For example, you might program your PC to automatically scan a dozen of your favorite national newspapers early each morning, but to search for and retrieve only those items and stories that relate to your list of approved subjects. For example, you might specify that you want to read about: France, Photography, Tennis, Laptop Computers, the U.N., Health & Diet, Theatre Reviews, or whatever else your particular interests might be. Delivery could be via satellite and transmitted directly into your PC. It's expected that the PC ideally suited for this function would be a handheld unit equipped with a pen-input stylus, a flat screen, and color capabilities.

While this is quite an intriguing scenario, it's still mainly only a possibility. However, a few firms, including Dow Jones Inc., have in fact introduced a modified, scaled down type version of a customized news product. These are being marketed mainly to businesses that want to follow specific industries, companies, and news items. Even CompuServe has a very modest type of customized news retrieval system via its Executive News Service option.

Finally, there's the Internet. If you haven't yet heard about the Internet, you probably will shortly. It's a worldwide computer network linking millions of people in over 60 countries, and has been growing at a phenomenal rate. The number of information resources on this "network of networks" is staggering. Of course, you need to know how to negotiate it, and be able to locate what you need. That brings us back to the problem of the Infoglut, and that, in turn, brings us to the main purpose of this book: helping you steer a clear path through these mountains of information so you can locate exactly what you need.

Introduction

Taking Advantage of the Information Explosion

It may come as a surprise to you, but for virtually any subject, facts and information are "out there"—by the truckload. Whether it is moviemaking, the wine industry, real estate investments, or baseball historical statistics, information and expertise are available—at no or low cost.

Perhaps you're a market researcher digging up forecasts on the growth of the computer software industry, a college student studying the latest advances in genetic engineering, a writer who needs facts about a new form of dream research, an entrepreneur interested in starting a health food store, or an activist investigating the pornography industry. Whatever your particular situation, this book will provide the knowledge, information sources, and strategies you need in order to quickly find top-quality advice and answers. With this know-how, you'll be able to get the kind of information that's normally available only to a select few.

As everyone knows, we are living in the age of information. Every day book and periodical publishers, government agencies, libraries, professional associations, conventions, private companies, research centers, and museums are adding to our store of knowledge. Unfortunately, most of us have little idea how to find the specific information we need, when we need it.

In this book you'll discover where to go and what to look for in searching for information on any subject. First, *key resources,* including many little-known information gold mines, are identified and described, and for each of these you will be given a contact address and phone number or other specific advice for locating the source.

Second, you'll be given strategies on how to go beyond the written sources and phone information services to learn from the experts themselves. Most people would assume that experts don't bother to talk to a lay information seeker. But nothing could be further from the truth. This book will show you not only how to find experts—"the sources behind the sources"— but also how to get them to freely share their knowledge with you.

Finally, this book will help you learn how to conduct an information search from beginning to end. You'll discover what the various steps of an information-finding project are—all the way from defining your problem to receiving a final "expert review" of your finished project. This process is summarized in the special "Recap" section in the back of the book.

WHY THIS BOOK

Some years ago I found myself in a new position where I had to learn how to find information on many subjects—fast. I had just landed a job at McGraw-Hill Inc., where my duties were to research and write in-depth analyses and reports for businesses and government agencies on a wide range of topics—from cutting energy costs to selecting the best computer and dozens of other technical subjects. With each of these projects, I'd start off knowing absolutely nothing about the topic. But in the course of a few short weeks I needed to turn out an accurate and authoritative report.

To create these analyses, I needed to have top-quality information at my immediate disposal. So I did some digging and began talking with professional information specialists, investigating little-used documents, and developing my own sources. I began to build a bank of information resources. Over the next few years, every time I'd find a valuable and easy-to-use information source, I'd add it to the bank. I also developed techniques for quickly finding experts and getting them to share their knowledge, which I'd also add to the bank.

My friends and family were intrigued when I described to them this process of finding information and quickly becoming knowledgeable on a subject. Their interest motivated me to create the course "You Can Be an Instant Expert," which I taught at the Learning Annex, an adult education program in New York City, for three years.

The people who took the class had varied backgrounds and reasons for being there. Many were businesspeople who wanted to sharpen their job skills and learn where to find the best information in their field. Some were writers who wanted to unearth new sources of expertise. College students took the class, too, hoping to add unexplored dimensions to their research and to learn to be more creative. Others took the class to learn how to dig up facts about a new field, in the hopes of starting their own business. And, confirming my own experience, students told me that they were amazed to discover that so much good information was available so easily and so cheaply. They were equally surprised at how available experts were, and how easy it could be to talk to them.

Sometimes I heard from people after they had taken the course. Here are some of their success stories: A detective novel writer found background information about countries where she set her stories. A director of research at a national television network found the right demographic statistics to back up his report on TV viewing trends. A student found free consumer assistance and resolved a complaint with an automobile manufacturer. A man found inexpensive business advice to assist him in starting a consulting firm in a high-technology field. A woman found out where to apply for a grant to get funding for an art-related project. An international marketing executive discovered how to find free industry forecasts instead of paying hundreds of dollars for them.

You undoubtedly will have your own success stories to tell. Perhaps you'll find consumer-oriented information you need to help you buy a home, manage your money, or raise your child. Or maybe you'll get important business information, aiding you in finding a new job, making investments, going public, or getting a loan. Some of you will have a need for obscure information that can be answered by offbeat sources—like the Association for Symbolic Logic or the Paint Research Institute!

HOW TO USE THIS BOOK

Here's a brief rundown on how this book works and what the different chapters will provide.

A preliminary section, "Getting Started," will help you define what information you're really after and organize your plan of attack. Part I identifies actual information sources and provides tips on how to best find and use each of them. It contains chapters covering the initial selection of information sources, including how to choose the right library for your needs and discover which sources to check once you get there; how to identify "supersources" on your topic, ranging from associations to museums and much more; how to tap into the huge storehouse of knowledge and data available from the U.S. government—much of it for free; how to locate the best information sources related to business; and, finally, how to perform computer searches, whether or not you actually own your own computer.

Each chapter presents many specific sources, along with suggestions for further avenues to try. You may want to highlight those that sound most interesting to you and appropriate for your needs so that you can later locate them quickly. Or scan the "Quickfinder" feature, which begins each resource chapter and lists every information source included in those chapters.

Part II moves into the second component of the information search—talking to the experts. You'll find out how to locate the nine types of expert, and what the pros and cons are of each type; how to make contact with the experts; and then how to get them to open up and share their knowledge. You'll find out that experts *will* talk to you—but it helps to have some strategies to increase their willingness to do so. We'll also examine ethics in finding information, the issue of information quality, and how to evaluate experts' information. Finally, you'll get advice on knowing how to tell when it's time to wind up your project and some tips on writing up your results if you choose to do so.

Part III shows how information sources and strategies work in action. Here you'll see how the information-finding process actually worked and what was uncovered in two sample projects. The first case study deals with finding information about opening a health club; the second one is about finding information about computer careers.

The book concludes with a recap of the six steps of an information-search project, an appendix that lists additional resources, and a comprehensive index, which will be helpful in targeting specific sources, techniques, and topics.

Naturally, a book like this cannot include every potential information source, but I believe that I've provided some of the best. The sources selected for this book have been carefully culled from among many. Those included were specifically chosen as being most useful for people who are not professionals in finding information. This means that, to qualify for inclusion, each source had to be easy to obtain and easy to use. Unless otherwise noted, each source also is free, inexpensive, or available for use at a public institution such as a library. You'll note that the cost of individual documents described in the book is generally not provided, since prices change so quickly. However, unless otherwise noted, no document mentioned costs over about $40—and the great majority are *much less or free*—unless available for use in a library, through some other inexpensive outlet, or by a special technique described in the book. I'd greatly appreciate hearing from readers who want to suggest other sources and information-finding strategies worth including in future editions. Write to me c/o HarperCollins, 10 East 53rd Street, New York, NY 10022.

When you've finished reading this book, I'd suggest keeping it handy so that you can use it as a ready reference guide. This way, whenever you need a fact, some advice, or information, you can find out where to look to get the answers you need.

One final note: If you must get information on a particular

INFORMATION SEEKER'S MAP

START

1 DEFINE YOUR PROBLEM

- √ What do you need?
- √ Why do you need it?
- √ What will you do with it?

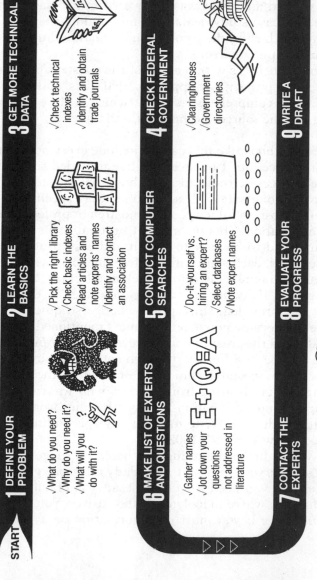

2 LEARN THE BASICS

- √ Pick the right library
- √ Check basic indexes
- √ Read articles and note experts' names
- √ Identify and contact an association

3 GET MORE TECHNICAL DATA

- √ Check technical indexes
- √ Identify and obtain trade journals

FINISH

√ Congratulate yourself!

Ronan

6 MAKE LIST OF EXPERTS AND QUESTIONS

- √ Gather names
- √ Jot down your questions not addressed in literature

E + Q = A

5 CONDUCT COMPUTER SEARCHES

- √ Do-it-yourself vs. hiring an expert?
- √ Select databases
- √ Note expert names

4 CHECK FEDERAL GOVERNMENT

- √ Clearinghouses
- √ Government directories

7 CONTACT THE EXPERTS

- √ Start with non-technical experts
- √ Identify yourself clearly
- √ Be persistent but polite

8 EVALUATE YOUR PROGRESS

- √ Have goals changed?
- √ New questions to ask?
- √ Untapped sources to contact?

9 WRITE A DRAFT

- √ Send to experts
- √ Get comments
- √ Final changes

subject *immediately,* be sure to take special note of the alternative "quick search" plan described on page 322. This will be of particular use to people pressed for time who need to identify the fastest way to find information.

Getting Started

Before plunging into your project, take a few minutes to consider your endeavor. Try to define for yourself exactly what kind of information you need, and why. What are your *reasons* for wanting to find this information? What are your overall goals? Try to be as *specific* as possible, even though it may be difficult to do so at this early stage. The more you can narrow your scope and break your task into subprojects, the easier your search will be, and the more likely your project will be a success. For example, say your goal is to find information on how to travel overseas inexpensively. With a little reflection, you can break that topic into its major components: cutting costs on overseas transportation, lodging, meals, car rental, shopping, currency exchange, and so on. Now you have some specific and concrete subtopics to zero in on in your research. If during your research you discover that your subject was too broad to adequately handle within the strictures of your plan, you can decide whether to choose one or more of your subtopics instead. (If you are not familiar enough with your subject at the outset to identify subdivisions, you'll find that you'll discover them once you begin your research.)

The first step in the information-gathering process is to find the very best *written* information sources in your field. Although some of your best findings will eventually come from talking to experts, you don't want to begin your project by contacting them. It's much better to first read and learn about your subject, and *then* speak with the experts. This way, when you do eventually talk to the authorities in the field, you'll be knowledgeable enough to ask the right questions and get the most out of your conversation.

Before you actually start your search, you should come up with a method for recording the information you'll be receiving from your written and "people" sources. Your approach to note taking and organization is important, because it will affect the course of your entire project. If you need advice in this area, see chapter 10. If, however, you feel confident enough to jump right into the information search, continue on to the first chapter.

PART I

Unlocking the Information Vault

1

Libraries

Zeroing in on the Best Resources

PEOPLE INFORMATION

BUSINESS AND INDUSTRY INFORMATION

Business Indexes

Company Directories

General Directories

SUBSIDIARIES AND DIVISIONS DIRECTORIES

(continued)

INTERNATIONAL BUSINESS DIRECTORIES

"INSIDER" DIRECTORIES

When most of us think of libraries, we think of books. But the library is a place where you can find an extraordinary variety of in-depth, timely information in nonbook formats ranging from fashion newsletters to company financial data to government research reports, and much more. You can even perform electronic information searches on "CD-ROMs," free! But before you go to the library, you'll need to know how to match the right type of library to your specific needs, and how to get the most out of the library once you get there.

SELECTING A LIBRARY

There are three basic types of library: public libraries, college and university libraries, and special libraries (which include corporate libraries). Let's look at each.

Public Libraries

The best public libraries for information gatherers are *large*, usually main branches, because these are most likely to contain an extensive reference collection. It's here in the reference section that you'll find some superb information-providing sources. (These sources will be identified and described later in this chapter.) If the only public library in your area is a very small one, you might want to look to one of the other types of libraries described in this section.

College and University Libraries

Academic libraries typically have more information sources than an average town's public library. Many are open to the public. The academic library's collection will normally reflect the majors and specialties of the particular institution.

TIP: How to Find an Academic Library
- Contact the Association of College and Research Libraries, American Library Association, 50 Huron Street, Chicago, IL 60611; 312-944-6780. At no charge, the association will help you find college and research libraries that specialize in your subject of interest.

Special Libraries

There are thousands of libraries around the country that specialize in a particular subject—astronomy, baseball, the environment, Asia, minorities, marketing, and countless other topics. Most of these libraries are open to the public—and even those that officially are not may still let you come in if you let the librarian know you are working on an important project. Working at one of these special subject libraries is like working in a gold mine where you are surrounded by resources that pertain to the specific subjects you need to find out about.

One particularly valuable type of special library is the *corporate library*. Corporate libraries contain a wealth of information on subjects related to a firm's special interests. Exxon's library, for example, has extensive information on energy, while CBS's library contains top-notch information on broadcasting. Unfortunately, many of these libraries allow access only to their company employees. But don't despair—sometimes you can get around the official policy. If you've identified a company library you want to use, call up the librarian, introduce yourself, and politely explain what kind of information you are trying to find, and why. Let the librarian know your project is a serious and important one, and explain that you've heard that the library has the resources you need. Describe specifically what you'll want to do at the library and what kind of materials you'll want to examine.

Often—but not always—you'll find that the librarian will allow you to come in and work. Of course, you won't be able to take anything out of the library. And when you get to the library, you should work on your own and not use up the corporate librarian's time, which must be dedicated to serving the company's own employees.

If you happen to know someone who works at a company that has a library you want to use, you should be able to gain entrance by using that person as a reference.

TIP: Identifying a Special Library
▪ Contact the Special Libraries Association, 1700 18th Street NW, Washington, DC 20009; 202-234-4700. Ask to speak with one of the "information specialists." These people will try to identify a special library in your area of interest. Another way to find a special library is to check a large library's reference department for one of these directories: *Subject Collections,* published by R. R. Bowker, or *Subject Directory of Special Libraries and Information Centers,* published by Gale Research. Both of these directories list thousands of special libraries.

Once you've identified the right library for your needs, the next step is to find the best information-providing sources kept at the library you select. But don't forget that the library staff is itself a major resource not to be overlooked.

TIPS: Getting the Most Out of Any Library
- If you've located a library that has the information you want, but it is not nearby, you can usually get a certain amount of information and answers by writing or calling with your specific question. You'll find librarians to be very helpful people!
- When you get to the library, remember to ask the reference librarian for assistance. That's what these people are there for! By enlisting their help, you can save yourself a lot of research time.
- If the library doesn't have a source you need, don't forget to ask for an interlibrary loan.
- Try calling your town library's reference department on the phone. At no charge, the library will try to find any fact you need. For example, you could ask, "What's the flying time from New York to Istanbul?" or "When was the clock invented?" Answering such questions by mail or phone is a public service that nearly every public library provides.

EASY STARTS: ALL-PURPOSE RESOURCES

Now we're ready to identify and describe some of the very best library information sources. We'll begin with a few basic—but excellent—sources and then progress to some very valuable lesser-known ones. All of the sources described in this section are typically found in the reference department. Note that today many libraries have these sources available not only in print, but electronically on CD-ROM disks. Use of these electronic sources can *vastly* reduce your initial research time. The end of this chapter examines these electronic resources in detail. Let's start off simply:

 Source: *New York Times Index*

An index to articles published in the *New York Times*. The user looks up key words such as a subject or a person's name, and the index provides a brief summary of all pertinent articles published, giving the date of publication and page. Supplements are issued twice every month. You'll find this index in practically every library.

The *New York Times* is a newspaper of record with historical significance. Checking its index is a quick and easy way to begin

an information search. Most likely, the librarian will provide you with the articles on microfilm. Sometimes the short summary of the article provided by the index itself will be all the information you need.

 Source: *Readers' Guide to Periodical Literature* (H. W. Wilson Company)

> The *Readers' Guide* indexes articles published in about 240 popular magazines such as *Newsweek, Health, Ms., Sports Illustrated,* and *Popular Science.* Supplements are issued monthly. You can find this guide at nearly every library. As with the *New York Times Index,* the user looks up key words to find articles on subjects he or she is interested in.

These familiar green volumes provide a quick way of finding back issues of popular magazines that have published articles on your subject of interest. You may not always get "inside" information from articles published in these general-interest magazines, but they can still be good information sources. And because these periodicals are so popular, you can usually find back issues of many of them right in the library.

TIP: Use the *Readers' Guide* to Understand a Technical Subject
- Because the magazines indexed in the *Readers' Guide* are read mainly by the general public, any description of a technical matter will be clearly defined and explained. This makes the guide especially helpful if your subject is technical and you don't quite understand it yet. The term "genetic engineering," for example, would be explained clearly to readers in a magazine like *Newsweek,* but probably would not be in a publication like *Applied Genetic News.*

 Source: *Business Periodicals Index* (H. W. Wilson Company)

> The *Business Periodicals Index* is an index to articles published in nearly 350 periodicals oriented toward business. Its scope is broad, ranging from advertising and marketing to real estate, computers, communications, finance, and insurance. Supplements are issued monthly. Almost all libraries have it.

The *Business Periodicals Index* is an extremely valuable index. Its name may mislead some people, because the guide actually indexes periodicals that contain information on topics beyond the scope of what most people consider simply "business." For example, it indexes articles from publications like the *Journal of Consumer Affairs, Human Resource Management, Telecommunications*, and *Automotive News*. "Trade" periodicals like these generally provide more specialized and in-depth information than the popular magazines indexed in the *Readers' Guide*, but at the same time the articles are usually not overly technical or hard to read. This is a nice balance for the information seeker who is not technically oriented or an expert in the field but still wants more than a superficial examination of a subject. I once used this index to find some excellent information about the topic of office ergonomics—how to design and furnish healthy and safe work areas.

 Source: *Subject Guide to Books in Print* (R. R. Bowker Company)

> *SGBIP* lists all new and old books—hardbound, paperback, trade, text, adult, and juvenile—that are currently in print, by subject. Virtually all libraries (and bookstores, for that matter) have it.

This is the standard guide for finding books in print on any subject. (Books "in print" are kept in stock by the publisher and can be ordered at a bookstore.) If you look under "Circus," for example, you'll find about twenty-five books; each entry includes the author's name, book title, date of publication, price, and publisher. There are accompanying volumes that list books by title and by author as well.

 Source: *Forthcoming Books* (R. R. Bowker Company)

> This guide lists books that have just been released or are projected to be released within five months. Supplements are issued bimonthly. You'll find this guide in large libraries and most bookstores.

Forthcoming Books is an intriguing source, as it identifies what books are about to be published in a given field. This can be especially useful when you are digging up information on a timely issue and you want to find the very latest books. (Note, however, that because books take a long time to produce, they will probably not be the best source of information on events occurring in the last few months or even year.) This source is good to use in conjunction with the *Subject Guide to Books in Print.*

TIPS: Finding Out-of-Print Books
▪ Strand Bookstore in New York City stocks 2.5 million books, and a large percentage of these are out-of-print books. Contact the store to see if it has a book you seek: 828 Broadway, New York, NY 10003; 212-473-1452.
▪ Book search companies and out-of-print specialty stores often advertise in the *New York Times Book Review* and other literary publications.

SPECIAL PERIODICAL INDEXES

 Source: H. W. Wilson Subject Indexes

The Wilson Subject Indexes are multivolume series that identify articles published within many major subject areas. There are different series for different fields (e.g., humanities, social science, science, art, business, education, agriculture, and law). To use these indexes, you consult the volumes devoted to your field of interest and look up specific subtopics. The index identifies which periodicals have published articles on the topic, and when. You'll find the Wilson indexes at medium-size and large libraries.

Two well-known indexes published by H. W. Wilson have already been described—the *Readers' Guide to Periodical Literature* and the *Business Periodicals Index*—but Wilson also indexes literature published in specific fields. For example, there is the *Education Index,* which I've used to locate articles published in education-oriented periodicals on the subject of personal computer use in schools.

Not only will the articles that you locate be of great assistance, but so will the names of the authors of those articles and the experts cited in the pieces. These are people that you'll want to speak with later on to obtain answers to your own particular questions.

The trick in using these guides is to figure out which subject index to consult. What you need to do is determine which subject area established by Wilson your topic falls into. For example, if you wanted to find out about growing tomatoes, that would be a food science question, and you'd check the *Biological and Agricultural Index*. If your subject were meditation, that would fall under psychology, and so you'd look in the *Social Science Index*. (As noted previously, I've found Wilson's *Business Periodicals Index* worth checking for almost any subject.)

Here are some samples of the major subtopics covered in the different Wilson indexes:

If Your Area of Interest Is	*The Wilson Guide to Check Is*
Fire, mineralogy, oceanology, plastics, transportation, and other applied scientific subjects	*Applied Science and Technology Index*
Architecture, art history, film, industrial design, landscape design, painting, photography	*Art Index*
Animal breeding, food science, nutrition, pesticides	*Biological and Agricultural Index*
Accounting, advertising, banking, economics, finance, investment, labor, management, marketing, public relations, specialized industries	*Business Periodicals Index* (see page 11)
Curriculums, school administration and supervision, teaching methods	*Education Index*
Astronomy, physics, and broad scientific areas	*General Science Index*
Archaeology, classical studies, folklore, history, language and literature, literary and political criticism, performing arts, philosophy, religion, theology	*Humanities Index*
Legal information, all areas of jurisprudence	*Index to Legal Periodicals*

| Anthropology, environmental science, psychology, sociology | *Social Sciences Index* |

There are two other very useful specialized subject indexes, not published by Wilson, worth mentioning. The **Engineering Index**, published by Engineering Information Inc., covers all aspects of engineering; and the **Public Affairs Information Service (PAIS) Bulletin** (published by Public Affairs Information Service Inc.) covers politics, legislation, international law, public policymaking, and related topics worldwide. You can find special subject indexes either at a large public library or at an appropriate special library (e.g., the *Index to Legal Periodicals* at a law library).

TIP: Start a Search Narrowly
- If you're gathering information on a topic that combines two subjects—e.g., *marketing* done by *museums* or *new technologies* in *videocassettes*—identify the narrowest approach to take. To find information on marketing by museums, I might look under "Museums" in the *Business Periodicals Index*. But it would not be a good idea to use the *Business Periodicals Index* and look under "Marketing," since I'd find too much information, and maybe none of it related to museums. If you don't find enough information by taking the narrower path, then you can always try the broader approach.

TIP: Spotting Hot Periodicals
- Use the periodical indexes described above to identify publications that are worth examining in depth. Take a look at the opening pages, where the magazines and journals that the index scans are listed. Reading this listing is a good way to identify the hottest and most relevant periodicals in your field of interest. Say your subject is the paper industry—you might spot the magazine *Pulp and Paper*. Another way of identifying the best publications is to note whether most of the articles you find when using an index were published in the same magazine or magazines. If so, those publications are also worth looking at in more depth. If you identify such a "hot" publication, try to locate the most recent issues and peruse these for valuable articles not yet indexed, or consider talking to the editors of the publication.

MAGAZINE AND NEWSLETTER DIRECTORIES

☑ **Sources:** *Ulrich's International Periodicals Directory*
Gale Directory of Publications
Standard Periodical Directory
Oxbridge Directory of Newsletters

There are periodicals and newsletters covering thousands of different subjects. The directories above identify tens of thousands of magazines, newsletters, newspapers, journals, and other periodicals. The most comprehensive of these directories, but the most difficult to use, is *Ulrich's*, which lists 126,000 periodicals in 554 subject areas. Two easier indexes to use are the *Gale Directory* and the *Standard Periodical Directory*. Virtually all libraries have one or more of these directories.

These are all excellent resources for tracking down specific periodicals covering a particular subject. The way these guides work is simple: You look up your subject, and the guide lists the magazines or newsletters published within the field. Entries typically include the name of the periodical, the publisher, address, and circulation.

TIP: Newspaper Feature Editors

▪ One particularly valuable section in the *Gale Directory* is its "newspaper feature editors" listing. This is a compilation of the names and phone numbers of the editors of the most popular newspaper features (e.g., art, automobiles, fashion, movies, real estate, society, sports, and women) appearing in daily newspapers with a circulation of 50,000 or more. It's superb for identifying subject experts, and regional publications.

There are loads of specialized publications being published around the United States. Even if your topic is extremely narrow, there may just be a periodical devoted to that subject alone. Let me give you a few examples. If you looked under "Folklore" in *Ulrich's*, you'd find *Folklore Center News*, and under "Motion Pictures" you'd see magazines like *Amateur Film Maker* and *Motion Picture Investor*—a newsletter that analyzes private and public values of movies and movie stock. Under the

BEVERAGES - BREWING

Michigan Beverage Journal
PUBLISHING CO.: Sponsor-Associated Beverage Pub., MBJ, Inc., 8750
Telegraph Rd., #104, Taylor, MI 48180 (313) 287-9140
PERSONNEL: Publ-Larry Stotz, Adv Dir-Ann Cook, Prom Dir-William Slone;
EDITORIAL DESCRIPTION: Covers merchandising, product information, news,
laws & regulations of beverage industry.
MISCELLANEOUS DATA: 1982 M 8 3/8 x 10 7/8 Sheetfed Color-4 p bind (Last
updated in Aug. 88)
CIRCULATION (BPA):
Total: 5,417
ADVERTISING: One Time   Annual   CPM: $201
  Full pg. b/w: $1,089 $973
  Full pg. 4/c: $1,942 $1,826
  1/3 pg. b/w: $457 $396

Michigan Beverage News
PUBLISHING CO.: Michigan Beverage News Inc., 27716 Franklin Rd.,
Southfield, MI 48034-2352 (313) 357-6397
PERSONNEL: Ed-Publ-David Brown, Adv Dir-Anne Platenik, Circ Mgr-Diane
Brown;
EDITORIAL DESCRIPTION: Reporting marketing, sales and other spirits,
wine and beer news.
MISCELLANEOUS DATA: 0026-2021 1939 BW $11.75 $.50/copy 10 1/4 x 14 1/4
Web 30pg. Color-4 c stock (Last updated in Nov. 87)
CIRCULATION (ABC, 100% controlled):
Total: 6,000
ADVERTISING: One Time   CPM: $259
  Full pg. b/w: $1,555
PRINTING CO.: Webco, Northville, MI

Mid-Continent Bottler
PUBLISHING CO.: Fan Publications, Inc., 10741 El Monte, Box 7406,
Overland Pk., KS 66207 (913) 341-0020
PERSONNEL: Ed-Publ-Floyd Sageser;
EDITORIAL DESCRIPTION: For and about soft drink bottlers in the mid-
continent area.
MISCELLANEOUS DATA: BM $9 $1.50/copy 8 1/2 x 11 Sheetfed 64pp. Color-4
(Last updated in July 88)
CIRCULATION (100% controlled):
Total: 3,220
ADVERTISING: One Time   CPM: $281
  Full pg. b/w: $905
LIST RENTAL: $35/M
PRINTING CO.: Jostens, 11000 Adams, Topeka, KS 66601

Modern Brewery Age
PUBLISHING CO.: Modern Brewery Age, 50 Day St., Box 5550, Norwalk, CT
06854 (203) 853-6015
PERSONNEL: Ed-Terri Finnegan, Publ-Mac Brighton;
EDITORIAL DESCRIPTION: Bimonthly magazine supplement.
MISCELLANEOUS DATA: 1933 W $65 $4/copy 8 1/4 x 11 Sheetfed Color-4
(Last updated in Nov. 87)
CIRCULATION (BPA, 100% controlled):
Total: 5,500
ADVERTISING: One Time   CPM: $254
  Full pg. b/w: $550

Nebraska Beverage Analyst
PUBLISHING CO.: Golden Bell Press, 2403 Champa St., Denver, CO 80205
(303) 296-1600
PERSONNEL: Ed-Mariette Bell, Publ-Allen Bell;
EDITORIAL DESCRIPTION: Complete price lists, new products, industry
news, legal notices and information for distilled spirits, beer &
wine.
MISCELLANEOUS DATA: 1934 M $7 $1.50/copy 8 3/8 x 10 7/8 Offset 14pp.
Color (Last updated in Feb. 88)
CIRCULATION:
Total: 4,500
ADVERTISING: One Time   CPM: $122
  Full pg. b/w: $550

New Brewer
PUBLISHING CO.: Institute for Fermentation, 734 Pearl, Boulder, CO
80302 (303) 447-0816
PERSONNEL: Ed-Virginia Thomas, Publ-Adv Dir-Charlie Papazian, Prom Dir-
Alan Dikty, Circ Mgr-Rob Cunov, Art Dir-David Bjorkman;
EDITORIAL DESCRIPTION: Technical Journal for micro-and Pub-Brewers
MISCELLANEOUS DATA: 0741-0506 1983 BM $48 $8/copy 8 1/2 x 11 Sheetfed
36pp. No Color c stock s bind (Last updated in Aug. 87)
CIRCULATION (100% controlled):
Total: 800
  Subscript.:   600
ADVERTISING: One Time   CPM: $937
  Full pg. b/w: $750
LIST RENTAL
PRINTING CO.: D&K Printing, Boulder, CO 80302

New Jersey Beverage Journal
PUBLISHING CO.: Gem Publishers Inc., 2400 Morris Ave., Union, NJ 07083
(201) 964-5060
PERSONNEL: Ed-Publ-Harry Slone, Adv Dir-Max Slone, Circ Mgr-Angel
Wolters,
EDITORIAL DESCRIPTION: Business publication for alcohol beverage
industry (spirits, wines, b
MISCELLANEOUS D

  Full pg. 4/c: $1,570
  1/3 pg. b/w: $380
  1/3 pg. 4/c: $1,110
LIST RENTAL $60/M
PRINTING CO.: Ranno Printing Co., 20 10 Maple Ave.,
NJ 07410

Observer
PUBLISHING CO.: Observer Corp., 226 N. 12th St., Ph
(215) 567-6221
PERSONNEL: Ed-Anthony West, Publ-James Curran,
EDITORIAL DESCRIPTION: The alcoholic beverage inc
For state operated liquor and distributors, restauran
etc.
MISCELLANEOUS DATA: 1936 BW $12 10 x 16 Web (L
CIRCULATION:
Total: 20,000
ADVERTISING: One Time   CPM: $89
  Full pg. b/w: $1,785

Ohio Beverage Journal
PUBLISHING CO.: Beverage Journal, 3 12th St., Wheeling,
232-7620
PERSONNEL: Ed-Publ-Adv Dir-Arnold Lazarus, Circ Mgr-Da
EDITORIAL DESCRIPTION: Edited for beverage alcohol reta
local & natl. industry news.
MISCELLANEOUS DATA: Former Title-Buckeye Beverage Jo
$1/copy 8 1/2 x 11 Sheetfed 48pp. Color-4 s bind (Last upd
July 88)
CIRCULATION (100% controlled):
Total: 7,200
ADVERTISING: One Time   CPM: $120
  Full pg. b/w: $870
PRINTING CO.: Boyd Press, 112 31st St., Wheeling, WV 26

Oklahoma Beverage News
PUBLISHING CO.: Beverage News, Inc., Box 1677, Wichit
263-0107
PERSONNEL: Ed-Chas Walters, Jr.;
EDITORIAL DESCRIPTION: Carries complete news cove
beverage industry with emphasis on legal and econor
MISCELLANEOUS DATA: 1959 M $6 $1/copy 8 1/2 x 1
(Last updated in Aug. 87)
CIRCULATION (100% controlled):
Total: 2,250
ADVERTISING: One Time   CPM:
  Full pg. b/w: $525
  Full pg. 4/c: $900

Patterson's California Beverage Journal
PUBLISHING CO.: Wolfer Printing Co., Inc., 1613 E. Gl
Glendale, CA 91206-2825 (213) 627-4996
PERSONNEL: Ed-Harry Bradley, Publ-Robert Good, Ad
Circ Mgr-Pearl Cooper;
EDITORIAL DESCRIPTION: Trade publication; covers alc
and pricing information.
MISCELLANEOUS DATA: Former Title-Patterson's Califor
Gazetteer, 1941 M $29.95 $5/copy 8 3/8 x 10 7/8 Web 40
stock p bind (Last updated in Apr. 86)
CIRCULATION (100% controlled):
Total: 10,145
ADVERTISING: One Time   CPM: $162
  Full pg. b/w: $1,645
PRINTING CO.: Wolfer Printing Co., 422 Wall St., Los Angele

Practical Winery Vineyard
PUBLISHING CO.: Don Neel, 15 Grande Paseo, San Rafael, C
479-5819
PERSONNEL: Ed-Stan Hock, Publ-Don Neel, Circ Mgr-F. Ne
Cobb;
EDITORIAL DESCRIPTION: Information on equipment and
winemaking and grape growing, marketing.
MISCELLANEOUS DATA: 0739-8077 1980 BM $8 $3.95/c
56pp 18% ads Color-2-4 c stock s bind (Last updated i
CIRCULATION (100% controlled):
Total: 2,500
  Newsstand: 200
  Subscript.:   2,125
  Internatl.:   175
ADVERTISING: One Time   CPM: $2
  Full pg. b/w: $605

Quarterly Review of Wines
PUBLISHING CO.: QRW Publishing, 24 Garfield Ave., Win
(617) 729-7132
PERSONNEL: Ed-Randy Sheahan, Publ-Prod Mgr-Richard
Lynch, Circ Mgr-Beth Hamilton, Art Dir-Lily Yamamoto;
EDITORIAL DESCRIPTION: For those interested in wines, res
selected spirits & beers & gourmet foods. The nation's seco
consumer wine magazine-dedicated to bringing the world's
wine writers to our readers.
MISCELLANEOUS DATA: 0740-1248 1978 Q $9.95 $2.95/cop
36pp Color-2-4 c stock s bind (Last updated in Nov. 87)
CIRCULATION:

category "Nutrition and Dietetics" you'd find loads of publications, including *Jewish Vegetarian*, published by the International Jewish Vegetarian Society of London.

 Source: *Magazines for Libraries* (R. R. Bowker Company)

> Another directory of publications. This one covers fewer periodicals (about 6,500), but provides much more in-depth information on each one.

This is an excellent and highly recommended directory for researchers. Although it does not cover the most obscure publications, it provides a superb analysis and review of the coverage and usefulness for those it does include. The directory is actually designed to assist librarians in deciding which magazines to obtain, so it is also an excellent tool for researchers who want to know which publications are considered the best in the field and how their scope compares.

TIP: Identifying the Right Periodical

▪ If your topic is *very* obscure, look up subjects that are a little broader. For example, while working on an information-finding project on the topic of "rebuilding school buses," I could not find any publications covering just that narrow topic, but I did find a magazine called *School Transportation News*. It seemed logical that such a publication might, at one time or another, have written an article on rebuilding school buses, so I telephoned the magazine and asked for the editorial department. An editor was happy to check the files, and sure enough, the magazine had published three different articles on that topic during the previous two years; the editor mailed me copies. So, if you are having trouble finding a periodical on a very narrow topic, try looking up some broader subjects whose scope may encompass it. You can always try calling a publication to find out if it has published an article on a particular topic during the last year or two.

TIP: Locating Hard-to-Find Periodicals
- Once you identify the specialized magazine or newsletter you need, how do you obtain it? Because there are so many special-interest and obscure periodicals, it's unlikely that even the largest library will have all the ones you seek. What you need to do is to contact the publisher of the periodical you're interested in (the address and phone number are listed in the directory) and request a sample copy or two. Then you can decide whether you want to subscribe or interview the writers and editors for information or find a library that specializes in the subject and contact the librarian to find out if the library subscribes to it (see pages 7–8 for tips on locating special libraries).

PEOPLE INFORMATION

 Source: Marquis Who's Who Series

The Who's Who volumes are the standard and most popular sources of biographical details on people of various accomplishments. The best-known of these books is *Who's Who in America,* which lists facts on prominent Americans. There are scores of more specialized Who's Who volumes, such as *Who's Who in Finance and Industry, Who's Who in the East,* and *Who's Who of American Women.* Virtually all libraries have *Who's Who in America.* Larger and specialized libraries have the other volumes.

Who's Who in America, the most popular of the Who's Who series, lists various information about prominent Americans—place and date of birth, schools attended, degrees awarded, special accomplishments, and current address. A caution in using these books is that the information is often furnished by the biographees themselves, so accuracy will depend on their truthfulness.

Large libraries have a master Who's Who index titled *Index to Who's Who Books.* With this guide you can look up a name and find out which, if any, of the fifteen or so Who's Who books includes a listing.

Source: *Current Biography* (H. W. Wilson Company)

This is a monthly magazine with articles about people prominent in the news—in national and international affairs, the sciences, arts, labor, and industry. Obituaries are also included. At the end of each year, the articles are printed in a single volume, and an index at the back helps users find biographies published during the current year and a few years back. Medium- and large-size libraries have the set.

Current Biography strives to be "brief, objective, and accurate, with well-documented articles." It may be more reliable than Who's Who, since its editors consult many sources of biographical data, rather than rely solely on the biographers' own accounts.

 Source: *Biography Index* (H. W. Wilson Company)

Biography Index scans more than 2,700 periodicals, many books, and various biographical sources like obituaries, diaries, and memoirs to identify and index sources of information on prominent people. You can find *Biography Index* in large libraries.

Checking *Biography Index* is a fast way to find articles and other sources of information on all sorts of people—from comedian Robert Klein to Buonarroti, Michelangelo.

 Source: *Biography and Genealogy Master Index* (Gale Research Company)

Biography and Genealogy Master Index is an index to biographical directories, providing information on more than 8.8 million current and historical figures. Five hundred sixty-five publications are indexed, including the various Who's Who volumes. Large libraries have this guide.

This source will tell you whether there is a directory or publication that lists biographical information on a historical or well-known figure. For example, if you looked up Bob Dylan, you'd find that biographical sketches could be found in *Baker's Biographical Dictionary of Musicians, Biography Index, The New Oxford Companion to Music, Who's Who in the World,* and elsewhere. Once you've located a directory, try to find a library that has it. (You might call the Special Libraries Association to help you identify a likely library.) Then write or call the library to find out if the person you need information on is listed in the directory.

 Source: *National Directory of Addresses and Telephone Numbers* **(Omnigraphics, Inc.)**

A listing of 115,000 addresses and phone numbers of various institutions such as government agencies, corporations, associations, retailers, hotels, restaurants, and more.

This is a handy and useful source for finding addresses and phone numbers of all sorts of popular organizations. It is not as comprehensive as directories devoted to a single type of institution but is still a useful research tool, because it is inexpensive and can be found in many bookstores.

 Source: *New York Times Obituaries Index*

An index to all the obituaries published in the *New York Times* from 1858 to 1978. Most libraries have it.

Obituaries published in the *Times* are a good source of information about well-known people. Usually the obituary will identify organizations and individuals that the person was affiliated with—these are fruitful leads for digging up more information.

(If you seek biographical information on someone who died after 1978, you can find obituary articles published in the *Times* by checking the regular *New York Times Index.* Look under

"Deaths" in the volume covering those issues published the year the person died.)

TIP: Check Periodical Indexes
▪ Other good library sources of biographical information on well-known individuals are the Wilson Subject Indexes (see page 13). Figure out which of these guides would most likely index periodicals covering the profession in which the person was active. For example, if you want to find information on someone who was well-known in the electronics industry, look up his or her name in the *General Science Index*.

BUSINESS AND INDUSTRY INFORMATION

Libraries can be particularly valuable to people seeking business information. Specialized periodical indexes, industry directories, and special business guides can provide you with important facts about companies and industries. (Many more business information sources, not found in libraries, are identified in chapter 4.)

The following is a selection of some leading and most broadly useful business library sources.

 Source: *Wall Street Journal Index*

An index to articles published in the *Wall Street Journal* and *Barron's*. There are two parts: a subject index and a company name index. Supplements are issued monthly. You'll find the *Wall Street Journal Index* in nearly all libraries.

This is one of the quickest and best ways to search for authoritative information on a particular industry, company, or business topic. Articles published in the *Wall Street Journal* are generally not too technical, yet they are in-depth and probing enough to provide very valuable information. Most libraries keep back issues of the *Journal* on microfilm, so you can often read the articles you find right at the library. Like the *New York Times Index*, the *Wall Street Journal Index* is itself a source of facts and information, because each entry typically contains a one-or two-line summary of the indexed article.

GAS
(see **Industrial Gases, Natural Gas**)

GASOLINE
Motor gasoline stocks in week ended Nov. 1 totaled 215,796,000 barrels; motor gasoline production totaled 42,532,000 barrels. 11/6-48;6

Motor gasoline stocks in week ended Nov. 8 totaled 215,821,000 barrels; motor gasoline production totaled 43,568,000 barrels. 11/14-53;3

Motor gasoline stocks for week ended Nov. 15 totaled 213,460 barrels; motor gasoline production totaled 45,913,-000 barrels. 11/20-51;3

Motor gasoline stocks in week ended Nov. 22 totaled 214,403,000 barrels; motor gasoline production totaled 45,038,000 barrels. 11/27-38;6

Energy futures prices plunged Nov. 27, with heating oil and gasoline contracts falling by as much as the permissible daily limit amid concern that the past few months' rally may be faltering. (Futures Markets) 11/29-20;3

GASOLINE STATIONS
(see **Service Stations**)

GEKAS, GEORGE
Can staggered filing of returns break up the processing logjam?; Rep. Gekas' bill would let returns claiming refunds be filed early, but would make returns--and taxes owed--due at the later of April 15 or the end of the filer's birth month. (Tax Report) 11/20-1;5

GENEALOGY
Beatrice Bayley Inc. mails postcards offering for $29.85 a 'Family Heritage Book' that promises to trace a family's genealogy; but many buyers have discovered that book contains not their lineage but simply a list of people with the same last names; complaints have led to investigations by the U.S. Postal Inspector and Wisconsin and Pennsylvania state officials. 11/4-27;3

GENERAL ACCOUNTING OFFICE
The SEC, responding to criticism from the General Accounting Office, proposed closing certain loopholes in its program for finding lost or stolen securities; proposal would force 19,000 brokerage firms and banks nationwide to become more active in the program. 11/22-6;4

GENERAL AGREEMENT ON TARIFFS & TRADE
The General Agreement on Tariffs & Trade finds the slowdown in trade is more serious than it expected; GATT estimated that the growth in trade for 1985 will be 2% to 3%, well below the forecasts of other analysts. 11/15-35;2

U.S. trade officials, impatient with opposition from India, Brazil, Egypt, Yugoslavia and Argentina, are prepared to call a vote in an effort to force the beginning of a new round of global trade negotiations under the General Agreement on Tariffs and Trade. 11/20-35;2

U.S. hopes for a new round of global trade talks are expected to get a boost in the upcoming meeting of the General Agreement on Tariffs & Trade; the talks sought by the U.S. are likely to be the most difficult and longest ever. 11/25-32;1

The Mexican government will begin negotiations to enter the General Agreement on Tariffs and Trade, closing another chapter in the country's longstanding debate over external economic policy. 11/26-35;4

Trade officials from 90 countries agreed unanimously to launch a new round of global trade talks next September; at the end of a four-day meeting delegates...

GHANA—Foreign Relations
Justice Department said a cousin of leader has secretly pleaded no contest to c on the U.S.; he was sent back to Ghana about 10 Ghanians 'of interest to the U.S.'

GIFTS
(see also **Illegal Payments**)
New Form 8283 for deducting non-cash c valued at more than $500 should be avai offices by the end of November. (Tax Report

Alexander Calder's widow received 1, from her husband's estate and valued them the $949,750 accepted by the IRS for est reflected 60% discount from retail value; b discounts of 18% to 25%, valued gifts at $2. billed Mrs. Calder for $459,419 more in Report) 11/20-1;5

When Judge Shirley Kram called lawye the pending litigation between Hanson Tr Corp., they were expecting a decision on fight; but judge wanted to know whether she a complimentary copy of a book written by represents Hanson. (Shop Talk) 11/21-33;3

Colleges find gifts such as racehorses a bet; property donations can cost dearly, be lots that slide into the sea. 11/25-1;4

GINNIE MAE
(see **Government National Mortgage Ass**

GIOVANNINI, ALFIO
Yugo Yearning: Editorial page article by nini on how Yugoslavia's latest car import, affect East-West trade. 11/20-30;4

GLICK, ALLEN
A government witness described how application to the Teamsters Central States led him into a partnership with organized Glick's testimony provided substance to a Senate subcommitteee in the late 1970s th fund had served for decades as 'the mob's b

GOING PRIVATE
Beatrice Cos. accepted Kohlberg Kr offer of $50 a share, or $6.2 billion, to after Kohlberg Kravis threatened to with buyout pact ever is set after board spurne a share, or $5.9 billion, from Dart Group 11/15-2;2 .

GOLD
New methods enable miners to step gold; the more developed process, heap le boost annual U.S. production to 2.3 milli year; second, less-developed technolgy, is thiobacillus ferrooxidans, which eats away s unreachable by cyanide solutions. 11/1-33;1

The U.S. dollar fell against most major fc cies after the release of several U.S. economic were more discouraging than the market ha on the Comex, gold fell to $324.70 an ounce.

Foreign-exchange traders are now convi jor nations are serious about lowering the banks' determination was underscored No reportedly intervened and old on the Comex

Source: *Funk & Scott Index* (Information Access Co., Inc.)

The *Funk & Scott Index* (or *"F&S"*) is a leading guide to published articles about industries and about company activities and developments. *F&S* indexes articles published in leading business periodicals such as *Barron's* and the *Wall Street Journal,* as well as more specialized industry publications like *Iron Age* and *Aviation Week.* Most large libraries and almost all business libraries have this index. *F&S* issues weekly and monthly supplements.

The *F&S Index* is an extremely *fast* and *helpful* tool for digging up information on specific industries and companies. This includes information on corporate acquisitions and mergers, new products, technology developments, forecasts, company analyses, and social and political factors affecting business. To find information about a particular *industry,* you can turn to the front of the book to find the industry's **SIC** code (**SIC** = Standard Industrial Classification, the accepted method of categorizing industry types using assigned reference numbers) and then check the appropriate section of the volume to find citations of articles that discuss a given issue within that industry.

This index is conveniently organized so that you can also look up the name of a particular firm and find references to relevant articles, with a brief description of each article's scope. For example, if I wanted to find out what kinds of developments and activities Liz Claiborne was involved in, I would find this citation.

Is starting a New Women's Casual Knit Sportswear Division, Liz & Co., Women Wear, 1/30/89 p. 2.

TIP: Finding Leading Industry Periodicals
- The front of the book lists all the periodicals indexed in *F&S,* which cover industries ranging from rubber to fertilizer. Since these periodicals have been selected by *F&S* for indexing, it's a good bet that they are leading trade publications. The description of each includes the title, frequency of publication, subscription price, and single-issue price. (Some are expensive, but many are moderately priced or even free.)

Note: Predicasts also publishes two companion international directories: *F&S Index Europe* identifies published information on companies operating in Western and Eastern Europe, and *F&S Index International* covers business activity in Canada, Latin America, Africa, Middle East, and Asia. Another popular volume from the same publisher is *Predicasts Forecasts,* which lists published forecasts for hundreds of different products, industries, and topics (for example, the estimated growth in the number of hospital beds through the 1990s and the increase in personal computers).

 Source: *Standard & Poor's Register of Corporations, Directors and Executives*

Standard & Poor's Register, or the "*S&P,*" is a leading industry directory of company information. The register consists of three volumes. Volume 1, *Corporations,* is a straight alphabetical listing of approximately 55,000 corporations, giving their addresses, phone numbers, names and titles of key officers and directors, subsidiaries, numbers of employees, and certain financial data like gross sales. Volume 2, *Directors and Executives,* is a listing of about 70,000 officers, directors, trustees, partners, and so on. The information provided about them includes date and place of birth, college attended, professional affiliations, and place of residence. Volume 3 is a set of indexes. You'll find the *S&P* volumes in large general libraries and in business libraries.

S&P is a very highly regarded source of information about companies. It and the Dun & Bradstreet volumes described below are considered leading industry directories.

 Source: Dun & Bradstreet *Million Dollar Directory*

The D&B *Million Dollar Directory* is composed of five volumes of information on over 160,000 companies with a net worth in excess of $500,000. The directory provides an alphabetical listing of company names, subsidiary relationships, headquarters, addresses, phone numbers, officers, numbers of employees, stock exchange numbers, SIC numbers, and annual sales. A cross-reference volume enables users to look up companies by geographical location or SIC code. Most large libraries and business libraries have Dun & Bradstreet.

2178   STANDARD & POOR'S REGISTER

Parch Agt—Edward Stone
Product Mgr—Fred Delp
Traffic Mgr—Evert Jackson
Mktg & Prod Mgr—Clarence Bowman
Qual Con Mgr—Robert W. Stratton
Accts—Hill, Barth & King, Salem, Ohio
Primary Bank—Farmers National Bank of Canfield
Sales $5.50Mil Employees 110
    *Also DIRECTORS —Other Directors Are:
John Tonti
PRODUCTS: Tool & die, metal stamping, assembly special machines
S.I.C. 3544; 3469; 3559

QUAKER OATS CO.
321 N. Clark St., Quaker Tower, Chicago, Ill. 60610
Tel. 312-222-7111

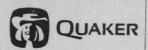

*Chrm & Chief Exec Officer—William D. Smithburg
*Pres & Chief Oper Officer—Frank J. Morgan
Exec V-P (Pres. Grocery Specialties Div)—Philip A. Marineau
Exec V-P (Diversified Grocery Products)—Douglas W. Mills
*Exec V-P (Intl Grocery Products)—Paul E. Price
Exec V-P (Pres-Fisher-Price Div)—R. Bruce Sampsell
Sr V-P (Human Resources)—Lawrence M. Baytos
*Sr V-P (Fin)—Michael J. Callahan
*Sr V-P (Law) & Secy—Luther C. McKinney
Sr V-P (U. S. Grocery Products Serv)—David R. Nogle
V-P & Assoc Gen Con Coun—John H. Calhoun
V-P (Tax)—Leland R. Chalmers
V-P (Dir-Latin America)—James F. Doyle
V-P & Gen Cor Coun—R. Thomas Howell, Jr.
V-P (Bus Devel & Cor Plan)—Terry G. Westbrook
V-P (Pres-Quaker Oats of Canada)—Jon K. Grant
V-P & Treas—Richard D. Jaquith
V-P (Dir-Europe)—Jose A. Rodriguez
V-P (Cor Affairs)—Deborah E. Kelly
V-P (Cor Adm Serv)—Richard E. Kozitka
V-P (New Areas)—William C. Trotter
V-P (Govt Rel)—Thomas F. Roeser
V-P (Inf Sys)—Ronald T. Brzezinski
V-P & Cont—Raymond C. Eggleston
V-P (Pres Pet Foods)—George J. Yapp
V-P (Cor Programs)—W. Thomas Phillips
V-P (Pres-Food Service Div)—Russell L. Jones
Accts—Arthur Andersen & Co., Chicago, Ill.
Sales $4.42Bil Employees 30,000
Stock Exchange(s): NYS, BST, PAC, MID, TOR, PSE
    *Also DIRECTORS —Other Directors Are:
Richard D. Harrison   Weston R. Christopherson
William J. Kennedy, III   Vernon R. Loucks, Jr.
Thomas C. MacAvoy   Donald E. Meads
G. G. Michelson (Mrs.)   Walter J. Salmon
William L. Weiss
PRODUCTS: Foods, pet foods & toys
S.I.C. 2032; 2038; 2041; 2043; 2045; 2047; 2051; 2052; 2099; 3942; 3944; 5411; 5621; 5945

QUAKER SALES CORP.
Cooper Ave., Johnstown, Pa. 15907
Tel. 814-536-7541
*Pres—Elvin W. Overdorff, Jr.
*V-P—Calvin Q. Overdorff
*Secy & Treas—Donald Overdorff
Accts—Martin, Waltman & Kotzan, Inc., Johnstown, Pa.
Primary Bank—Johnstown Bank & Trust Co.
Primary Law Firm—Kaminsky, Kelly, Wharton & Thomas
Sales Range: $5—8Mil Employees: 100
    *Also DIRECTORS
BUSINESS: Road & paving contractors & supplies
S.I.C. 1611; 5085

QUAKER STATE CORP.-SOUTHEAST REGION
(Subs. Quaker State Corporation)
5500 S. Cobb Dr., Smyrna, Ga. 30080
Tel. 404-799-7212
*Chrm & Chief Exec Officer—Jack W. Corn
*Pres & Chief Oper Officer—Homer M. Ellenburg
*Exec V-P (Admin) & Secy—Maurice G. Erwin
V-P (Coml Sales)—Ennis Mobley
V-P (Sales)—Robert E. Hardesty
V-P (Purch)—Patricia Woodall
Treas—K. Joe Sutton
*Asst Treas—Conrad A. Conrad
Compt—William H. Fields, Jr.
Accts—Coopers & Lybrand, Pittsburgh, Pa.
Primary Bank—National Bank of Georgia
Primary Law Firm—Smith, Eubanks & Smith, P.C.
Sales $53.60Mil Employees: 250
    *Also DIRECTORS —Other Directors Are:
W. B. Cook
Quentin E. Wood

QUAKER STATE CORPORATION
255 Elm St., Oil City, Pa. 16301
Tel. 814-676-7676

*Chrm—Quentin E. Wood
*Pres & Chief Exec Officer—Jack W. Corn
*Vice-Chrm—Roger A. Markle
Exec V-P—James D. Berry, III
*Exec V-P—Jonathan B. Cook
V-P, Secy & Coun—Gerald W. Callahan
*V-P (Fin) & Chief Fin Officer—Conrad A. Conrad
V-P (Research)—Embert H. DeLong
V-P (Distr)—Homer M. Ellenburg
V-P (Mfg)—William C. Helsley
V-P & Treas—R. Scott Keefer
V-P (Sales)—William E. Marshall
V-P & Cont—John R. Sedlacko
V-P (Mktg)—Earl V. Swift
Public Rel Mgr—Benton H. Faulkner
Purch Mgr—William E. Kingsley
Mktg Dir (Motor Oil)—Richard L. Pennington
Accts—Coopers & Lybrand
Revenue: $847.95Mil Employees: 4,400
Stock Exchange(s): NYS, BST, MID, PSE
    *Also DIRECTORS —Other Directors Are:
Lee R. Forker   Thomas A. Gardner
H. Bryce Jordan   W. Craig McClelland
Kenton E. McElhattan   William J. McFate
Delbert J. McQuaide
PRODUCTS: Lubricants, fuels, other automotive aftermarket products, quick lube serv. centers; ins., truck & auto lights; coal
S.I.C. 5172; 2992; 5013

QUAKER STATE MINIT-LUBE, INC.
(Subs. Quaker State Corporation)
1385 W. 2200 S., Salt Lake City, Utah 84119
Tel. 801-972-6667
*Chrm—Roger A. Markle
*Vice-Chrm—John P. Pearson
*Pres & Chief Oper Officer—Jeffrey J. O'Neill
Exec V-P & Cor Coun—David E. Neff
Exec V-P (Mktg)—Paul G. Remund
V-P (Fin) & Cost—Kirk A. Umphrey
V-P (Hallmark Ina)—Wanda M. Hall
V-P & Asst Cont—Kerry A. Scovill
V-P (Oper)—Kay D. Olsen
*Secy & Treas—Conrad D. Morgan
Accts—Coopers & Lybrand, Salt Lake City, Utah
Primary Bank—Key Bank
Primary Law Firm—Jones, Waldo, Holbrook & McDonough
Sales: $21Mil Employees: 1,500
    *Also DIRECTORS —Other Directors Are:
Jack W. Corn   Quentin E. Wood
PRODUCTS: Franchisor & operator of fast lube service centers
S.I.C. 5141; 5172; 5812

QUALCORP, INC.
(Affil. Penn Central Federal Systems Co.)
Shelter Rock Rd., Danbury, Conn. 06810
Tel. 203-796-5000
Pres—W. Derek Buckley
Sr V-P (Sys)—Joseph A. Savarese
Sr V-P (Serv)—Allen R. Schwartz
V-P (Admin)—Phyllis F. Zappala
Chief Fin Officer—D. Joseph Gersuk
Accts—Deloitte Haskins & Sells, New York, N. Y.
Sales: $50Mil Employees: 700
PRODUCTS: Quality assurance service & equip.
S.I.C. 3829; 3825

QUALHEIM, INC.
1225 14th St., Box 368, Racine, Wis. 53401
Tel. 414-634-6671
*Chrm & Pres—Ellen A. Qualheim
*V-P (Mktg)—Robert F. Karis
Secy & Treas—Julane Nelson
Purch Agt—Garrett Schutz
Accts—Robert G. Berkley, Racine, Wis.
Primary Bank—M&I Bank of Racine
Primary Law Firm—Reinhart, Boerner, Van Deuren, Norris & Rieselbach
Sales: $1Mil Employees: 20
    *Also DIRECTORS
PRODUCTS: Electric coml. vegetable cutters, coml. can & bottle crushers, glass washers
S.I.C. 3556; 3565; 3589

QUALI-TECH MACHINE & ENGINEERING CO.
330 Bond St., Elk Grove Village, Ill. 60007
Tel. 312-439-1311
*Chrm & Pres—Paul Carson, Jr.
*V-P—Barbara L. Carson

*Also DIRECTORS —Other Directors Are:
Herbert Portes
BUSINESS: Construction, metal work, oil field service
S.I.C. 1629; 1389; 1791; 3799; 3441; 3448; 3469

QUALITAD SALES CORP.
Quality Lane, Rutland, Vt. 05701
Tel. 802-773-9141
*Chrm & Pres—Daniel Bernhardt
*V-P—A. Bernhardt
Sales Range: $2—5Mil Employees: 50
    *Also DIRECTORS
PRODUCTS: Plastic trays & containers
S.I.C. 3089

QUALITEX, INC.
19 Industrial Lane, Providence, R. I. 02919
Tel. 401-751-5727
*V-P & Treas—Mauro Primo
*V-P (Mfg)—David E. Monti
*V-P (Sales)—Nancy Monti
*Secy—Jonathan Cole
*Purch Agt—Joe Riccittelli
Accts—Laventhol & Horwath, Providence, R. I.
Primary Bank—Hospital Trust National Bank
Primary Law Firm—Edwards & Angell
Sales Range: $20—30Mil Employees: 30
    *Also DIRECTORS
PRODUCTS: Extruded rubber thread
S.I.C. 3069; 2241

QUALITONE
(Div. Biscayne Holdings, Inc.)
4931 W. 35th St., Minneapolis, Minn. 55416
Tel. 612-927-7161
Pres—Lane Burger
Exec V-P—Max Harada
V-P (Mktg & Sales)—Joel Wernick
V-P (Fin)—James Anderson
Per Dir—Cleo DeBina
Purch Agt—Thomas McGregor
Sr Engr—Katsumi Tanaka
Mktg Mgr—David Wessell
Audiology—Dawn Galloway
Employees: 170
PRODUCTS: Hearing aids & audiometers
S.I.C. 3842; 3825

QUALITONE INDUSTRIES, INC.
696 Locust St., Mount Vernon, N. Y. 10552
Tel. 914-668-1135
Pres—Robert Karns
Gen Mgr—David Cutler
Sales Range: $2—5Mil Employees: 10
PRODUCTS: Phonograph needles
S.I.C. 3679

QUALITROL CORP.
(Subs. Danaher Corporation)
1385 Fairport Rd., Fairport, N. Y. 14450
Tel. 716-586-1515
*Pres—John R. Becker, Jr.
V-P (Mktg & Sales)—Daniel F. McNulty
*Treas—P. W. Allender
*Secy—M. T. Lynch
Cont—David E. Winterton
Accts—Arthur Andersen & Co., New York, N. Y.
Primary Bank—National Westminster Bank USA
Primary Law Firm—Skadden, Arps, Slate, Meagher & Flom
Sales: $10Mil Employees: 150
    *Also DIRECTORS —Other Directors Are:
Mitchell P. Rales   Steven M. Rales
PRODUCTS: Liquid level gauges controls, thermometers, high temperature alarms, pressure relief devices, pressure electrical switches
S.I.C. 3824; 3492; 3613; 3643

QUALITY ALUMINUM CASTING CO.
1242 Lincoln Ave., Waukesha, Wis. 53187
Tel. 414-542-0731
*Chrm—Gregory E. Pauly, New Holstein, Wis.
*Pres & Chief Exec Officer—C. C. McMullen
V-P (Qual Con & Tech Support)—P. C. Gottgetreu
V-P (Mfg)—John Nebeo
V-P—Paul Thompson
Treas—David J. Rutkowski
Purch Mgr—C. R. Fahl
Mgr Ind Rel—Robert Swanson
Accts—Arthur Young, Milwaukee, Wis.
Primary Bank—M&I Marshall & Ilsley Bank
Sales: $11.50Mil Employees: 200
    *Also DIRECTORS —Other Directors Are:
J. W. Blakey   James Butler
Gilbert A. Harter   Jeff Pauly
Theodore Pauly
PRODUCTS: Aluminum alloy castings: lost foam molded, permanent molded, cold-set molded, heat & machined
S.I.C. 3365; 3363

QUALITY ARCHITECTURAL PRODUCTS, INC.
16804 S. Gridley Pl., Box 549, Cerritos, Calif.
Tel. 213-402-7884
*Chrm & Pres—Warren R. Olson
*V-P (Fin, Data Proc & Cr) & Treas—John A. Olson
*Secy—Virginia L. Olson
Purch Agt—Dav...
Engr...

This well-known directory is especially helpful for finding information on smaller firms, because it includes companies that are worth only $500,000. The *Million Dollar Directory* is one of the most popular of Dun & Bradstreet's industry directories.

D&B's other business guides include a directory of international firms, a directory of biographical data about principal officers and directors of 12,000 leading companies, a directory of ranking of company size within industrial categories and states, and a directory that traces the structure and ownership of multinational corporations.

 Source: Ward's Business Directory (Gale Research)

Ward's Directory is a five-volume set that provides information on 135,000 U.S. public and private companies worth more than $500,000. Volumes 1–3 list companies alphabetically, volume 4 is organized geographically by state, and volume 5 classifies businesses by their 4-digit SIC code, and then ranks them by sales. Data provided include name, address, city, SIC code, sales, number of employees, name of chief executive, year founded, and type of firm (e.g., private, public, subsidiary, or division).

Ward's is a very interesting and useful directory. Unlike other popular company directories, *Ward's* provides various *rankings* in its listings. For example, *Ward's* lists the largest pharmaceutical firms, and ranks firms geographically and by other categories. *Ward's* also claims that more than 90 percent of the firms in its directory are privately held—data on these companies are harder to find than for public firms.

 Source: *Hoover's Handbook* (The Reference Press)

Hoover's Handbook provides one-page profiles of 500 major enterprises around the world, arranged alphabetically. For each listing, the directory provides an overview, history, names of top executives, address, phone, fax, major divisions and subsidiaries, rankings, names of competitors, stock price history, and other data.

A relatively new entry to the company directory field, Hoover's has made quite a name for itself by being the first to offer a company directory at a bargain price. While the preceding competitors' books cover many more firms, they cost well into the mid-hundreds of dollars, but you can get your own copy of the *Hoover's Handbook* for just $27.95 at many bookstores. Note that Hoover's also publishes a World Business edition as well, which covers international firms.

 Source: Moody's *Manuals* (Dun & Bradstreet)

Moody's *Manuals* provide a great deal of background and detail on specific companies. Typical information provided includes company history, structure, capital, lines of businesses and products, properties, subsidiaries, names of officers and directors, income statement, balance sheet, financial and operating data, and various stock charts and tables.

Much of the information provided in Moody's comes from documents that public companies are required to file by the Securities and Exchange Commission (SEC). The *Manuals* are a particularly good source for tracing the history of a large company.

 Source: *Business Rankings* (Brooklyn Public Library/Gale Research Company)

A collection of 3,500 citations of ranked list of companies, for various categories. Also included is a salary list for over 150 occupations.

This directory helps answer the question "who's number one" in a certain field. It is actually a compilation of information that the Brooklyn Public Library scans in its daily duties gleaned from scores of reference sources.

 Source: *Thomas Register of American Manufacturers*

Thomas Register tells you who manufactures what product, and where the manufacturer is located. There are three sets of volumes. One set consists of sixteen volumes and is organized alphabetically by product. It lists manufacturers' names and addresses. A companion two-volume set lists 145,000 U.S. companies in alphabetical order, providing addresses, phone numbers, asset ratings, and other information. These two volumes also include a trademark index at the back. A third set of volumes provides more than 10,000 pages of actual catalog data from about 1,800 companies. Most libraries keep a set of *Thomas Register*.

Thomas Register is a very useful resource. Volume 1 of the first set starts with a listing of abacus manufacturers, and the last volume ends with a listing of manufacturers of Zonolite (a form of insulation). If you look up radiation detectors, you'll find about twenty-five manufacturers—about the same number of firms that manufacture poultry netting. Although *Thomas Register* does not list every manufacturer of a product, it is still an extraordinarily comprehensive directory.

> **TIP:** To find more obscure manufacturers, check trade magazines that publish an annual buyers' guide. These are special issues devoted to listing manufacturers and suppliers.

 Source: *Findex: The Directory of Market Research Reports, Studies and Surveys* (Find/SVP)

> *Findex* is a guide to published, commercially available market and business research. Topics covered include chemicals, fuels, consumer durables, consumer nondurables (e.g., food), plastics, construction, data processing, retailing, health care, transportation, media, business, and finance. This directory is commonly found in corporate libraries, but not in many public libraries.

An extremely useful and valuable tool for business research. By using this directory, you can find out, for example, that there is a market research study that analyzes the Mexican market for mini-computers and microcomputers. Another entry describes a study on vodka drinkers in the United States. The information in this guide will be precious to many—but you'll have to pay for it. Most of the market studies listed cost between $500 and $8,000.

TIP: Getting Market Research Reports
- Use your ingenuity to best use this valuable, though expensive and sometimes hard-to-find, guide. First, try to get into a corporate library that has it (see pages 7–8 for advice on how to do this). Or pick up a similar guide, which is free and published in magazine format by Find/SVP, called *The Information Catalog* (see page 131). Once you locate a market research study you want, call the producer of the report directly to find and talk to the experts there for information rather than buy the study outright. Often you can order an executive summary and table of contents for no charge. Sometimes that information alone can be of assistance.

 Source: *The Wall Street Transcript* (Richard A. Holman)

The Wall Street Transcript is a verbatim transcript of roundtable discussions conducted by the publication's editors with CEOs and industry leaders. It is published weekly and covers industries ranging from aerospace to waste management.

This source can be a bit difficult to wade through and its indexing system is cumbersome, but it is unusual and intriguing. It provides actual transcripts of conversations of business leaders on developments within their industry, covering topics such as major strategic thrusts of leading companies, technology developments, and other factors influencing the industry.

 Source: *Organization Charts* (Gale Research)

Contains organization charts for over 200 businesses and organizations around the United States. Also provides detailed listings of department and division names and, where available, identification of subsidiary and parent companies.

A unique source for researching a corporation's structure and organization. According to the publisher, the data were compiled from public sources and then verified with the specific companies.

TIP: Another interesting business source that may come in handy is *Companies and Their Brands* (and *International Companies and Their Brands*), published by Gale Research. It identifies which companies are behind which trade names (e.g., Band-Aid is the trade name of Johnson & Johnson's adhesive bandages).

SUBSIDIARIES AND DIVISIONS DIRECTORIES

One of the most difficult tasks of business researchers is discovering linkages between corporate parents and their subsidiaries and divisions. The following sources will help identify connections.

 Source: *America's Corporate Families* (Dun & Bradstreet)

A description of 11,000 U.S. parent companies and their 60,000 subsidiaries and divisions. Includes any firm worth more than $500,000, conducting business from two or more locations, and having a controlling interest in one or more subsidiaries.

This is a very useful tool for finding out the subsidiaries and divisions a corporation operates and for finding names of division vice presidents and managers. Each listing provides names, addresses, sales, and the industry of each division and subsidiary listed. Volume 2 in this set is titled *International Affiliates*, which provides data about companies with foreign parents and U.S. subsidiaries. These directories are designed to be rather easy to use.

 Source: *Who Owns Whom* (Dun & Bradstreet)

Lists connections among companies. Parent firms are listed in alphabetical order.

Not as easy to use as *America's Corporate Families,* but it may still be worth checking to dig up hard-to-find information. Separate directories cover North America; Australia and the Far

East; United Kingdom and Republic of Ireland; and Continental Europe.

 **Source: *Directory of Corporate Affiliations*
(National Register Publishing)**

> Lists data on 3,700 U.S. parent companies and 30,600 divisions, subsidiaries, and affiliates and 12,650 outside the United States.

An easier directory to use than *Who Owns Whom*, but not as simple to use as *America's Corporate Families*.

INTERNATIONAL BUSINESS DIRECTORIES

Today's business world is global, and researchers can no longer confine themselves to finding facts on firms and industries that operate within the boundaries of the United States. The following is a selected listing of some of the most useful directories of information on companies in other parts of the world. If you have trouble finding any of these at your local public library, try visiting a nearby university's business school library.

 Source: *Major Companies of Europe* (Graham & Trotman, London)

> A three-volume set that provides facts about companies in Western Europe and the United Kingdom. Information provided includes company name, address, names of top executives, trade names, company activities, subsidiaries, sales, profit, and number of employees.

This is a straightforward directory, broken down into three volumes. Volume 1 contains information on 3,000 firms located in the European Community (EC), volume 2 lists data on 1,300 British firms, and volume 3 lists information about 1,400 firms located in Western Europe that are not part of the EC.

Source: *Japan Company Handbook* (Toyo Keizai Inc.)

> Provides financial information on all Japanese companies listed in the first and second sections of the Tokyo, Osaka, and Nagoya stock exchanges. Approximately 2,000 firms are covered.

This directory is considered the leading sourcebook for finding out about Japanese companies. It is filled with loads of useful data, including company descriptions, profit and loss statements, breakdown of sales by categories, methods for raising funds, in-depth financial statements, balance sheets, company outlooks, stock price graphs, and more. Amazingly, with so much data provided for each firm, the handbook is still very easy to use and read and is accompanied by clear explanatory material.

 Source: *Principal International Business* (Dun & Bradstreet)

> Lists data on 50,000 firms in 143 countries around the world. Companies are selected for inclusion based on their size and prominence. This directory provides names, address, sales, year founded, names of top executives, number of employees, and type of industry.

This is a very useful source if you need to get some basic information on any major company located anywhere around the world. The directory makes it easy to find firms by providing both an alphabetical and industry index.

TIP: If you need to find facts on a lesser-known company or one that is in a smaller country, I'd suggest visiting a good university business school's library and simply sit and browse for a while at the business directory reference section. There you will likely find a variety of directories that cover firms operating in *just one specific country*. (By the way, you'll also likely find there many *state directories* as well—compilations of data about firms operating within an individual state. These are often published by chambers of commerce or state economic development offices.)

"INSIDER" DIRECTORIES

 Source: *Directories in Print* **(Gale Research Company)**

This directory describes over 15,500 different types of specialized directories, covering subjects such as banking, agriculture, law, government, science, engineering, education, information science, biography, arts and entertainment, public affairs, health, religion, hobbies, and sports. You can find this guide, published annually, at most large public libraries.

This excellent source unearths an amazingly diverse range of specialized directories. (A directory is any kind of reference book that tells readers where they can find sources of information within a specific field.) Here are some samples of the directories indexed in this "ultimate" directory: *Special Libraries of Israel, Computer Software Applications in Oceanography, Bicycle Resource Guide, Major Companies of Europe, American Indian Painters, Index of Stolen Art,* and *Free Things for Teachers.* A detailed subject index is provided at the back of the book, so all you need to do is look up the topic of your choice, and *Directories in Print* refers you to a particular directory, giving you its name, publisher and address, phone number, specialties, and other details.

TIP: Getting the Directory You Want

▪ Many of the directories listed in this guide are cheap or moderately priced, but certain ones are expensive and are best used at a library. To find a library that has a directory you need, contact the Special Libraries Association (see page 8) and find out which libraries specialize in your topic of interest. Then, just call or write the library to see if it has the guide. If it does, you can then ask the librarian there to look up what you need.

For example, let's say you need information on whether a particular food is kosher. Checking the guide, you'll locate a directory called *Kosher Directory: Directory of Kosher Products and Services.* To get this directory, you could write to the address listed and purchase it or you could contact the Special Libraries Association to find a library devoted to Jewish studies. Such a library may have this directory, and you could ask the librarian there to look up the food and supply you with the answer.

★7622★
AMERICAN COUNCIL ON CONSUMER INTERESTS—
MEMBERSHIP LIST
American Council on Consumer Interests
Stanley Hall, Room 240
University of Missouri
Columbia, MO 65211   Phone: (314)882-3817
Number of listings: 2,000. **Frequency:** Biennial, odd years.
Price: Available to members only.

★7623★
AMERICAN GROUP PSYCHOTHERAPY ASSOCIATION—
MEMBERSHIP DIRECTORY
American Group Psychotherapy Association
25 E. 21st Street, 6th Floor
New York, NY 10010   Phone: (212)477-2677
Covers: 3,500 physicians, psychologists, clinical social
workers, psychiatric nurses, and other mental health
professionals interested in treatment of emotional problems by
group methods. **Entries include:** Name, office or home
address, highest degree held, affiliate society of which a
member. **Arrangement:** Alphabetical. **Indexes:** Geographical.
Pages (approx.): 160. **Frequency:** Reported as biennial;
previous edition 1984; latest edition summer 1987. **Price:**
$25.00. **Other formats:** Cheshire labels, $65.00 per thousand;
pressure-sensitive labels, $75.00 per thousand.

American Humane Agency Directory *See* **Directory of**
Animal Care and Control Agencies (7747)

★7624★
AMERICAN SOCIETY OF ACCESS PROFESSIONALS—
MEMBERSHIP DIRECTORY [Freedom of information]
American Society of Access Professionals
2001 S Street, N. W., Suite 630
Washington, DC 20009   Phone: (202)462-8888
Covers: Over 300 individuals concerned with the methods,
procedures, and techniques of administering statutes
pertaining to the availability of records or information contained
therein, including freedom of information, privacy protection,
open meetings, and fair credit reporting laws. **Entries include:**
Name, address, phone, affiliation. **Arrangement:** Alphabetical.
Indexes: Geographical. **Pages (approx.):** 35. **Frequency:**
Annual, winter. **Editor:** Clifford M. Brownstein. **Price:** Available
to members only.

American Society of Association Executives—
Convention & Exposition Managers Section Directory
See Who's Who in Association Management **(8281)**

American Society of Association Executives—Directory
See Who's Who in Association Management **(8281)**

★7625★
AMERICAN SOCIETY OF JOURNALISTS AND
AUTHORS—DIRECTORY
American Society of Journalists and Authors
1501 Broadway, Suite 1907
New York, NY 10036   Phone: (212)997-0947
Covers: Over 750 member freelance nonfiction writers.
Entries include: Writer's name, home and office addresses
and phone numbers, specialties, areas of expertise; name,
address, and phone of agent; memberships; books; periodicals
to which contributed; awards; employment history.
Arrangement: Alphabetical. **Indexes:** Subject specialty, type
of material written, geographical. **Pages (approx.):** 90.
Frequency: Biennial, October/November of even years.
Former title(s): Society of Magazine Writers - Directory of
Professional Writers (1975); American Society of Journalists

and Authors - Directory of Professional Writers. **Price:** $50.0
Other formats: Mailing labels.

★7626★
AMERICA'S HIDDEN PHILANTHROPIC WEALTH:
TOMORROW'S POTENTIAL FOUNDATION GIANTS
Taft Group
5130 MacArthur Boulevard, N.W.
Washington, DC 20016   Phone: (202)966-708(
Covers: 300 small family foundations with the potential t
become billion dollar philanthropies. Published in four loos
leaf editions covering 75 foundations each. **Entries inclu**
Foundation name, location, analysis of wealth, philanthr
interests, study of the conditions leading to expansion
future giving interests, biography, giving history, ir
relationship information. **Indexes:** Individuals are alphab
foundations are geographical; grants are by cat
Frequency: Annual; suspended indefinitely. **Price:**
each edition, postpaid; $197.00 per set.

★7627★
AMERICA'S NEWEST FOUNDATIONS: THE
SOURCEBOOK ON RECENTLY CREATED
PHILANTHROPIES
Taft Group
5130 MacArthur Boulevard, N. W.
Washington, DC 20016   Phone: (202)966-
Covers: Over 500 foundations created since 1980 that prov
grants to charitable organizations. **Entries include:** Foundati
name, address, phone, name and title of contact, curre
charitable and geographic preference, previous recipient an
grant types, assets. **Arrangement:** Alphabetical. **Indexes:**
Personal name, type of grant, giving interest, recipient location.
Frequency: Annual, February. **Editor:** Ben Lord. **Price:** $89.95.
Other information: Former publisher, Public Service Materials
Center.

★7628★
ANIMAL ORGANIZATIONS & SERVICES DIRECTORY
Animal Stories
16787 Beach Boulevard
Huntington Beach, CA 92647
Covers: Over 400 national and state organizations involv
animal protection and welfare; also lists veterinary and m
organizations such as clinics, pet insurance comp
zoological societies, pet transporting and other service
fancier clubs, consultants, and publishers of magazine:
newsletters concerned with animals. **Entries include:** Nai
organization, address, phone, branch offices, year establis
key personnel, membership information, objectives, descrip
of materials available by mail. **Arrangement:** Classified by t
of organization or service. **Indexes:** Alphabetical. **Pag**
(approx.): 230. **Frequency:** Biennial, fall of odd years. **Edito**
Kathleen A. Reece. **Advertising accepted.** Circulation 5,00(
Price: $16.95, plus $1.50 shipping.

Annotated Directory of Exemplary Family Based
Programs *See* Annotated Directory of Selected
Family-Based Service Programs **(7629)**

★7629★
ANNOTATED DIRECTORY OF SELECTED FAMILY-
BASED SERVICE PROGRAMS
National Resource Center on Family Based Services
Oakdale Hall, Room N240
University of Iowa
Iowa City, IA 52319   Phone: (319)335-4
Covers: 275 social service programs nationwide involving
family-centered services and operating out of public
voluntary agencies. **Entries include:** Name, address, pho

**Source: *1993 Directory of Country Environmental Studies*
(WRI Publications)**

An annotated bibliography of 350 environmental assessments of the developing world. Data include assessments of 130 countries with studies covering topics such as biological diversity, land use, forestry, food and agriculture, population and health, pollution, and more.

 **Source: *World Directory of Environmental Organizations*
(California Institute of Public Affairs)**

Covering more than 2,600 organizations in over 200 countries, this directory provides detailed descriptions and contact information for key national governmental and non-governmental organizations. In addition to the listings, this directory has a number of extra features, including a timeline, glossary, "who's doing what" analysis, description of U.N. programs, and more. The book is a cooperative project of The California Institute of Public Affairs, the Sierra Club, and the International Union for Conservation of Nature and Natural Resources.

These two sources can be helpful to anyone researching environmental issues and needs a place to start looking for data. Other places to find good environmental reference sources would be *Directories in Print, The Encyclopedia of Associations*, and *Research Centers Directory*. Also, the publisher of these three guidebooks (Gale Research, Detroit, MI) lists several environmental reference directories in its catalog.

 Source: *Research Centers Directory* (Gale Research Company)

An annual directory of 13,000 university, government, and other nonprofit research organizations. Major subjects span agriculture, business, education, government, law, math, social sciences, and humanities. You'll find this guide in university and other academically oriented libraries.

The *Research Centers Directory* provides a wealth of information on who's conducting research on what subjects around the country. You'll find an incredible diversity of studies being conducted. Some examples of the research organizations listed in this directory: the Alcohol Research Group, the National Bureau of Economic Research, the International Copper Research Association, the Birth Defects Institute, the Center for Russian and East European Studies . . . you get the idea.

I recently used this guide when I was researching the topic of "rebuilding rather than replacing automobiles." By checking the directory, I found a research institute associated with a university in Detroit that was conducting a study on just that topic.

The directory is easy to use. You just look up your subject, and the directory refers you to a particular research center. It provides the center's name, a contact person, the address, the phone number, a description of the activities conducted, and the organization's publications.

 Source: *Foundation Directory* (Foundation Center)

The *Foundation Directory,* published by the Foundation Center, is a guide that can help you find the right foundation to apply to in order to obtain funding and grants. Many libraries have it.

This guide is only one of many directories and publications published by the Foundation Center. The Foundation Center maintains information on over 27,000 active foundations and supports a national network of 170 library reference collections made available for free public use. The biggest collections are located in New York City, Washington, D.C., Cleveland, and San Francisco. These libraries provide important reference tools, such as sample application forms and the annual reports, tax information, and publications of foundations.

The center publishes a variety of helpful information sources, including specialized directories that tell you where to get grants for projects that cover subjects like public health, the aged, minorities, museums, and so on. For more information on the Foundation Center's publications and to locate a foundation library collection near you, contact: The Foundation Center, 79 Fifth Avenue, New York, NY 10003; 212-620-4230.

n 2 — Biological Sciences, Conservation, Ecology   Entry 986

ment grants, and foundations. Staff: 2 research professionals, 8 supporting professionals, 2 technicians, 1 other.

Research Activities and Fields: tress effects on natural ecosystems, integrated pest management, acid rain, solar energy, and behavioral, agricultural, community, and population ecology. Maintains 16 quarter-acre animal enclosures, aviaries, and a database on precipitation chemistry. Offers field ecology courses.

Publications and Services: Research results published in scientific journals. Provides graduate and undergraduate training.

★983★
MIAMI UNIVERSITY
INSECT COLLECTION
Department of Zoology   Phone: (513) 529-5454
Oxford, OH 45056   Founded: 1910
Dr. D.L. Deonier, Curator

Governance: Integral unit of Department of Zoology at Miami University. Supported by parent institution. Staff: 2 research professionals, 2-5 supporting professionals, 1 technician, 1 other.

Research Activities and Fields: Systematics, behavior, and ecology of aquatic insects, primarily Diptera, Ephydridae, and Chironomidae. Maintains an extensive collection of shore flies and rearing facilities for aquatic insects.

Publications and Services: Research results published in professional journals and published symposia. Maintains a library on entomology; Marian Winner, librarian.

★984★
MIAMI UNIVERSITY
INSTITUTE OF ENVIRONMENTAL SCIENCES
Oxford, OH 45056   Phone: (513) 529-5811
Gene E. Willeke, Director   Founded: 1969

Governance: Integral unit of Miami University. Supported by parent institution, U.S. government, and local governmental agencies. Staff: 3 research professionals, 1 supporting professional, 1 other.

Research Activities and Fields: Environmental sciences, including studies on river restoration techniques, hazardous and toxic substances, acid precipitation, environmental history, ecological dynamics, conservation, land use planning, water quality, community environmental planning, and energy. Produces environmental media, especially tape and slide programs. Offers a master's degree in environmental sciences.

Publications and Services: Research results published in scientific and technical journals and project reports. Maintains a library.

★985★
MIAMI UNIVERSITY
RT A. HEFNER ZOOLOGY ----

Left margin fragments:
54-2955

ported by
profession-

tudies and
ed species,
Mountains.
on, factors
ces. Main-
he Ozark

rofessional
on at the

76-5772

phis State
taff of the

ield work
rveys and

: journals.

TORY
37-5771

gricultur-
ota State
essionals,
; scholar.

, animal
ants and
tics, and

**Source: *National Directory of Nonprofit Organizations*
(Taft Group)**

Data on over 140,000 nonprofit organizations. Directory provides addresses, phone numbers, annual income, IRS status, and activities.

Included in this interesting directory are organizations such as hospitals, museums, conservation organizations, alumni organizations, and many other types of nonprofits.

 Congressional Information Service Indexes

Check university or large public libraries for any of the following comprehensive statistical directories published by the Congressional Information Service: ***American Statistics Index,*** for sources of government statistics; ***Index to International Statistics,*** for sources of foreign statistics; ***Statistical Reference Index,*** for sources of U.S. nongovernment statistics.

Together these guides index more than 1,600 sources of statistical information.

 Source: The Yellow Pages

Don't forget this familiar resource. You can use the yellow pages to find manufacturers, dealers, and all types of service firms. It is a great and underestimated source of information! Large libraries have the yellow pages of most of the bigger cities, and you can use these listings to supplement what you get out of *Thomas Register* (see page 28). The Manhattan yellow pages alone constitute an immense source of information on products and services. (Large libraries usually have the white pages of the major cities too.)

TIP: What do you do if you need international phone directories?
- Most large libraries contain a selection of white and yellow pages from major cities around the world. But if you don't see the region you want, you can call an organization based in New York City called Worldwide Books, which specializes in locating and obtaining phone books from around the world. Their toll-free phone number is 800-792-2665.

CD-ROMs IN LIBRARIES

One of the most powerful and valuable offerings at today's public and academic libraries is computer terminals equipped with CD-ROM disks and drives. CD-ROMs look similar to audio CDs, and, like them, contain codes created by lasers. The key difference between the two, though, is that the CDs you use in your stereo play music, while the CD-ROM databases in a library contain and "play" information. The storage capacity of a CD-ROM is enormous: about 550 MB, or the equivalent of about 250,000 pages!

The information that you may find in a CD-ROM disk varies enormously. For example, there are CD-ROMs today that contain abstracts of articles published in hundreds of popular newspapers and magazines; the full text of articles from business and trade periodicals, excerpts from U.S. government reports, scholarly literature in psychology, company financial filings, and so on.

The nice thing about library CD-ROMs is not only are they free, but you don't need to be a computer expert to use them. They are designed to be fairly simple to search, and, to a large degree, self-explanatory. Typically, to search any library CD-ROM database you'd follow these basic steps (simplified here for clarity):

- Choose the appropriate database
  When you sit down at a CD-ROM terminal, the computer screen typically displays the title of the CD-ROM database currently "ready" to be searched. You can choose to search that particular database or (if the system allows) hit a key to view other available CD-ROM titles. You may also be able to hit another key to read a description of the various databases available. Or, there may be print literature next to the terminal that describes each of them. In any case, the first step is to make sure that you've selected a CD-ROM that is relevant to your information search.

- Decide on a search method
  You may be given a choice as to the the *kind* of search you can perform. Typically, this includes either choosing an option to "browse" an already created list of subject terms, or to enter your own "key

words" to try and match items contained in the database. (A fuller discussion of "key word" database searching can be found in Chapter 5.)

- Search the database
  If you choose to browse subject terms, you then scan through an alpha-betical list of already created index terms and "mark" one or more terms that seem most relevant. If you choose to enter key words, you simply type in the word or words. In either case, the system then checks the database and informs you how many items (e.g., article abstracts, report titles, or whatever else the particular CD-ROM contains) were matched to your search.

- View results
  After you find out how many items matched your search, you then normally can "view" a display listing those items. So, for example, say you were searching a newspaper abstract database for articles on the country of Borneo, and the system located twelve items. You could then view those abstracts, one at a time. Normally, you can also print out those items on an attached printer.

  If you need additional background on databases and computer searching, take a look at Chapter 5, which deals with this subject in detail.

TIP: Don't get CD-ROM database terminals confused with a library's "online catalog."
- While both workstations may appear alike, an online catalog contains only information on the *holdings* of the particular library you're working at. A full CD-ROM workstation, however, contains disks that include bibliographies, abstracts, or the full text of articles and/ or reports from many sources, not necessarily just those found in that library.

Systems Available

What kind of CD-ROMs are available at libraries, and how do they differ? Although today there are several major vendors of CD-ROM systems that you might encounter, only a few are truly widespread, and we'll examine those here:

InfoTrak

InfoTrak is the brand name of a series of CD-ROMs produced by a firm called Information Access Company of Foster City, California. That firm pioneered the placement of consumer-oriented CD-ROMs in public libraries with the introduction of its computerized indexing systems in 1986. Today, you may find any or all of these specific InfoTrak products at a public or academic library:

- Academic Index
  Indexes approximately 400 scholarly and general-interest journals, including substantial abstracts for most titles. Also provides 6 months coverage of the *New York Times*.

- Business Index
  Abstracts 700–850 journals, plus *The Wall Street Journal, The New York Times, The Asian Wall Street Journal,* and *The Financial Times of Canada*.

- General Periodicals Index
  Indexes and abstracts 1,100 business and general-interest periodicals, as well as *The New York Times, The Wall Street Journal,* and the *Christian Science Monitor*.

- Government Publications Index
  An index to the monthly catalog of the government printing office.

- Health Index
  An index to over 160 core publications on health, fitness, nutrition, and medicine.

- Health Reference Center
  Provides the full text of 150 titles on health, fitness, nutrition, and medical issues. Includes 100 consumer-oriented magazines and 500 medical educational pamphlets.

- Investext
  Indexing and the full text of company and industry research reports prepared by over 60 leading Wall Street firms, as well as regional and international brokerage and financial firms.

- LegalTrac
  An index to over 800 legal publications. Sources include all major law reviews, 7 legal newspapers, law specialty publications, and bar association journals.

- Magazine Index Plus
  Indexes 400 general-interest magazines most frequently found in public libraries, plus the current two months of *The New York Times* and *The Wall Street Journal.*

- Magazine ASAP Plus
  Provides the full text of articles found in 100 titles selected from Magazine Index Plus.

- National Newspaper Index
  Indexes 5 national newspapers combined in one source. Covers indexing of *The New York Times, The Wall Street Journal, Christian Science Monitor, Washington Post, Los Angeles Times.*

Note how the CD-ROMs differ not only in the subjects they cover, but also in their *level* of coverage, i.e., indexing, abstracts, or full text. Indexed databases only provide the most basic bibliographic data (e.g., title, author, date, name of source, page number) so you can track down the original source yourself. Abstracts give you a short summary of the original piece, which may run as short as a few lines or as much as a couple of paragraphs. This may or may not be enough information to satisfy you. Finally, full-text databases provide the complete text of the original item. In those cases, you normally then have no need to obtain the original item.

University Microfilms

University Microfilms Inc., or UMI (Ann Arbor, Michigan), with its "ProQuest" system is another major provider of CD-ROMs in libraries. Here is a list of some of its most popular databases:

- ABI/INFORM
  Provides 150 word abstracts from articles published in major leading business periodicals.

- Business Dateline
  Provides the full text of articles from 350 regional business journals.

- Newspaper Abstracts
  Provides indexing (and brief abstracts) for 8 major national newspapers: *The New York Times, The Atlanta Constitution, The Boston Globe, Chicago Tribune, Christian Science Monitor, Los Angeles Times, The Wall Street Journal,* and *The Washington Post.*

- Newspapers Fulltext
This database provides the full text of *American Banker, Atlanta Constitution and Atlanta Journal, Christian Science Monitor, The New York Times, San Francisco Chronicle, USA Today, The Wall Street Journal,* and *The Washington Post.*

- *New York Times* Ondisc
Provides the full text of articles printed in *The New York Times.* Updated monthly.

- Periodical Abstracts
Abstracts hundreds of popular magazine articles.

InfoTrak and ProQuest are not the only CD-ROM systems you may encounter in a library. Other major vendors include H. W. Wilson and SilverPlatter.

Search Tips

Although, as mentioned earlier, it is not all that difficult to search a library CD-ROM, it's still true that conducting a *good* search is something of both an art and a science. If you are inexperienced in performing searches, you may be disappointed in your results. If you're not sure what you are doing, your search may turn up irrelevant results, too many, or none at all. Here are a few basic tips and techniques you can follow to help your CD-ROM searches go smoothly and efficiently.

- Always make sure that the CD-ROM you are searching contains the type of information you are seeking! While it seems obvious that you wouldn't pick up a book titled *Consumer's Guide to Healthy Living* if you were researching facts on the furniture industry, it's easy to mistake one CD-ROM for another, since they don't as prominently display their contents in as familiar a fashion. Note the name of the specific CD-ROM you are searching, and if you have the opportunity, read (in print or on screen) a description of the database.

- Find out how far back in time the CD-ROM's coverage extends. CD-ROM database "backfiles" vary widely: some go back five years, while others include data for only one year. Obviously, if you are searching for reports on an incident that occurred three years ago in a CD-ROM whose backfile is only one year, you're not going to find much!

- Find out how timely the CD-ROM is, and determine whether it is timely enough for your purposes. A CD-ROM's timeliness is usually measured by its "update frequency." Most vendors update their products on a monthly basis; however, some update theirs more or less frequently.

Update frequency is not as straightforward as it sounds, and can be misleading. For example, say you were searching a newspaper article database in late June, and the CD-ROM vendor claimed a monthly update frequency. What would be the *most recent* date of an article that you would expect to be able find in that database?

The answer depends on many factors. Let's look at a worst case—but not at all atypical—scenario. Say that the vendor updates its file at the beginning of every month. That means that the last update sent to the library would have been in early June. Clearly, then, you're not going to find any articles published during June. But just because the library received an update in June doesn't mean that that disk necessarily will contain articles through the end of May. There is a "lag-time" that database vendors work with, which reflects the time it takes them to get data from the original sources keyed into the CD-ROM. So a disk received at a library in early June may still not have articles from, say, the last two weeks of May.

Adding potential further delays is the fact that sometimes, a workstation hasn't even been loaded with the latest version of a CD-ROM. This can occur for a number of reasons, such as the library not receiving it on time, or simply that the librarians have been too busy to getting around to loading it. I have had several experiences of sitting down at a CD-ROM terminal to discover that it had been two months or more since an updated disk was installed.

The lesson here is simply this: find out the date of the last reload of the CD-ROM, and take that into account accordingly. Often the reload date is displayed on the initial screen display when you first "open" the CD-ROM. If you don't find it there, you might ask a nearby librarian if he or she knows. If you still can't get an answer, you can "test" the CD-ROM by searching for occurrences of articles on some recent event.

Since CD-ROM timeliness is inherently limited, what do you do if you need the *very latest* information on a subject? Don't rely on CD-ROMs! You'll need to supplement your research with more timely sources: either by going "online" and searching databases updated on a weekly or daily basis (see Chapter 5 for more on this) or by doing your research the "old fashioned" way, by poring through the most recent print copies of the newspapers, journals, etc., that are relevant to your research!

- Plan your search "strategy." While there's nothing wrong with "playing" around on a CD-ROM system and experimenting with different key words and search terms, a little foresight and planning is likely to pay off with superior results. Take a few moments and, with a pen and pad, write a couple of sentences that best describe what you are searching for. Isolate the most critical ("key") words in those sentences and use them to create your search. If you need help doing this, ask a nearby librarian for assistance. Most have become something of an expert at database searching, and one of their main jobs is to help people like you use these systems efficiently. Librarians are very helpful people, and you are paying for them—so use their services!

- Practice, practice, practice. The more you do CD-ROM searching, the better you'll get. These amazing devices are free—so search to your heart's content and improve your skills!

What if the library you use doesn't have any CD-ROMs? Well, then they're behind the times! Your best bet then is to find the *largest* library in your area, as the bigger ones usually have the most electronic resources. If there is a college or university library nearby, it will almost certainly have several CD-ROMs available for searching.

2

Selected Supersources

The Cream of the Crop

QUICKFINDER: SELECTED SUPERSOURCES

The resources described in this chapter are the cream of the information-source crop. They range from museums to the federal government to bookstores to other storehouses of information, but they all have a few things in common. Each contains information on an enormous scope of subjects. Each can easily be tapped for answers and advice. And each provides answers for no charge or dirt cheap.

✔ Source: Associations

Perhaps the single best resource discussed in this book, associations offer a bountiful harvest of information. They are staffed by knowledgeable and helpful people whose job is to provide information about their field to those who need it.

There are thousands of associations, one for nearly every conceivable purpose and field of interest: the Chocolate Manufacturers Association of the U.S.A., the International Barbed Wire Collectors Association, the Laughter Therapy Association, the American Association for Career Education, the Committee to Abolish Legal Sized Files, the Tin Research Institute, even the Flying Funeral Directors of America—for funeral directors who own and operate their own planes. And naturally there is the Star Trek Welcommittee—an association whose reason for being is to answer fans' questions about the "Star Trek" TV series.

Associations have helped me out more times than I can remember. A couple of occasions stand out: One time I needed to find out the "average life of a flag." Well, naturally a group called the North American Vexillological (a fancy word for the study of flags!) Association had the answer. (Flag life depends on the material and height flown.) Another time, a city agency was seeking advice on how to stop the local water pipes from leaking. To the rescue with an answer was the American Water Works Association, of Denver, Colorado.

Associations can also be a quick source of industry statistics and news. For example, if you want to find out how the sales of potatoes were last year, you need only inquire of the Potato Association of America or, if you prefer, the National Potato Promotion Board.

How to Find:

To find the name of an association that deals with your area of interest, call or write to the American Society of Association Executives (an association of associations!) at 1575 Eye Street, NW, Washington, DC 20005; 202-626-2723, and it will help identify the right one for you. Or look up your subject in the priceless *Encyclopedia of Associations*, published by Gale. Nearly all libraries have it. (Gale publishes companion volumes on international organizations, as well as local and regional associations.)

Often, the *Encyclopedia of Associations* lists more than one association that sounds promising. In such cases, try contacting the largest one first, as it will most likely have the most resources to help you. To compare the size of different associations, examine the published data on the size of the association's staff and the number of members. Many libraries often contain the companion volumes to the *Encyclopedia of Associations: International Associations* and *State and Regional Associations*.

Unlocking the Information Vault

annual; (3) IFTF Perspectives (newsletter), irregular; also publishes papers and research reports.

★5851★ WORLD FUTURE SOCIETY (WFS)
4916 St. Elmo Ave.   Phone: (301) 656-8274
Bethesda, MD 20814   Edward S. Cornish, Pres.
Founded: 1966. **Members:** 30,000. **Staff:** 20. **Local Groups:** 80.
Individuals interested in forecasts and ideas about the future. Formed "to contribute to a reasoned awareness of the future and the importance of its study, without advocating particular ideologies or engaging in political activities; to advance responsible and serious investigation of the future and to promote development of methods for the study of the future; to facilitate communication among groups and individuals interested in studying or planning for the future." Is developing services for professional forecasters and planners, including a register, special studies sections, and professional activities. Offers chapter activities in various U.S. cities as well as in Toronto, ON, Canada and London, England; sponsors book service; maintains library; offers specialized education service. **Publications:** (1) Future Survey, monthly; (2) The Futurist, bimonthly; (3) Futures Research Quarterly; also publishes books and Resource Catalog. **Convention/Meeting:** biennial - 1985 Aug. 8-9, Washington, DC.

★5852★ WORLD FUTURES STUDIES FEDERATION (WFSF)
2424 Maile Way, Office 720
University of Hawaii   Phone: (808) 948-6601
Honolulu, HI 96822   James A. Dator, Sec.Gen.
Founded: 1973. **Members:** 521. Institutions, scholars, policymakers, and individuals involved in futures studies. Promotes futures studies and innovative interdisciplinary analyses. Serves as a forum for the exchange of information and opinions through national and international research projects. Conducts regional colloquia and seminars. Maintains extensive collection of correspondence, monographs, serials, audiovisual materials, and books on social, political, economic, and environmental futures-related topics. **Publications:** (1) Newsletter, quarterly; (2) World Conference Proceedings, biennial; also publishes seminar papers. **Convention/Meeting:** biennial - next 1986.

★5853★ AMERICAN SOCIETY OF GAS ENGINEERS (ASGE)
P.O. Box 936   Phone: (312) 532-5707
Tinley Park, IL 60477   Charles R. Kendall, Exec.Dir.
Founded: 1954. **Members:** 600. **Local Groups:** 10. Professional society of engineers in the field of gas appliances and equipment. **Publications:** (1) Digest, quarterly; (2) Membership Directory, annual. **Formerly:** (1975) Gas Appliance Engineers Society. **Convention/Meeting:** annual technical conference.

INSTITUTE OF GAS TECHNOLOGY
See Index

★5854★ AMERICAN GENETIC ASSOCIATION (Genetics) (AGA)

Urbana, IL.

★5857★ NATIONA'
(NCGR)
2855 Telegraph Ave
Berkeley, CA 94705
Founded: 1980. St
and professional org
conservation and u:
resource conserva
information, techni
diversity of geneti
microorganisms requ
the problems, issues
use of genetic resou
continues, the U.S.
quality of life due
pharmaceutical and
including the producti
to initiate statewide
publish newsletter.
Committees: Adviso
Resources; Douglas-
Programs: California

TOMATO GENETICS
See Index

★5858★ U.S. AN
P.O. Box 15426
San Francisco, CA 9
Founded: 1972. S
the encouragemen
documentation sta
distinctive genetic
and cell samples
nitrogen. Offers
18,000 volume l
Review. Publicat
Register, quarterly

GEOCHEMISTRY
See Geoscience

★5859★ AMERIC
156 Fifth Ave., Suit
New York, NY 10.01
Founded: 1852.
educators, and oth
research in geograp
sponsored research

> **TIP:** Sometimes associations produce reports and studies that are of interest to researchers. However, these can be expensive to purchase, and you may only need a single statistic or data from just a portion of the study. Try contacting either the association's library or, if the association publishes a magazine, the publication's editor. Sometimes the staffers at those departments won't mind finding the report and reading you the significant information you need. (Staff in marketing or publications-ordering departments may only agree to sell you the entire study.)

✔ Source: Conventions

Every day, hundreds of conventions and professional conferences are held around the country—the National Accounting Expo, the American Academy of Sports Physicians, the Beekeepers Convention, and the Nuclear Power Expo, to name a few. Conventions are especially good sources of information on fast-changing subjects, like computer technology. The seminars and talks presented at these conventions reflect the state of the art in a profession or field. Often brand-new products are displayed and ground-breaking research is presented.

How to Find:

Consult the *Directory of Conventions* (Successful Meetings, New York City)—found at large libraries. Or check an "upcoming events" column in a relevant trade publication. (I recently found the convention I needed on computer printers by consulting a popular computer magazine's "events to watch" column.) Another way to find a convention on your subject is to find an association. Nearly all associations hold conventions.

Typically, two major activities take place at such conventions: technical presentations by authorities in the field and product exhibits by vendors who set up booths to try and sell their wares to the conference attendees. Although it is often inexpensive or free to visit the exhibition hall, it may run into the hundreds of dollars to sign up for the technical information sessions. However, there *is* a way you can tap into the information presented there *without* actually attending.

Here is the secret to tapping into convention information. If you find one that interests you, write and request a free "preliminary program." These programs typically describe the technical seminars to be held at the convention and provide the names and affiliations of the speakers or panelists. These speakers are *excellent* people to speak with to obtain information.

Here's an example of how I utilized this strategy. Once I had to research the subject of asbestos removal from school building insulation. I discovered that a convention of school administrators was being held the following month in Texas. Although I could not attend the convention, I wrote away for the preliminary program. Inside the program, I spotted a description of a planned technical session on asbestos removal. The description included the name of the speaker and the name of his school district. It was then an easy matter to contact that person to set up an information interview. I was then able to obtain his expertise and information for free instead of paying hundreds of dollars to hear him speak.

It's worth noting that programs from *past* conventions as well as for upcoming ones are often available.

Another way to obtain convention information without actually attending is to request a "conference proceedings," a transcript of the technical sessions published after the conference is over. Conference proceedings vary in cost and occasionally are expensive. Sometimes tape recordings of the technical sessions are available too.

If you are interested in actually attending a conference in your area, call your city's convention and visitors bureau or the chamber of commerce. They should be able to provide you with a list of upcoming conventions.

✔ Source: Scientists' Institute for Public Information

If you have a scientific question for which you need to get a quick answer, the Media Resource Center at the Scientists' Institute for Public Information may be able to help you. The center can handle just about any scientific inquiry—from toxic wastes to cancer treatments. They've even answered the question as to whether it really is ever hot enough to fry an egg on the sidewalk! (It *is* possible—depending not only on the temperature but the construction of the sidewalk.) Although the center is designed to serve journalists, the staff will help other researchers as well.

How to Find:

Call the center toll-free at 800-223-1730; in New York, call 212-661-9110.

 Source: New York Public Library

The New York Public Library is a tremendous source of all kinds of information. The library's **mid-Manhattan branch** is especially rich in information and regularly answers reference inquiries from around the country. Its collections include the fields of art, business, education, history, literature and language, and science. In addition, it contains an extensive picture collection. Other specialties of the New York Public Library include the Schomburg Center for Research in Black Culture, the Early Childhood Resource and Information Center, and the Job Information Center. There is also the **Performing Arts Research Center,** which answers written or phone inquiries regarding music, dance, and theater at no charge. (Because the New York Public Library handles so many requests, you may have to be patient if you telephone and get a busy signal.)

How to Find:

Contact the mid-Manhattan branch at 455 Fifth Avenue, New York, NY 10016; 212-340-0849. Contact the Performing Arts Research Center at the New York Public Library, 111 Amsterdam Avenue, New York, NY 10023; free reference numbers are as follows: dance, 212-870-1657; music, 212-870-1650; theater, 212-870-1639. For other questions contact the library's public relations office at 8 West 40th Street, New York, NY 10018; 212-221-7676.

Pages 54 through 64 list some of the best and most widely used government information sources. Be sure to read through chapter 3 for details on many more resources available from various federal agencies.

☑ **Source: Library of Congress**

The U.S. Library of Congress in Washington, D.C., is the largest library in the world. Its collection includes 20 million volumes and pamphlets, over a million technical reports, 3.5 million maps, 34 million manuscripts, and 8.5 million photographs, negatives, prints, and slides. The library is also known for its collection of rare books and foreign publications. It sometimes can be tricky to use the Library of Congress' vast resources; not only because there is so much information available, but also because the Library's policy discourages phone reference usage by the public when materials are available on a more local level. However, it will assist users when it can help in researching topics unique to the Library. Some of these areas include copyright, legislative research, and international law.

One division that may be of help is the library's Telephone Reference Service. If the librarian has time, he or she will try to locate any obscure facts or information you have been unable to find elsewhere, and may be located at the Library of Congress.

How to Find:

You can contact the library's Telephone Reference Service at the Correspondence Section of the Library of Congress, Washington, DC 20540; 202-707-5522.

Another excellent resource is the Library of Congress's photo-duplication service. The service will search the library's books, technical reports, maps, manuscripts, and photographic materials to find what you need, and send you photocopies. Turn-around time can run to 4 to 6 weeks, but you can't beat the price —you pay only for photocopying, copyright fees, and postage ($10 minimum charge).

How to Find:

Contact the Library of Congress, Photoduplication Service, Washington, DC 20540; 202-707-5640.

A very useful and interesting publication series of the Library of Congress is its *LC Science Tracer Bullets*. These are twelve- to sixteen-page pamphlets covering popular science-oriented topics that identify key information sources, such as introductory textbooks, general books, conference proceedings, government publications, journals, articles, technical books, associations, and more. Subjects have included: *Japanese Technology, Inventions and Inventors; The History of Technology;* and *Fiber Optics.*

How to Find:

Contact the Library of Congress, Science Reference Section, Science and Technology Division, 10 First Street SE, Washington, DC 20540; 202-707-5639.

Finally, there is the Library of Congress's Performing Arts Library. The Library will try to answer, at no cost, any question regarding the performing arts—dance, music, theater, motion pictures, broadcasting, puppetry, circus, costuming, stage sets, and arts management and administration.

How to Find:

Contact the Performing Arts Library, JFK Center for the Performing Arts, Washington, DC 20566; 202-707-6245.

You can keep up with some of the Library of Congress' publishing activities by obtaining a catalog called *New from CDS,* which is the Library of Congress' Cataloging Distribution Service.

How to Find:

Contact the Library of Congress, Cataloging Distribution Service, Washington, DC 20541; 202-707-6100.

TIP: England's equivalent to the Library of Congress is the British Library, with millions of documents ranging from books and maps to worldwide conference proceedings to sheet music from around the globe. The time-span of coverage ranges from the first items printed with movable type before 1501 to the present. Much of this invaluable material is available online or through an inter-country lending system. This is truly one of the world's great depositories of information.

Contact the British Library Document Supply Centre, Boston Spa, Wetherby, West Yorkshire, LS23 7BQ, United Kingdom. Phone: 44-937-546049; fax: 44-937-546236.

✔️ Source: Government Printing Office (GPO)

The U.S. government is the largest publisher in the world. A mind-boggling amount of information pours out of Washington, D.C., daily. Tens of thousands of books, pamphlets, and magazines are published each year by federal departments and agencies. Topics span nearly all areas of human endeavor—from starting a business to finding a mortgage to getting rid of acne. Documents are typically concise and very readable, and they are specifically aimed at the general, nontechnical public. They are prepared by experts in the various federal departments and agencies whose job is to keep the public informed. Best of all, the information is free or dirt cheap. The only caution in using these documents is to check the issue dates. Although many documents are timely and up to date, sometimes older ones are offered too.

There are a number of ways to dig out the publications on your subject of interest. One way is to contact a specific department directly. The following chapter lists many of the information specialties of the departments and provides addresses and phone numbers.

A typical approach to finding government documents available from the GPO is through consulting *The Monthly Catalog of U.S. Government Publications*. Use the subject index in the back of each volume to identify published literature on your topic of interest. Each listing provides helpful information such as the office that issued the document, the price, and ordering instructions. You can obtain monthly catalogs directly from the Superintendent of Documents or at a medium- or large-size library.

A simpler and quicker way to find publications directly available from the GPO is to order its *Subject Bibliography Index*. The index is a listing of 240 major subject categories for which specific catalogs of bibliographies have been created. The index represents over 15,000 different pamphlets, booklets, guides, and periodicals. You circle which bibliography you'd like to get and send in the form, and the information is then sent to you, along with price information.

How to Find:

Contact the Superintendent of Documents, U.S. Government Printing Office, Washington, DC 20402; 202-783-3238. The GPO takes MasterCard or Visa telephone orders and checks payable to: Superintendent of Documents, Government Printing Office.

TIPS: Government Depository Libraries and Bookstores

- There are 1,400 designated libraries around the United States that are legally required to store government documents and provide the public with free access. Ask the Government Printing Office to send you a free "Government Depository Library" directory, which tells where these libraries are located, what kinds of documents they store, and how to use them.
- You can also ask for a listing of GPO bookstores, which are government bookstores located in most major cities. These carry the most popular of the government's published materials.

 Source: National Technical Information Service (NTIS)

The National Technical Information Service (NTIS) provides access to the results of both U.S. and foreign government-sponsored research and development (R&D) and engineering activities. This includes more than 60,000 summaries of U.S. and foreign government-sponsored R&D and engineering activities annually, complete technical reports, and access to software and databases produced by federal agencies.

A collection of more than a million technical reports on completed government research is made available. NTIS is the central source for the public sale of U.S. government-sponsored research and development and engineering reports, as well as foreign technical reports. Dozens of technical areas are covered, including aeronautics, biological sciences, energy, materials, and medicine. A couple of sample research reports: "General Aviation Aircraft Noise Problem: Some Suggested Solutions" and "World Trade in Fruits and Vegetables: Projections for an Enlarged European Community." Many reports are gathered from sources around the world. Some are expensive, but others are very moderately priced. Here is a sample of some of the different ways you can tap into this information:

■ NTIS publishes weekly newsletters that abstract its research summaries. These newsletters can be expensive, however.

■ NTIS makes available "Published Searches"—already completed computer searches of abstracts of technical reports in over 3,000 subject areas gathered from both NTIS sources as well as twenty-three other international sources. Searches usually yield 100 to 200 individual summaries for each topic.

■ NTIS's Center for the Utilization of Federal Technology (CUFT) keeps U.S. industry aware of government R&D and engineering efforts that have special potential or are at a breakthrough stage. Publications include: *Federal Technology Catalog*, containing more than 1,000 summaries of government technologies and resources in twenty-three subject fields, with full telephone or other contact sources for further information.

■ A superb guide is the *Directory of Federal Technology Resources*, which guides readers to hundreds of federal agencies, laboratories, and engineering centers willing to share their expertise, equipment—and sometimes even their facilities.

■ Many NTIS databases (a database is a collection of information on one particular subject, like energy or agriculture; see Chapter 5) are available on-line (through computers) from popular commercial database vendors. See Chapter 5 for more information on how to tap into these databases.

How to Find:

Contact the National Technical Information Service, Springfield, VA 22161; 703-487-4650. For a complete description of all of NTIS's print sources and computer databases, ask for the free publication *NTIS Products and Services Catalog*. Another catalog, titled *CD-ROMs & Optical Disks* lists the agency's CD-ROM products.

☑ **Source: Bureau of the Census**

Do you want to know which neighborhoods have the highest concentration of elderly people? How many men in Latin America own TV sets? Which sections of Wyoming are the wealthiest?

The U.S. Bureau of the Census can supply you with figures on these and countless other data-oriented questions. Major areas covered include agriculture, business, construction, foreign nations, foreign trade, geography, governments, housing, manufacturing, mineral industries, people, retail trade, service industries, and transportation.

You can obtain a listing of the names of subject data experts at the bureau and their phone numbers by ordering an especially useful and free pamphlet titled "Telephone Contacts for Data Users." This publication will tell you, for example, who the expert is for statistics on religion, or for foreign-owned U.S. firms.

How to Find:

Contact the User Training Branch, Data User Services Division, Bureau of the Census, Washington, DC 20233; 301-763-4100. Or call the Public Information Office at 301-763-4040.

Another excellent source is the *Census Catalog & Guide*. This is a clear and comprehensive 400-page book that lists and describes census products, services, and programs, and provides complete ordering information. A useful subject index and contents identify sources on topics including: agriculture, business, foreign trade, population, transportation, and much more. Remember—much of the Bureau of the Census's products and services are free or inexpensive. An excerpt from the 1989 catalog's list of sources for statistics within the federal government is on page 62.

How to Find:

Available from the Superintendent of Documents, U.S. Government Printing Office, Washington, DC 20402; 202-783-3238. Stock number 003-024-07009-0.

Finally, you should know that during the last few years the Bureau of the Census has been making quite an effort to transform much of its print data into low-priced electronic databases. Two excellent guides to these resources are a booklet called *Census, CD-ROM and You*, which lists and describes Census products on CD-ROM, and *CENDATA: The Census Bureau Online*, a non-technical manual that describes where one can find Census data online, what kind is available, and how to best use it. Contact the Data User Services division phone number, listed above.

Source: *Statistical Abstract of the United States*

The bible for statistics of all types is the *Statistical Abstract of the United States*, published annually. The kinds of statistical data you can find in this guide are extremely diverse—the number of eye operations performed, murder victims by weapons used, consumer price indexes, new business failure rates, retail sales of men's fragrances, pottery imports, railroad accidents, consumption of ice cream, and much more.

This book is the standard summary of statistics on the social, political, and economic organization of the United States. Major sections include: population; vital statistics; immigration and naturalization; health and nutrition; education; law enforcement; courts and prisons; geography and environment; parks and recreation; elections; state and local government finances and employment; federal government finances and employment; national defense; veterans' affairs; social insurance and human services; labor force, employment, and earnings; income expenditure and wealth; banking, finance, and insurance; business enterprise; communications; energy; science; transportation; agriculture; forests and forest products; fisheries; mining and mineral products; construction and housing; manufacturers; and comparative international statistics.

How to Find:

You can order this guide from the Superintendent of Documents, U.S. Government Printing Office, Washington, DC 20402, 202-783-3238, or you can find a copy at GPO bookstores and at nearly all libraries.

 Source: United States General Accounting Office (GAO)

The United States GAO is an independent, nonpolitical agency that serves as the investigative agency for Congress and carries out investigations and makes recommendations. The GAO publishes findings in reports and testimony transcripts that are available to the public for free. These reports cover fields such as education, health, housing, justice, defense, technology, and more. Recent reports have included: "Air Pollution: Uncertainty

Assistant Secretary for Public Affairs,* U.S. Dept. of Health and Human Services, Room 647-D, Humphrey Building, 200 Independence Avenue, S.W., Washington, D.C. 20201 Information: 202/245-1850. Locator: 202/245-6296

Administrator for Health Resources and Services, U.S. Dept. of Health and Human Services, 5600 Fishers Lane, Park Lawn Building 14-05, Rockville, MD 20857. Information: 301/443-2216. Publications: 301/443-2086

Alcohol, Drug Abuse, and Mental Health Administration, U.S. Dept. of Health and Human Services, 5600 Fishers Lane, Rm. 12C15, Rockville, MD 20857. Information/Publications: 301/443-3783. Alcohol: 301/443-4733. Drug Abuse: 301/443-6245. Mental Health: 301/443-4536 or 3600. Substance Abuse Prevention: 301/443-0373

Centers for Disease Control, U.S. Dept. of Health and Human Services, 1600 Clifton Road, N.E., Atlanta, GA 30329. Information: 404/639-3311. Public Affairs: 404/639-3286

Food and Drug Administration, U.S. Dept. of Health and Human Services, 5600 Fishers Lane, Rockville, MD 20857. Information: 301/443-2404. Publications: 301/443-3170

Health Care Financing Administration, U.S. Dept. of Health and Human Services, 330 Independence Avenue, S.W., Washington, D.C. 20201. Public Affairs: 202/245-6113. Publications: 301/597-2618

Health Resources and Services Administration U.S. Dept. of Health and Human Services, 5600 Fishers Lane, Rockville, MD 20857. Public Affairs: 301/443-2086

Indian Health Service, Office of Tribal Affairs, U.S. Dept. of Health and Human Services, 5600 Fishers Lane, Room 6A-07, Rockville, MD 20857. Director's Office: 301/443-1083

National Center for Health Statistics, U.S. Dept. of Health and Human Services, 3700 East-West Highway, Hyattsville, MD 20782. Information: 301/436-8500

National Institutes of Health, U.S. Dept. of Health and Human Services, 9000 Rockville Pike, Bethesda, MD 20892. Information/Publications: 301/496-4000

Office of the Surgeon General, Office of Communications, 725 H, U.S. Dept. of Health and Human Services, 200 Independence Avenue, S.W., Washington, D.C. 20201. Information: 202/245-6867

Public Health Service,* Office of Public Affairs, Office of the Assistant Secretary, U.S. Dept. of Health and Human Services, 200 Independence Avenue, S.W., Washington, D.C. 20201. Public Affairs: 202/245-6867

Social Security Administration, U.S. Dept. of Health and Human Services, Office of

Research and Statistics and International Policy, Room 912, Universal North Building, Publications: Room 209, 4301 Connecticut Avenue, N.W., Washington, D.C. 20008. Information/Publications: 202/282-7138

Housing

Assistant Secretary for Community Planning/Development, U.S. Dept. of Housing and Urban Development, 451 7th Street, S.W., Washington, D.C. 20410. Information: 202/755-6270

Assistant Secretary for Housing, U.S. Dept. of Housing and Urban Development, 451 7th Street, S.W., Washington, D.C. 20410. Information: 202/755-6600

Immigration

Immigration and Naturalization Service, U.S. Department of Justice, 425 I Street, N.W., Washington, D.C. 20536. Office of Information: 202/633-4316. Statistics Office: 202/633-3053

Income and Taxation

Internal Revenue Service, Statistics of Income Division, U.S. Dept. of Treasury, 1111 Constitution Avenue, N.W., Washington, D.C. 20224. Information/Publications: 202/376-0216

Office of the Secretary, Public Affairs Office, U.S. Dept. of the Treasury, Room 1500, 15th Street and Pennsylvania N.W., Washington, D.C. 20220. Information: 202/566-2041

Office of Tax Analysis, U.S. Dept. of the Treasury, Room 4217, 15th Street and Pennsylvania Avenue, N.W., Washington, D.C. 20220. Information: 202/566-5374. Publications: 202/566-5282

International

United Nations, D.C. 2 1628, Statistical Office, United Nations, New York, NY 10017. Information: 212/754-4562

Labor and Employment

Bureau of Labor Statistics,* U.S. Dept. of Labor, Washington, D.C. 20212. Information/Publications: 202/523-1221. Locator: 202/523-6666. Latest BLS data: 202/523-9658. CPI detail: 202/523-1239. PPI detail: 202/523-1765

Employment and Training Administration, Office of Public Affairs, U.S. Dept. of Labor, 200 Constitution Avenue, N.W., Room S2322, Washington, D.C. 20210. Information/Publications: 202/523-6871

Miscellaneous

Commission on Civil Rights, 1121 Vermont Avenue, N.W., Washington, D.C. 20425. Locator: 202/376-8177

Executive Office of the President, Office of Management and Budget, Washington, D.C. 20503. Information: 202/395-3000.

Public Affairs: 202/395-3080. Publications: 202/395-7332

National Archives and Records Administration, 7th and Pennsylvania Avenue, N.W., Washington, D.C. 20408. Information/Locator: 202/523-3218

National Technical Information Service, U.S. Dept. of Commerce, 5285 Port Royal Road, Springfield, VA 22161. Information/Orders: 703/487-4650

Science and Technology

National Oceanic and Atmospheric Administration, Office of Public Affairs, U.S. Dept. of Commerce, Room 6013, 14th and Constitution Avenue, N.W., Washington, D.C. 20230. Information/Publications: 202/377-8090

Energy Information Administration,* National Energy Information Center, EI-20, U.S. Dept. of Energy, 1000 Independence Avenue, S.W., Washington, D.C. 20585 General Information: 202/586-8800

Bureau of Mines, U.S. Dept. of the Interior, 4900 LaSalle Road, Avondale, MD 20782. Information: 301/436-7966

Office of Public Information, Bureau of Mines, U.S. Dept. of the Interior, 2401 E Street, N.W., Washington, D.C. 20241. Information: 202/634-1004

U.S. Geological Survey, Public Affairs Office U.S. Dept. of the Interior, 503 National Center, Reston, VA 22092. Information/Publications: 703/648-6892

National Science Foundation, Office of Legislative and Public Affairs, 1800 G Street, N.W., Washington, D.C. 20550. Information: 202/357-9498

Transportation

Federal Highway Administration, Office of Public Affairs, U.S. Dept. of Transportation, 400 7th Street, S.W., Room 4210, Washington, D.C. 20590. Information/Publications: 202/366-0660

Materials and Transportation Bureau, Information Services Division (BMT-11), Office of Operations/Enforcemen U.S. Dept. of Transportation, 400 7th Street, S.W., Washington, D.C. 20590 Information: 202/426-2301

National Highway Traffic Safety Administration, Office of Public Affair U.S. Dept. of Transportation, 400 7th Street, S.W., Washington, D.C. 20590. Information: 202/366-9550

Urban Mass Transportation Administration, Public Affairs Office, U.S. Dept. of Transportation, 400 7th Street, S.W., Room 9328, Washington, D.C. 20590. Information: 202/366-4040

Veterans

Veterans Administration, 810 Vermont Avenue, N.W., Washington, D.C. 20420. Information: 202/233-2563

Exists in Radon Measurements," "Hazardous Wastes: Contractors Should Be Accountable for Environmental Performance," "Failed Thrifts: The Resolution Trust Corporation's Working Capital Needs," "Medical Device Recalls: An Overview and Analysis 1983–1988," "In-Home Services for the Elderly," and "Non-Traditional Organized Crime."

How to Find:

Requests for copies of GAO reports and testimony are available from the U.S. General Accounting Office, P.O. Box 6015, Gaithersburg, MD 20877; 202-512-6000.

 Source: State Government

Your state government can be an excellent resource for a variety of topics. Subject expertise varies from state to state, but typically you can find information on most of these topics:

Aeronautics	Environment
Aging	Fish and game
Agriculture	Food
Air resources	Handicapped
Alcoholism	Hazardous materials
Archives	Health
Arts	Highways
Banking	Housing
Child labor	Labor
Child welfare	Land
Civil rights	Mental health
Commerce	Natural resources
Community affairs	Occupational safety
Consumer affairs	Parks and recreation
Criminal justice	Taxation
Disabled	Tourism
Disaster preparedness	Transportation
Drug abuse	Veterinary medicine
Economic opportunity	Water resources
Education	Women
Energy	

How to Find:

Consult a library copy of the *State Executive Directory,* published by Carroll Publishing Company. This guide provides a detailed listing of the various offices in each state and a listing of state personnel—names, titles, and phone numbers. A subject index makes it easy to locate who in your state can be of assistance to you. (This directory also lists state historic preservation offices and legislative reference numbers.) You'll find the directory at large libraries. Or check the name of the state in your phone book to find the division you need (in many cities, government listings are separated into a special blue-pages section).

TIP: Consumer and Legal Advice
▪ Your State Attorney General's Office can answer many questions about your legal rights as a citizen of your state. Typical questions handled by this office relate to subjects like tenant-landlord disputes, buying a car, mail-order fraud, investment fraud, and so forth. The expertise of this office varies from state to state. Check the blue pages in the phone book under "State Government" to locate the address and phone of your state's Attorney General.

✔ **Source: Colleges and University Faculty Experts**

College and university faculty members can provide information on topics ranging from architecture to international relations as well as other subjects taught at academic institutions. A computer database established in 1993 at the State University of New York (SUNY) in Stony Brook called ProfNet is a network of college public information officers located at over 300 campuses around the country. It was established to serve as a clearinghouse of over 300,000 faculty.

Journalists and other researchers can contact ProfNet to pose a question for the faculty experts. For example, not too long ago, a reporter from *The New York Times* used the network to try to locate an expert on computers and children. Another recent use was by a *Boston Globe* staffer who was looking for someone in the forefront of research in electric vehicles. ProfNet is free, so you should be sensitive to making queries as straightforward as possible, and not overusing this service.

How to Find:

You can call ProfNet toll-free at 800-PROF-NET. It is also available on the Internet computer network (see Chapter 5 for an explanation of the Internet) at: PROFNET @sunysb.edu.

 Source: Doctoral Dissertations

An unusual but potentially very valuable source of information is published and unpublished doctoral dissertations. These may provide you with information unavailable elsewhere.

How to Find:

You can locate dissertations on your subject by contacting University Microfilms International in Ann Arbor, Michigan. Through a computerized system called Datrix II, this firm can search more than 500,000 dissertations to find one that covers your subject of interest. If any are located, a copy can be sent to you directly. A modest fee is charged for the service. University Microfilms can also send you a subject index of its dissertations. Contact them at 300 North Zeeb Road, Ann Arbor, MI 48106; 800-521-0600.

 Source: Museums

There are museums for loads of topics—antiques, whaling, theater, and much more—and many museums have libraries that take written and telephone inquiries on subjects in their specialty areas. For example, the Museum of Radio and Television in New York City, which has a holding of over 40,000 radio and television programs and advertising broadcasts, will tackle any information query relating to a broadcasting matter. Questions it has handled include: Who produced "The Ed Sullivan Show"? and When did the "I Love Lucy" show premiere? (You can contact the Museum at 25 West 52nd Street, New York, NY 10019; 212-621-6600. The staff takes research questions by fax: 212-621-6700. And the museum is open to the public.) (P.S. Marlo Lewis co-produced "The Ed Sullivan Show" along with Ed Sullivan himself in the 1950s. "I Love Lucy" premiered October 15, 1951, on CBS.)

TIP: You can obtain transcripts of many news, documentary, and public policy broadcasts from Journal Graphics. The firm provides transcripts from "60 Minutes," "48 Hours," "Nova," "Frontline," "Adam Smith's Money World," "Oprah Winfrey," "Nightline," and many other broadcasts. Transcripts are modestly priced, and rush service is available. For more information, or to obtain a catalog of transcripts by topic, contact: Journal Graphics, 1535 Grant Street, Denver, CO 80203; 303-831-9000.

How to Find:

To find a museum that matches your subject of interest, take a look at the *Official Museum Directory,* which lists 7,000 institutions. These include art, history, nature, and science museums, as well as more specialized museums—museums of agriculture, antiques, architecture, audiovisual materials and film, the circus, clocks and watches, electricity, fire fighting, forestry, furniture, guns, hobbies, industry, logging and lumber, mining, money and numismatics, musical instruments, philately, religion, scouting, sports, technology, theater, toys and dolls, transportation, typography, whaling, and woodcarving.

The directory provides the museum's name, address, phone number, officers, collections, research fields, facilities, activities, and publications. It's published by the R.R. Bowker Co., New Providence, New Jersey, and can be found at many libraries.

One museum with extensive resources on a number of different subjects is the Smithsonian Institution in Washington, D.C. Its specialties include art, history, air and space, zoology, horticulture, and marine life. You can pose a question on any of these or related topics, and the museum will try to answer it. The service is free. Write: The Smithsonian Institution, Washington, DC 20560.

 Source: Specialized Bookstores

The yellow pages of some of the larger cities group bookstores into specific subject areas. For example, if you get hold of a copy of New York City's yellow pages (check any large library), you'll see bookstores devoted solely to art and sculpture, astrology, automobiles, China, cooking, health and nutrition, the occult, philosophy, religion, science fiction, theater, travel, and women.

Remember too that the people who work at these bookstores are good sources of information themselves.

 Source: Private Companies

One last "everything" source to keep in mind—private companies. Sometimes firms publish free pamphlets and guides related to their industry or products. For example, Prudential-Bache offices offer free advice on money management; Evenflo (Ravenna, Ohio), a maker of products for babies, provides free information and advice to expectant mothers about exercise, nutrition, and child care; and Delsey Luggage (Jessup, Maryland) provides tips on proper packing. Try to identify large firms that sell a product or service related to your subject. You may then want to call the public affairs department of these firms to inquire whether any free materials are available.

Also, individuals who work at companies can naturally be excellent persons to interview on their subjects of expertise. See chapters 6–8 on finding and interviewing experts for more information.

INFORMATION-FINDING TOOLS

Here are a few sources and strategies that will help make any information search easier.

 Source: Toll-Free Phone Number and Address Directories

Below are very useful and inexpensive paperback books that can save you time and money when you're making information-finding phone calls.

The *National Directory of Addresses and Telephone Numbers* (Omnigraphics Inc.), which not only lists organizations with toll-free numbers but also gives names, addresses, phone numbers, and fax numbers of frequently contacted organizations, such as the media, service firms, and financial institutions. You'll find this guide at many bookstores.

Finally, AT&T publishes two of its own directories of toll-free numbers: *AT&T Toll Free 800 Numbers,* which is geared for consumers, and the *AT&T Toll Free 800 Directory for Business*. Both are reasonably priced and can be ordered by contacting: AT&T 800 Directory, P.O. Box 44068, Jacksonville, FL 32232; 800-426-8686.

✔ Source: Grammar Hot Lines

If you plan to write up the results of your information-gathering project, you can obtain free assistance from "grammar hot lines," which are staffed by volunteers from colleges and universities around the country. These people are standing by, waiting anxiously for your questions on spelling, usage, diction, punctuation, or any other emergency grammar aid you may require.

These grammar experts are extremely knowledgeable and unfailingly helpful. I recently called with a question on whether it was proper to use the article *a* or *an* in front of a word beginning with the letter *h*. I was immediately informed that *a* is to be used if the *h* is pronounced, *an* if the *h* is silent. Another question I recently asked related to this sentence: "Lamps, chairs, as well as one table, (is) (are) necessary . . ." The answer is *are*.

State/School	Hours Available	Phone Number
Alabama:		
Auburn University	M–Th: 9–noon; 1–4; F: 9–noon; reduced summer hours	205-826-5749
Jacksonville State University	M–F: 8–4:30	205-231-5409
University of Alabama	M, Th: 8:30–4; T, W: 6 p.m.–8 p.m.; F: 9–1; summer hours, 8:30–1	205-348-5049
Arizona:		
Arizona State University	M–F: 8–5	602-967-0378
Arkansas:		
University of Arkansas	M–F: 8–noon	501-569-3162

California:

Moorpark College	M–F: 8–noon, Sept.– June	805-529-2321
Consumnes River College	M–F: 9–11:45 a.m. fall and spring semesters; 24-hour recorder	916-686-7444

Colorado:

University of Southern Colorado	M–F: 9:30–3:30; reduced hours May 15–Aug. 25	303-549-2787

Delaware:

University of Delaware	M–Th: 9–noon, 1–5, 6–9; F: 9–noon, 1–5	302-451-1890

Florida:

University of West Florida	M–Th: 9–5; occasional evening hours; summer hours vary	904-474-2129

Georgia:

Georgia State University	M–Th: 8:30–5; F: 8:30–3; evening hours vary	404-651-2906

Illinois:

Eastern Illinois University	M–F: 10–3; summer hours vary	217-581-5929
Oakton Community College	M–F: 10–2, Sept.– May; summer hours vary	708-635-1948
Illinois State University	M–F: 8–4:30	815-224-2720
Illinois Valley Community College	M–F: 8–4	815-224-2720

Triton College	M–Th: 8:30 a.m.–9 p.m.; F: 8:30–4; Sa: 10–1	312-456-0300

Indiana:

Indiana University	M–Th: 9–4	317-274-3000
Ball State University	M–Th: 9 a.m.–8 p.m.; F: 9–5; May–Aug., M–F: 11 a.m.–2 p.m.	317-285-8387
Purdue University	M–F: 9:30–4; closed May, Aug., and mid-Dec.–mid-Jan.	317-494-3723

Kansas:

Emporia State University	M–Th: noon–5; W: 7 p.m.–9 p.m.; summer hours vary	316-343-5380

Louisiana:

University of Southwestern Louisiana	M–Th: 8–4; F: 8–3	318-231-5224

Maryland:

University of Maryland	M–F: 10–noon, Sept.–May	301-455-2585
Frostburg State University	M–F: 10–noon	301-689-4327

Massachusetts:

North Shore Community College	M–F: 8:30–4	617-593-7284
Northeastern University	M–F: 8:30–4:30	617-437-2512

Michigan:

C. S. Mott Community College	M–Th: 8:30–3:30; F: 8:30–12:30; T, W: 5:30 p.m.–8 p.m.; summer hours vary	313-762-0229

Western Michigan University	M–F: 9–4; summer hours vary	616-387-4442
Lansing Community College	M–F: 9–4	517-483-1040

Missouri:

Missouri Southern State College	M–F: 8:30–4:30	417-624-0171
University of Missouri	M–F: 9–4	816-276-2244

New Jersey:

Jersey City State College	M–F: 9–4:30; summer, M–Th: 8–5	201-547-3337/3338

New York:

York College	M–F: 1–4	718-739-7483

North Carolina:

Methodist College	M–F: 8–5	919-488-7110
East Carolina University	M–Th: 8–4; F: 8–3; T, Th: 6	919-757-6728/6399

Ohio:

Raymond Walters College	Answering machine tapes requests— long-distance calls returned collect	513-745-5731
University College, University of Cincinnati	M–F: 9–10, 1–2	513-475-2493
Cincinnati Technical College	M–Th: 8 a.m.–8 p.m.; F: 8–4; Sa: 9–1	513-569-1736
Cuyahoga Community College	M–F: 1–3; Su–Th: 7–10 p.m.; 24-hour answering machine	216-987-2050

| Wright State University | M–F: 9–4 | 513-873-2158 |
| Ohio Wesleyan University | M–F: 9–noon; 1–4, Sept.–May | 614-369-4431 |

Oklahoma:

| Southern Nazarene University | M–F: 9–4; June–Aug., call | 405-491-6328 405-354-1739 |

Pennsylvania:

| Cedar Crest College | M–F: 10–3, Sept.–May | 215-437-4471 |
| Lincoln University | M–F: 9–5; summer hours vary | 215-932-8300 |

South Carolina:

The Citadel Writing Center	M–F: 8–4; Su–Th: 6 p.m.–10p.m.	803-792-3194
University of South Carolina	M–F: 8:30–5	803-777-7020
Converse College	T–Th: noon–5	803-596-9613

Texas:

Amarillo College	M–Th: 8 a.m.–9 p.m.; Fri: 8–3; Su: 2–6	806-374-4726
University of Houston	M–Th: 9–4; F: 9–1; summer hours, M–Th: 10:30–4	713-221-8670
San Antonio College	M–Th: 8 a.m.–9 p.m.; F: 8–4	512-733-2503

Virginia:

| Northern Virginia Community College | M–Th: 10–2 | 703-450-2511 |
| Tidewater Community College | M–F: 10–noon; afternoon hours vary; reduced summer hours | 804-427-7170 |

Wisconsin:

Northeast Wisconsin Technical Institute	M–Th: 8:30 a.m.–8 p.m.; F: 8–4	414-498-5427
University of Wisconsin	M–Th: 9–4; F: 9–noon	608-342-1615

Canada:
Alberta:

Grant MacEwan Community College	T–F: 12:30–3:30	403-441-4699

New Brunswick:

University of New Brunswick	Variable hours	506-459-3631

You can receive a free annual update of this list by sending a self-addressed stamped envelope to Grammar Hotline Directory, Writing Center, Tidewater Community College, 1700 College Crescent, Virginia Beach, VA 23456; 804-427-7100.

✔ **Source: Advertisements**

Granted, it's an offbeat idea, but one worth considering—especially if other sources don't pan out. Place an advertisement, and describe as specifically as possible what kind of information you're looking for and why. (You sometimes see such ads as "author's queries" in popular book review sections.) You may be pleasantly surprised at the response you receive—people do like to help! A friend of mine placed an ad in a large city newspaper requesting input from collectors of "snow dome" paperweights, and she received about fifty responses!

If you've found a trade publication covering your subject, try placing the ad there so that you can reach a specific audience. Otherwise, a daily newspaper is fine—and the bigger the better.

Ads can be an especially good way to find out if anyone has information on a particular person or to find users of a product or customers of a firm.

3

The U.S. Government
Mining for Information Nuggets

The U.S. government is a gold mine of information. Although many government publications and services have been eliminated during the last few years, an awesome amount of advice, data, and information is still available. The expertise is all there for the taking—if you know how to find what you need.

Because the government is so huge, it is impossible to describe in a single chapter (or book, for that matter) anywhere near the full amount of information available. However, to give you a feel for what's available, this chapter lists some of the most popular and helpful information sources and provides you with a head start on digging out information from each of the thirteen U.S. *departments* (Department of Justice, Department of Transportation, and so on) and a select number of the government's smaller independent *agencies* (Federal Communications Commission, Environmental Protection Agency, and so on). For each one, an address, main phone number, and public affairs phone number are provided. Then, to alert you to specific subjects that the department or agency covers and information sources available, the following two descriptive listings are provided:

Scope Includes

This is a sample of some of the subjects that are covered within the department or agency. Because each department and agency may deal with hundreds or thousands of different areas, only a sample of those judged to be of greatest appeal to the largest number of readers are included.

In addition, for each *department* (but not for the smaller independent agencies) names of key offices that cover the sampled subjects are provided. If there are higher divisions in the department that the key office reports to, these are also identified, in parentheses. For example:

☑ **Department of the Interior**

18th and C Streets NW
Washington, DC 20240
Main number: 202-343-7220
Public affairs: 202-343-6416

Scope Includes

Archaeology. Key Office: Archaeology Division (Cultural Resources, National Park Service)
Fish and Wildlife. Key Office: U.S. Fish and Wildlife Service

---

Note that the Archaeology Division reports directly to the larger division Cultural Resources, which is part of the National Park Service. The U.S. Fish and Wildlife Service does not fall under any larger divisions.

Rich Resources

Under this heading you will find specific offices and divisions within a department or agency that have been identified as sources of the very best and most useful information. An address and phone number are provided for each one.

For information on	*Check*
Agriculture	Department of Agriculture
Air travel/flight	National Aeronautics and Space Administration
Arts and literature	National Foundation on the Arts/ National Endowment for the Arts

Astronomy	National Aeronautics and Space Administration
Broadcasting	Federal Communications Commission
Business	Small Business Administration; *see also* chapter 4, "Business Information"
Consumer information	General Services Administration; Consumer Product Safety Commission; Department of Health and Human Services; Federal Trade Commission
Crime	Department of Justice
Education	Department of Education
Energy	Department of Energy
Engineering	Department of Commerce/ National Bureau of Standards
Environment	Environmental Protection Agency; Department of Commerce/National Oceanic and Atmospheric Administration
Food and nutrition	Department of Agriculture
Foreign affairs	Department of State
Health and medicine	Department of Health and Human Services
Housing and real estate	Department of Housing and Urban Development
Humanities	National Endowment for the Humanities
International affairs	Department of State; Department of Defense
Labor and employment	Department of Labor

Minority concerns	Department of Commerce; Department of Education; Department of the Interior; Department of Housing and Urban Development
Natural disasters	Federal Emergency Management Agency
Natural resources	Department of the Interior
Taxes	Department of Justice
Transportation	Department of Transportation
Travel	Department of State

TIP: Guides to Government Information
- If you want to get a much fuller understanding of the structure and offices of the federal government, I'd recommend you check out some of the special publications described at the end of this chapter. These are specifically designed to provide detailed listings of government offices and to examine their organizational structure.

AFTER YOU LOCATE AN AGENCY

What do you do if you find a department or agency that covers a subject you are interested in? There are several ways to track down the information you need, but the key is to zero in on as specific an individual or subagency as possible in making contact. Here, in order of preference, are the ways I recommend going about getting what you need:

1st choice. Contact a "rich resource" office—a source that has *already been identified for you* as providing excellent information.

2nd choice. If you've found a specific "key office" that sounds appropriate to your needs, call the main number and ask to be connected to that office. Then you can ask whether there are publications or find out if there is an expert who specializes in your topic.

If you *don't* find a "rich resource" or "key office," you can then try calling the public affairs/information number of the department or agency and pose your question. However, although you should be able to obtain information on publications available, it's hard to zero in on an expert by placing a call to a department's or agency's main public information number. You may be more successful if you take one of the more "targeted" routes first.

Finally, you can dig out more specialized subdivisions and offices by examining one of the guides to government information described at the end of this chapter. These locater sources will help you find out if there is a division, bureau, or office that has the specific answers you seek.

TIP: Government Phone Information
- Because personnel and departments in Washington often change, it's very possible that some of the phone numbers listed below will be outdated by the time you read this. If you dial a number that is no longer accurate, simply call 202-555-1212 and ask the operator to give you the "locater" telephone number for the specific department you are trying to reach.

DEPARTMENTS

 Department of Agriculture

14th Street and Independence Avenue SW
Washington, DC 20250
Main number: 202-720-8732
Public affairs: 202-720-4623

Scope Includes

Animal and Plant Health. Key Office: Animal and Plant Health Inspection Service (Marketing and Inspection Services)

Consumer Affairs. Key Office: Office of the Consumer Advisor (Office of the Assistant Secretary, Food and Consumer Services)

Family Nutrition. Key Office: Family Nutrition Programs (Food and Consumer Services)

Food Safety and Inspection. Key Office: Food Safety and Inspection Service (Marketing and Inspection Services)

Human Nutrition. Key Office: Human Nutrition Information Service (Food and Consumer Services)

Veterinary Medicine. Key Office: Veterinary Services (Animal and Plant Health Inspection Service, Marketing and Inspection Services)

Rich Resources

The USDA's Extension Service can provide you with information that links research, science, and technology to the needs of the people, where they live and work. There are more than 3,100 county offices located around the country.

Contact: USDA Extension Service, Washington, DC 20250; 202-720-0987, to find a local office. Or check your phone book's government blue-page listing under "Agriculture."

The USDA's Food and Nutrition Information Center can provide you with information or educational materials on human nutrition and food. The center lends books and audiovisual materials to specified borrowers, makes photocopies of journal articles, and provides comprehensive reference services such as computer searches.

Contact: Food and Nutrition Information Center, National Agricultural Library, U.S. Department of Agriculture, Beltsville, MD 20705; 301-504-5755.

The Human Nutrition Information Service will answer your questions about the nutrient composition of food—calories, fat content, vitamins and minerals, food consumption and dietary levels of the population.

Contact: Human Nutrition Information Service, U.S. Department of Agriculture, Hyattsville, MD 20782; 301-436-7725.

The Home Economics and Human Nutrition unit publishes information on managing a household, providing nutritious meals, managing resources such as money and energy, planning and caring for clothing, improving personal and community relationships, and providing an attractive, safe, and healthy home environment.

Contact: Home Economics and Human Nutrition, Extension Service, U.S. Department of Agriculture, 301-436-7725 (see above, Human Nutrition).

The National Agricultural Library is a great information source. Its specialties include botany, poultry, forestry, veterinary medicine, chemistry, plant pathology, livestock, zoology, and general agriculture topics. The library provides reference service by mail or phone. You can request the "Bibliography Series," which lists topics on which bibliographic citations are available—"Indoor Gardening," "Pesticide Safety," "The U.S. Poultry Industry," and so on.

Contact: The National Agricultural Library, U.S. Department of Agriculture, Beltsville, MD 20705; 301-504-5755

 Department of Commerce

14th Street and Constitution Avenue NW
Washington, DC 20230
Main number: 202-482-2000
Public affairs: 202-482-3263
Free reference: 202-482-2161

Scope Includes

Business Outlook Analyses. Key Office: Business Outlook Division (Associate Director for National Analyses and Projections, Bureau of Economic Analysis)

Economic and Demographic Statistics. Key Offices: Associate Director for Demographic Fields (Bureau of the Census); Associate Director for Economic Fields (Bureau of the Census)

Engineering Standards. Key Office: National Engineering Laboratory (National Bureau of Standards)

Imports and Exports. Key Office: International Trade Administration

Minority-Owned Business. Key Office: Minority Business Development Agency

Patents and Trademarks. Key Office: Assistant Commissioner for External Affairs (Patent and Trademark Office)

Technology. Key Office: Assistant Secretary for Productivity (Technology and Innovation, Under Secretary for Economic Affairs)

Travel. Key Office: Office of the Under Secretary (U.S. Travel and Tourism Administration)

Weather and Atmosphere. Key Office: National Oceanic and Atmospheric Administration

Rich Resources

The Department of Commerce is filled with sources of information about business. Chapter 4, which is devoted to business information, discusses some of the best of these. Here are other offices of the department that provide helpful materials and assistance:

The Minority Business Development Agency provides business management and technical assistance for members of minorities. Personal counseling is available, sometimes for free. The main office will give you a regional location near you.

Contact: Minority Business Development Agency, U.S. Department of Commerce, Washington, DC 20230; 202-482-1936.

The National Computer Systems Laboratory publishes free and inexpensive newsletters that examine computing issues that range from security to networks to buying software. It has a limited capacity for answering technical questions, however.

Contact: National Computer Systems Laboratory, B151 Technology Building, National Bureau of Standards, Gaithersburg, MD 20899; 301-975-3587.

The National Institute of Standards and Technology is devoted to the science of measurement and develops standards. It has a staff of experts in areas such as manufacturing engineering, chemical engineering, electronics, and electrical engineering. Also covered are radiation, building technology, applied mathematics, chemical physics, analytic chemistry, and computer science and technology. A good publication to get is "Co-operative Research Opportunities at NIST," which includes a directory that identifies the bureau's experts and gives their phone numbers.

Contact: U.S. Department of Commerce, National Institute of Standards and Technology, Research Information Center, Gaithersburg, MD 20899; 301-975-3058.

The National Oceanic and Atmospheric Administration will try to answer your questions about climate, earth and ocean sciences, the environment, and marine life. It will also refer you to other agencies and to published information.

Contact: NOAA Central Library, 1315 East-West Highway, Silver Spring, MD 20910; 301-713-2600.

 Department of Defense

The Pentagon
Washington, DC 20301-1400
Main number: 703-545-6700
Public affairs: 703-697-5131

Scope Includes

Atomic Energy. Key Office: Assistant to the Secretary, Atomic Energy (Research and Engineering)

Foreign Country Security. Key Office: Assistant Secretary, International Security Affairs

Mapping. Key Office: Defense Mapping Agency

Military History. Key Office: U.S. Army Center of Military History (Department of the Army)

Nuclear Operations and Technology. Key Office: Defense Nuclear Agency

Tactical Warfare. Key Office: Deputy Undersecretary, Tactical Warfare Programs

Rich Resources

The Department of Defense publishes about 150 "foreign area studies," which are in-depth studies of a particular country's social, economic, political, and military organization and are revised every three to five years. These are clothbound books, usually a few hundred pages long and very detailed. They are designed for the nonspecialist. Prices are very reasonable.

Contact: Superintendent of Documents, U.S. Government Printing Office, Washington, DC 20402; 202-783-3238.

The U.S. Army Military History Institute answers thousands of inquiries per year on military history. The institute has an extensive collection of unofficial documents such as personal papers. You can call or write with your question.

Contact: Historical Reference Branch, U.S. Army Military History Institute, Carlisle Barracks, PA 17013-5008; 717-245-3611.

 Department of Education
400 Maryland Avenue SW
Washington, DC 20202
Main office: 202-708-5366
Public affairs: 202-401-1577

Scope Includes
Adult Education. Key Office: Assistant Secretary for Vocational and Adult Education
Bilingual Education. Key Office: Office of Bilingual Education and Minority Language Affairs
Civil Rights. Key Office: Assistant Secretary for Civil Rights
Educational Statistics. Key Office: Center for Statistics (Assistant Secretary for Educational Research and Improvement)
Elementary and Secondary Education. Key Office: Assistant Secretary for Elementary and Secondary Education
Handicapped. Key Office: Director, National Institute of Handicapped Research
Higher Education. Key Office: Assistant Secretary for Postsecondary Education
Libraries. Key Office: Library Programs (Assistant Secretary for Educational Research and Improvement)
Special Education. Key Office: Assistant Secretary for Special Education and Rehabilitative Services

Rich Resources

The Office of Educational Research and Improvement (OERI), Education Information Branch, disseminates statistics and other data related to education in the United States and other nations. OERI conducts studies and publishes reports regarding all kinds of educational data. Past publications include "The Condition of Education," "Hispanic Students in American High Schools," and "Faculty Salaries."

Contact: OERI, U.S. Department of Education, 555 New Jersey Avenue, Washington, DC 20208; 800-424-1616.

Education Resource Information Center (ERIC) provides users with ready access to literature dealing with education through abstracting journals, computer searches, document reproductions, and other means. There are sixteen subject-specialized clearinghouses: adult, career, and vocational; counseling and personnel; educational management; elementary and early childhood; handicapped and gifted children; higher education; information resources; junior colleges; languages and linguistics; reading and communication skills; rural education and small schools; science, mathematics, and environmental; social studies/social science; teacher education; tests, measurement, and evaluation; urban education. These clearinghouses answer more than 100,000 written and telephone inquiries per year.

Contact: ERIC, U.S. Department of Education, 555 New Jersey Avenue, Washington, DC 20208; 202-219-2289.

 Department of Energy

Forrestal Building
1000 Independence Avenue SW
Washington, DC 20585
Main number: 202-586-5000
Public affairs: 202-586-6827

Scope Includes

Coal Liquids, Gas, Shale, Oil. Key Office: Deputy Assistant: Oil, Gas, Shale and Coal Liquids (Assistant Secretary for Fossil Energy)

Conservation. Key Office: Assistant Secretary for Conservation and Renewable Energy

Energy Emergencies. Key Office: Assistant Secretary for International Affairs and Energy Efficiencies

Fusion Energy. Key Office: Office of Fusion Energy (Office of Energy Research)

Inventions. Key Office: Invention Licensing Appeals Board (Office of Small and Disadvantaged Business Utilization)

Nuclear Energy. Key Office: Assistant Secretary for Nuclear Energy

Nuclear Physics. Key Office: Office of High Energy and Nuclear Physics (Office of Energy Research)

Radioactive Waste. Key Office: Office of Civilian Radioactive Waste Management

Rich Resources

DOE's Office of Scientific and Technical Information has information on nearly any energy-related topic. The scientists on the staff may be able to help you with a question, or even run a free computer search on the "EDB"—Energy Data Base—the world's largest database on energy.

Contact: Technical Services Division, OSTI, P.O. Box 62, Oak Ridge, TN 37831; 615-576-1301.

The Energy Information Administration provides energy information and referral assistance to the public. The best publication to ask for is "The Energy Information Directory," which is a list of government offices and experts. Topics in its subject index include appliances, buildings, coal, dams, diesel fuel, fusion power, ocean energy, safety, solar energy, and vehicles. The directory refers the user to a specific government office, describes the function of that office, and provides the name of a contact person. The publication is free and published semiannually. The EIA also publishes a free newsletter.

Contact: National Energy Information Center, Energy Information Administration, U.S. Department of Energy, EI-231 Forrestal Building, Washington, DC 20585; 202-586-8800.

The Conservation and Renewable Energy Inquiry and Referral Service is an information clearinghouse on energy conservation and short-term renewable energy (e.g., solar, wind, and ocean). The service will answer questions or refer you to an expert. Various free pamphlets and books are available.

Contact: Conservation and Renewable Energy Inquiry and Referral Service, P.O. Box 8900, Silver Spring, MD 20907; 800-523-2929.

 Department of Health and Human Services

200 Independence Avenue SW
Washington, DC 20201
Main number: 202-690-7000
Public affairs: 202-690-7850
Locater Service: 202-619-0257

Scope Includes

The department's Public Health Service division has key offices devoted to the following medical and health-related subjects:

AIDS. Key Office: AIDS Hotline (Assistant Secretary for Health), 800-342-AIDS

Alcohol Abuse. Key Office: National Institute on Alcohol Abuse and Alcoholism (Alcohol, Drug Abuse, and Mental Health Administration)

Diseases. Key Office: Office of Public Affairs, Centers for Disease Control

Drug Abuse. Key Office: National Institute on Drug Abuse (Alcohol, Drug Abuse, and Mental Health Administration)

Drug Research. Key Office: Office of Drug Research and Review (Food and Drug Administration)

Family Planning. Key Office: Office of Family Planning (Office of Population Affairs)

Food Safety. Key Office: Center for Food Safety and Applied Nutrition (Food and Drug Administration)

Minority Health. Key Office: Office of Minority Health (Assistant Secretary for Health)

Occupational Safety. Key Office: National Institute for Occupational Safety and Health

Smoking. Key Office: Office on Smoking and Health
Statistical Data. Key Office: National Center for Health Statistics
Toxic Substances. Key Office: Agency for Toxic Substances and Disease Registry
Veterinary Medicine. Key Office: Center for Veterinary Medicine

The department's National Institutes of Health include:

National Cancer Institute

National Eye Institute

National Heart, Lung and Blood Institute

National Institute of Arthritis and Musculoskeletal and Skin Diseases

National Institute of Child Health and Human Development

National Institute of Diabetes and Digestive and Kidney Diseases

National Institute of Dental Research

National Institute of Environmental Health Sciences

National Institute of Neurological and Communicative Disorders and Stroke

In the Office of Human Development Services, you can find these offices:

Administration for Children, Youth, and Families

Administration for Native Americans

Administration on Aging

Administration on Developmental Disabilities

President's Committee on Mental Retardation

Other major divisions of HHS include:

Family Support Administration

Health Care Financing Administration

Social Security Administration

Rich Resources

The Office of Disease Prevention and Health Promotion's (ODPHP) National Health Information Center provides information on virtually all health-oriented questions ranging from weight control to rare disorders. Up-to-date expertise and literature are available on most health problems, including alcoholism, allergies, arthritis, birth defects, cancer, child diseases, dental problems, depression, drug addiction, genetic diseases, high blood pressure, poisoning, and sexually transmitted diseases.

Contact: Telephone the Information Center at its toll-free number, 800-336-4797.

The National Center for Health Statistics provides expert advice and statistical data relating to health matters, including illness, disabilities, and hospital and health care utilization and financing. You can call to talk to an expert or write to receive a publication—many are free. This center can also help you track down vital statistics—records on births, deaths, marriages, and divorce. You will be provided with the vital statistics office to contact in the proper state.

Contact: National Center for Health Statistics, U.S. Department of Health and Human Services, 6525 Belcrest Road, Hyattsville, MD 20782; 301-436-8500.

The department maintains clearinghouses of information on special health concerns, including:

Aging

Contact: Office of Program Development, Administration on Aging, U.S. Department of Health and Human Services, 330 Independence Avenue SW, Room 4661 Cohen Building, Washington, DC 20201; 202-619-0011.

Family Planning

Contact: National Clearinghouse for Family Planning Information, Office of Family Planning, U.S. Department of Health and Human Services, P.O. Box 30436, Bethesda, MD 20814.

Mental Health

Contact: National Institute of Mental Health, Public Inquiry Branch, 5600 Fishers Lane, Room 15C05, Rockville, MD 20857; 301-443-4513.

The National Institute for Occupational Safety and Health (NIOSH) publishes a variety of free reports and publications. You can talk to a staff expert who specializes in a particular hazard (e.g., asbestos, formaldehyde).

Contact: NIOSH Publications, 4676 Columbia Parkway, Cincinnati, OH 45226; 513-533-8326.

The National Library of Medicine is the world's largest medical library, with over 4 million items. Specialties include the health sciences and, to a lesser degree, chemistry, physics, botany, and zoology. The library will assist you by checking its resources or by referring you to another organization.

Contact: U.S. Department of Health and Human Services, National Institutes of Health, National Library of Medicine, Bethesda, MD 20894; 301-496-6308.

A free catalog of the department's publications is available from the Public Information Division, 301-496-4143.

The U.S. Office of Consumer Affairs, located in HHS, will try to tell you who can help you with a consumer complaint.

Contact: U.S. Office of Consumer Affairs, HHS 1009 Premier Building, Washington, DC 20201; 202-634-4319.

 Department of Housing and Urban Development

451 7th Street SW
Washington, DC 20410
Main number: 202-708-1422
Public affairs: 202-708-0980

Scope Includes

Block Grants. Key Office: Office of Block Grant Assistance (Assistant Secretary for Community Planning and Development)

Elderly Housing. Key Office: Office of Elderly and Assisted Housing (Assistant Secretary for Housing, Federal Housing Commissioner)

Energy Conservation. Key Office: Solar Energy and Energy Conservation Bank

Fair Housing. Key Office: Assistant Secretary for Fair Housing and Equal Opportunity

Indian/Public Housing. Key Office: Assistant Secretary for Public and Indian Housing.

Urban Studies. Key Office: Office of Urban and Community Studies (Assistant Secretary for Policy Development and Research)

Rich Resources

HUD's Library and Information Services will answer housing-related questions or will refer people with housing questions to the correct department.

Contact: HUD Library and Information Services, U.S. Department of Housing and Urban Development, Room 8141, 451 7th Street SW, Washington, DC 20410; 202-708-2370.

HUD User is a service that will try to locate research reports sponsored by the department and help you get them. Many of these reports are inexpensive.

Contact: HUD User, P.O. Box 6091, Rockville, MD 20850; 301-251-5154 or 800-245-2691.

The Housing Information and Statistics Division can provide various housing statistics free, as well as answer inquiries. Topics on which statistics are generated include mortgages, neighborhoods, construction, and prices.

Contact: Housing Information and Statistics Division, U.S. Department of Housing and Urban Development, 451 7th Street SW, Washington, DC 20410; 202-755-7510.

Finally, the Department of Housing and Urban Development has a hot line for discrimination complaints: 800-669-9777.

Department of the Interior

18th and C Streets NW
Washington, DC 20240
Main number: 202-208-3100
Communications: 202-208-6416

Scope Includes

Archaeology. Key Office: Archaeology Division (Cultural Resources, National Park Service)

Fish and Wildlife. Key Office: U.S. Fish and Wildlife Service

Geology. Key Office: Geologic Division (U.S. Geological Survey)

Mapping. Key Office: National Mapping Division (U.S. Geological Survey)

Minerals. Key Office: Minerals Information (Bureau of Mines, U.S. Geological Survey)

Native Americans. Key Office: Bureau of Indian Affairs

Natural Resources. Key Office: Natural Resources (National Park Service)

Water. Key Office: Water Resources Division (U.S. Geological Survey)

Rich Resources

Do you want to know how to place reservations to go to Yosemite? When the Cherry Blossom Festival is being held? The best time to visit Shenandoah National Park to see the peak foliage? The National Park Service's public inquiries office answers such questions and provides information on national parks. Written or telephone inquiries are accepted.

Contact: National Park Service, Public Inquiries Office, P.O. Box 37127, Washington, DC 20013-7127; 202-208-6843.

The Department of the Interior's Natural Resource Library will try to answer phone or mail inquiries on matters related to natural resources, including conservation, public lands, native Americans, the environment, and fish and wildlife. The library also publishes bibliographies on areas of current interest ranging from the survival of the Florida panther to pollution problems in wildlife areas.

Contact: Natural Resources Library, U.S. Department of the Interior, 18th and C Streets NW, Washington, DC 20240; 202-208-5815.

The Bureau of Indian Affairs will help you obtain information about native Americans—their culture and their relationship with the federal government.

Contact: Bureau of Indian Affairs, Public Affairs Office, U.S. Department of the Interior, MS 2620, 18th and C Streets NW, Washington, DC 20245; 202-208-5116.

 Department of Justice

10th Street and Constitution Avenue NW
Washington, DC 20530
Main number: 202-514-2000
Public affairs: 202-514-2007

Scope Includes

Antitrust. Key Office: Antitrust Division (Office of the Associate Attorney General)

Civil Rights. Key Office: Civil Rights Division (Office of the Associate Attorney General)

Drug Enforcement. Key Office: Drug Enforcement Administration (Federal Bureau of Investigation)

Immigration. Key Office: Immigration and Naturalization Service (Office of the Deputy Attorney General)

Justice Statistics. Key Office: Bureau of Justice Statistics (Office of the Deputy Attorney General)

Juvenile Justice. Key Office: Office of Juvenile Justice and Delinquency Prevention (Office of the Deputy Attorney General)

Prisons. Key Office: Bureau of Prisons (Office of the Deputy Attorney General)

Rich Resources

A special division of the Bureau's National Institute of Justice is its National Criminal Justice Reference Service (NCJRS). NCJRS provides the latest criminal justice findings via databases, reference and referral sources, publications, audiovisual materials, and more. Membership in NCJRS is free.

The U.S. Government

Contact: National Institute of Justice, NCJRS, Box 6000, Department AFA, Rockville, MD 20850; 800-851-3420 (in Washington, D.C., 301-251-5500).

A relatively new program from the department is the Justice Statistics Clearinghouse. Among the services offered by the clearinghouse are: responding to statistical requests (e.g., how many burglaries occurred in the past year), providing information about JSC services, suggesting referrals to other sources, and conducting custom literature searches of the NCJRS database.

TIP: If your research requires investigation of federal courts, you should get hold of a book called *The Sourcebook of Federal Courts*, which provides contact information and search advice for each of the 295 U.S. District, 184 U.S. Bankruptcy, and 13 Federal Records Center courts. The 672-page directory is reasonably priced and can be ordered from: BRB Publications, 1200 Lincoln, #206, Denver, CO 80203; (800) 929-4981.

Contact: Telephone the Justice Statistics Clearinghouse at its toll-free number, 800-732-3277 (in Washington, D.C., 301-251-5500).

The bureau also publishes its free *Bureau of Justice Statistics Bulletin*. The bulletin identifies key individuals within the department and their area of expertise, and lists various free studies and reports.

Contact: Bureau of Justice Statistics, U.S. Department of Justice, 633 Indiana Avenue NW, Washington, DC 20521; 800-732-3277 (in Washington, D.C., 301-251-5500).

The FBI's "Uniform Crime Reports" is a reliable set of criminal statistics used in law enforcement operations and management. It covers such areas as crime trends in the United States by state, city, and county; number of types of crime; statistics on officers; and so forth. The division will answer inquiries from the public on these statistics. It also publishes the annual *Crime*

*Sub-national or otherwise limited BJS data are
available on this topic. Indicated staff can disc
availability of data and methodological difficu
in obtaining national data on the topic.

in the United States, available from the U.S. Government Printing Office.

Contact: Uniform Crime Reports, Federal Bureau of Investigation, Washington, DC 20535; 202-324-5015.

 Department of Labor
200 Constitution Avenue NW
Washington, DC 20210
Main number: 202-219-6666
Public affairs: 202-219-7316

Scope Includes

Employment Training. Key Office: Employment and Training Administration

Labor-Management Relations. Key Office: Bureau of Labor-Management Relations and Cooperative Programs

Labor Statistics. Key Office: Bureau of Labor Statistics

Occupational Safety and Health. Key Office: Occupational Safety and Health Administration

Pension and Welfare Benefits. Key Office: Pension and Welfare Benefits Administration

Productivity and Technology. Key Office: Office of Productivity and Technology

Veterans' Employment. Key Office: Assistant Secretary for Veterans' Employment and Training

Women. Key Office: Public Affairs, Women's Bureau

Rich Resources

The Bureau of Labor Statistics publishes statistical data on employment, prices, wages, living conditions, and productivity. Other specialties include state economic statistics, industry statistics, consumer expenditures, economic growth projections, and occupational outlooks. A special free directory, "Telephone Contacts for Data Users," identifies the bureau's experts and specialties. Also available free is a periodical titled *Bureau of Labor Statistics News.*

Contact: U.S. Department of Labor, Statistics, Inquiries and Correspondence Branch, Washington, DC 20212; 202-606-5900.

The Occupational Safety and Health Administration will answer general inquiries regarding health and safety in the workplace. It also publishes various pamphlets and materials. A helpful guide is "All about OSHA," which lists its regional offices.

Contact: OSHA Publications, OSHA Publications Distribution Office, U.S. Department of Labor, Room N-3101, Washington, DC 20210; 202-219-8151.

 Department of State

> 2201 C Street NW
> Washington, DC 20520
> Main number: 202-647-4000
> Public affairs: 202-647-6575

Scope Includes

African Affairs. Key Office: Bureau of African Affairs

Arms Control. Key Office: Arms Control Matters (Special Presidential Advisors)

Canadian and European Affairs. Key Office: Bureau of European and Canadian Affairs

East Asian and Pacific Affairs. Key Office: Bureau of East Asian and Pacific Affairs

Human Rights. Key Office: Bureau of Human Rights and Humanitarian Affairs

Inter-American Affairs. Key Office: Bureau of Inter-American Affairs

International Environmental Affairs. Key Office: Bureau of Oceans and International Environmental and Scientific Affairs

International Narcotics. Key Office: Bureau for International Narcotics Matters

Near Eastern and South Asian Affairs. Key Office: Bureau of Near Eastern and South Asian Affairs

Nuclear and Space Arms Negotiations. Key Office: Office of Negotiations on Nuclear and Space Arms with the Soviet Union

Passport Inquiries. Key Office: Passport Information Inquiries (Deputy Assistant Secretary, Passport Services)

Prisoners of War/Missing in Action. Key Office: POW/MIA Matters (Office of Vietnam, Laos and Cambodia Affairs, Bureau of East Asian and Pacific Affairs)
Refugees. Key Office: Bureau for Refugee Programs
Visa Inquiries. Key Office: Office of Public and Diplomatic Liaison (Deputy Assistant Secretary, Visa Services)

Rich Resources

The Department of State maintains a staff of "Country Desk Officers," experts who specialize in the workings of an individual country. You can speak with the authority of your choice and find out about a particular country's political and economic conditions and other related matters.

Contact: Country Officers, Department of State, Washington, DC 20520; 202-647-6575.

The department also publishes short "background note" booklets that contain information on about 170 countries' social, economic, political, and military organization. These booklets are designed for the nonspecialist. They are inexpensive and provide both a cultural and historical overview.

Contact: Superintendent of Documents, U.S. Government Printing Office, Washington, DC 20402; 202-783-3238.

The State Department publishes many free short periodicals too. To get a list of what is available, order the document "Selected State Department Publications."

Contact: Public Information Service, Room 4827, U.S. Department of State, Washington, DC 20520; 202-647-6575.

An especially useful publication, reasonably priced, is the "Diplomatic List," a listing of foreign diplomatic representatives in Washington, D.C., and their addresses.

Contact: Superintendent of Documents, U.S. Government Printing Office, Washington, DC 20402; 202-783-3238.

The State Department publishes "Foreign Consular Offices in the U.S.," which lists country consulates, their addresses, phone numbers, and personnel. You can obtain help on questions you have about a particular country by contacting its consulate. The British consulate, for example, reports that it receives questions such as: Where is the county of Middlesex, England, located? How can I trace my relatives? How can I find information about what the British law says regarding divorce? How can I get information on the fashion industry in your country?

Contact: Superintendent of Documents, U.S. Government Printing Office, Washington, DC 20402. Or check the white pages of a major city phone book to find the consulate you seek.

 Department of Transportation

400 7th Street SW
Washington, DC 20590
Main number: 202-366-4000
Public affairs: 202-366-4570

Scope Includes

Automobile Safety. Key Office: Auto Safety Hot Line, 800-424-9393

Aviation Safety. Key Office: Office of Aviation Safety (Federal Aviation Administration)

Aviation Standards. Key Office: Associate Administrator for Aviation Standards (Federal Aviation Administration)

Boating. Key Office: Office of Boating, Public and Consumer Affairs (U.S. Coast Guard)

Hazardous Materials Transportation. Key Office: Office of Hazardous Materials Transportation (Research and Special Programs Administration)

Highway Safety. Key Office: Office of Safety and Traffic Operations Research and Development (Federal Highway Administration)

Mass Transit. Key Office: Urban Mass Transportation Administration

Railroad Safety. Key Office: Associate Administrator for Safety (Federal Railroad Administration)

Shipbuilding. Key Office: Associate Administrator for Shipbuilding, Operations and Research

Vehicle Accident Statistics. Key Office: National Center for Statistics and Analysis (Associate Administrator for Research and Development, National Highway Traffic Safety Administration)

Vehicle Crashworthiness. Key Office: Office of Crashworthiness Research (Associate Administrator for Research and Development, National Highway Traffic Safety Administration)

Rich Resources

The department's library will try to answer your questions related to transportation. Topics it covers include accident prevention, automobile safety, boating information, bus technology, driver education, energy, environmental research, highway research, mass transit, pollution, railroad information, traffic safety, and transportation for the handicapped.

Contact: U.S. Department of Transportation Library, Room 2200, M-493.3, 400 7th Street SW, Washington, DC 20590; 202-366-0746.

A separate branch of the library can assist you with inquiries regarding air travel:

Contact: U.S. Department of Transportation Library, FOB-10A, M-493.2, 800 Independence Avenue SW, Washington, DC 20591; 202-267-3115.

 Department of the Treasury

15th Street and Pennsylvania Avenue NW
Washington, DC 20220
Main number: 202-622-2000
Public affairs: 202-622-2041

Scope Includes

Coin and Medal Production. Key Office: Office of Production (Operations, U.S. Mint)

Currency Production. Key Office: Office of Currency Production and Stamp Printing (Operations, Bureau of Engraving and Printing)

Currency Research and Development. Key Office: Office of Research and Technical Services (Operations, Bureau of Engraving and Printing)

Customs. Key Office: Office of Public Affairs, U.S. Customs Service

Savings Bonds. Key Office: Public Communications Branch, U.S. Savings Bonds Division

Secret Service Protection. Key Office: Office of the Director, U.S. Secret Service

Taxpayer Assistance. Key Office: Office of the Taxpayer Ombudsman (Office of the Commissioner, Internal Revenue Service)

Tax Return Investigation. Key Office: Office of Criminal Investigation (Internal Revenue Service)

Rich Resources

The U.S. Customs Service publishes various free leaflets and newsletters. For example, "Customs Hints—Know Before You Go" explains customs privileges for returning U.S. residents and lists prohibited and restricted imports. Other publications cover importing pets and wildlife, cars, and alcoholic beverages.

Contact: U.S. Customs Service, 1301 Constitution Avenue NW, Washington, DC 20229; 202-927-1320.

You can contact experts from the U.S. Customs Service, who can answer questions about import rules and regulations for scores of different commodities.

Contact: U.S. Customs Service, Department of the Treasury, 6 World Trade Center, Room 425, New York, NY 10048; 212-466-5550.

If you have questions about your taxes, you'll likely find the answer you need in the Internal Revenue Service's publication number 910. Inside you'll find out about all of the services and publications available to help you prepare a tax return.

Contact: Telephone IRS Information at its toll-free number, 800-829-1040.

SELECTED ADMINISTRATIVE AGENCIES

 Consumer Product Safety Commission

Washington, DC 20207
Main number: 301-504-0580
Public affairs: 301-504-0580

Scope Includes

Fire and thermal burn hazards, product safety assessment, mechanical hazards, injury information, electrical shock hazards, safety packaging, chemical hazards.

Rich Resources

The Consumer Product Safety Commission publishes a number of free pamphlets and reports on product safety, mostly devoted to specific products, such as wood stoves or toys. It also has a toll-free number that you can call if you have a complaint about a hazardous product or if you want to report an injury resulting from a consumer product.

Contact: Consumer Product Safety Commission, Washington, DC 20207; 800-638-2772.

 Environmental Protection Agency

401 M Street SW
Washington, DC 20460
Main number: 202-260-2090
Public affairs: 202-260-4361

Scope Includes

Air and radiation, pesticides and toxic substances, acid deposition, environmental monitoring and quality assurance, solid waste and emergency response, water, noise control.

Rich Resources

The EPA supports a staff of experts who specialize in subjects such as air quality, drinking water, noise, radiation, and toxic substances. A free headquarters telephone directory will identify exactly the person you need. In this directory you can look up the name and telephone number of the Director of the Office of Solid Waste, the Director of Acid Deposition, and so on.

Contact: U.S. Environmental Protection Agency, 401 M Street SW, Washington, DC 20460; 202-260-4361.

 Federal Communications Commission

1919 M Street NW
Washington, DC 20554
Main number: 202-632-7000
Public affairs: 202-632-7000

Scope Includes

Cable television, broadcast stations, radio regulation.

Rich Resources

The FCC publishes some helpful documents, among them "The Information Seekers Guide," issued by the Consumer Assistance and Small Business Division. That division provides personal assistance and publishes free bulletins regarding communication issues (including cable television and other broadcasting matters).

Contact: Federal Communications Division, Consumer Assistance and Small Business Division, Office of Congressional and Public Affairs, 1919 M Street NW, Washington, DC 20554; 202-632-7000.

The FCC Library is a good source of information on various telecommunications issues.

Contact: FCC Library, 1919 M Street NW, Washington, DC 20554; 202-632-7100.

 Federal Emergency Management Agency

Federal Center Plaza
500 C Street SW
Washington, DC 20472
Main number: 202-646-2500
Public affairs: 202-646-4600

Scope Includes

Arson information, flood insurance, fire education, fire statistics, nuclear attack protection, radioactive hazards, earthquake research.

Rich Resources

FEMA publishes a catalog of free publications covering various issues related to emergency preparedness. Subjects range from shelter design to earthquakes, winter storm safety tips, and so forth.

Contact: FEMA, 500 C Street SW, Washington, DC 20472; 202-646-3484.

 Federal Trade Commission
Pennsylvania Avenue and 6th Street NW
Washington, DC 20580
Main number: 202-326-2000
Public affairs: 202-326-2180

Scope Includes

Advertising practices, competition and antitrust matters, consumer protection, financial statistics.

Rich Resources

The Federal Trade Commission can provide information and advice regarding consumer problems and complaints, especially in areas such as deceptive advertising and unordered merchandise.

Contact: FTC, Correspondence Branch, Room 692, Pennsylvania Avenue and 6th Street NW, Washington, DC 20580; 202-326-2508.

 General Services Administration
7th and D Streets SW
Washington, DC 20407
Main number: 202-708-5082
Public affairs: 202-501-0705

Scope Includes

Consumer information, government audits and investigations, fraud hot line, federal property, purchasing of equipment and supplies, information management, public buildings management.

Rich Resources

The GSA's Consumer Information Center publishes an extremely useful free quarterly catalog that describes more than 100 free and inexpensive consumer pamphlets and guides available from the government.

These pamphlets are very practical and helpful. "Ideas into Dollars," for example, provides advice on patenting, financing, and marketing a new invention or product. It lists various sources of assistance such as universities, government offices, inventors, and associations. "Occupational Outlook Quarterly" provides descriptions of new occupations, salary figures, job trends, and a lot of helpful advice.

Contact: Consumer Information Center, P.O. Box 100, Pueblo, CO 81009.

The *Consumer Resource Handbook* describes how and where to go to get help in resolving complaints and problems with companies. The handbook provides a complaint contact person at more than 1,000 well-known companies and gives advice on how to get help from a wide variety of sources, such as third-party resolution organizations, better business bureaus, media programs, municipal consumer offices, licensing boards, and federal agencies. The handbook is free.

Contact: Consumer Information Center, P.O. Box 100, Pueblo, CO 81009; 719-948-3334.

The Washington headquarters of the Consumer Information Center may be able to help you further.

Contact: Consumer Information Center, General Services Administration, 18th and F Streets NW, Room G-142, Washington, DC 20405; 202-501-1794.

HEALTH

FDA Consumer. Interesting articles for consumers based on recent developments in the regulation of foods, drugs, and cosmetics by the Food and Drug Administration. **Annual subscription—10 issues.** (FDA) **252W. $12.00.**

Fitness Fundamentals. A "must" for anyone starting to exercise. Discusses how to set up a program and monitor your progress. 7 pp. (1987. PCPFS) **129W. $1.00.**

How to Take Weight Off Without Getting Ripped Off. Discusses weight reduction and products, fad diets, and other diet aids; and provides tips on a sensible weight loss program. 4 pp. (1985. FDA) **529W. Free.**

Indoor Tanning. How tanning devices work, and why they can be as hazardous to your health as tanning outdoors. 4 pp. (1988. FTC) **422W. 50¢.**

Quackery—The Billion Dollar "Miracle" Business. How to protect yourself from health fraud. Discusses how bogus remedies for cancer, arthritis, and the "battle of the bulge" can hurt you much more than help. 4 pp. (1985. FDA) **530W. Free.**

Who Donates Better Blood For You Than You? Discusses the advantages of donating blood to yourself before undergoing planned surgery. 3 pp. (1988. FDA) **531W. Free.**

Drugs & Health Aids

Anabolic Steroids: Losing at Winning. Discusses the dangerous side-effects and reactions of these popular muscle-building drugs. 5 pp. (1988. FDA) **532W. Free.**

Comparing Contraceptives. Discusses effectiveness and possible side effects of nine types of birth control with a comparison chart and statistics on use. 8 pp. (1985. FDA) **533W. Free.**

A Doctor's Advice on Self-Care. There are more over-the-counter drugs available now than ever before which can cure, prevent and diagnose illnesses. The U.S. Commissioner of Food and Drugs tells how to use them safely and effectively. 7 pp. (1989. FDA) **534W. Free.**

Do-It-Yourself Medical Testing. Medical self-tests are available today for everything from eyesight to pregnancy to high blood pressure. Explains how some tests are used, how they work, and their accuracy. 7 pp. (1986. FD)

Food and Drug Interactions. How some commonly used drugs affect nutritional needs. How some foods affect drug actions; and how to avoid ill effects. 4 pp. (1988. FDA) **549W. Free.**

Myths and Facts of Generic Drugs. What they are and how they may save you money. Also corrects some common misconceptions about generic prescriptions. 3 pp. (1988. FDA) **536W. Free.**

Some Things You Should Know About Prescription Drugs. Even prescription drugs can be dangerous. Here's tips for safe use. 4 pp. (1983. FDA) **537W. Free.**

X-Ray Record Card. Wallet-sized card for recording X-ray examinations. (1980. FDA) **538W. Free.**

Medical Problems

AIDS. How AIDS is spread, how to prevent it, and what to do if you think you've been infected. 2 pp. (1988. FDA) **539W. Free.**

Breast Exams: What You Should Know. Eighty percent of breast lumps are not cancer. How to check for lumps, how doctors examine them, and treatments available. 17 pp. (1986. NIH) **540W. Free.**

Chew Or Snuff is Real Bad Stuff. Poster/booklet for teenagers describing dangers from smokeless tobacco including cancer, gum disease, stained teeth, and more. (1988. NIH) **542W. Free.**

Clearing the Air: A Guide to Quitting Smoking. No-nonsense tips on kicking the habit. 32 pp. (1985. NIH) **543W. Free.**

The Colon. While this part of the body is not generally discussed, it performs important functions and is the site of many problems, such as colitis, diverticulitis, and cancer. 6 pp. (1985. FDA) **544W. Free.**

Dizziness. Explains the various causes, diagnostic tests, and treatments for people suffering from dizzy spells. 27 pp. (1986. NIH) **130W. $1.00.**

Facing Surgery? Why Not Get a Second Opinion? Answers these and other questions of the prospective patient. Includes a toll-free number for locating specialists.

National Aeronautics and Space Administration

300 East Street SW
Washington, DC 20546
Main number: 202-358-0000
Public affairs: 202-358-1750

Scope Includes

Aeronautics and space technology, life sciences, astrophysics, earth sciences, solar system exploration, space shuttle payload, Mars observer program, microgravity science, upper atmosphere research, solar flares.

Rich Resources

NASA's Industrial Application Centers are designed to provide assistance in solving technical problems or meeting information needs. The centers offer on-line computer retrieval to 2 million technical reports in the NASA database and to more than fifty times that many reports and articles in 250 other computer databases. Topics covered include: aerospace, energy, engineering, chemicals, food technology, textile technology, metallurgy, medicine, electronics, surface coatings, oceanography, and more. The Centers operate on a cost-recovery basis.

Contact: To find the Center closest to you, write or phone NASA, Technology Utilization Office, 800 Elkridge Landing Road, Linthicum Heights, MD 21090; 410-859-5300.

Do you want to know how work is progressing toward development of a plane that can fly to Japan in two hours? Curious about the atmosphere on Venus? The NASA headquarters library will try to answer questions you have on flight and space. It can also send you documents from its collection or tell you where to obtain them.

Contact: NASA Headquarters Library, 300 East Street SW, Washington, DC 20546; 202-358-0168.

You can obtain an overview and a full description of several useful reports and information services available from NASA by getting a very valuable catalog called *NASA STI Products and Services at a Glance.*

Contact: NASA Access Help Desk, NASA Center for Aerospace Information, PO Box 8757, Baltimore, MD 21240; 301-621-0390.

NASA also makes its inventions available to the public for licensing. For more details, see page 147.

 National Archives and Records Administration

NARA, Washington DC 20408
Main number: 202-501-5400
Public Affairs: 202-501-5525

Scope Includes

Naturalization records, census data, military records, land records, passenger lists, passport applications, selected vital statistics.

Rich Resources

One popular use (among many others) of the National Archives is researching genealogy records. Although major projects need to be performed in person in Washington, DC, a reference services department will answer phone questions about holdings and furnish copies of documents for a modest fee. A useful bibliography is the *Archives' Select List of Publications.*

Contact: Reference Services Branch, National Archives and Records Administration, Washington DC 20408; 202-501-5400.

 National Foundation on the Arts and the Humanities

Arts: 1100 Pennsylvania Avenue NW
Washington, DC 20506
Main number: 202-682-5400
Public affairs: 202-682-5400

Humanities: 1100 Pennsylvania Avenue NW, Room 406
Washington, DC 20506
Main number: 202-606-8438
Public affairs: 202-606-8438

Scope Includes

Literature, museums, folk arts, visual arts, dance arts, music arts, theater arts and musical theater, opera, media arts (film, radio, TV), history, language, and so on.

Rich Resources

Program specialists at the National Endowment for the Arts may be able to help you with questions on design arts, expansion arts, folk arts, interarts, literature, media arts, museums, and visual arts.

Contact: National Endowment for the Arts, Old Post Office Building, Nancy Hanks Center, 1100 Pennsylvania Avenue, Washington, DC 20506; 202-682-5400.

The Division of Research Programs of the National Endowment for the Humanities will refer you to a division that can help you track down an answer to a humanities-related question, including inquiries related to history, philosophy, languages, linguistics, literature, archaeology, jurisprudence, the arts, ethics, and comparative religion. You can call the division directly or send for a booklet that will help you identify the expert you need.

Contact: Division of Research Programs, Room 318, National Endowment for the Humanities, 1100 Pennsylvania Avenue NW, Washington, DC 20506; 202-606-8200.

 National Science Foundation

1800 G Street NW, Room 527
Washington, DC 20550
Main number: 202-357-9498
Public affairs: 202-357-9498

Scope Includes

Atmospheric/astronomical and earth-ocean sciences, mathematical and physical sciences, arctic and antarctic research, anthropology, engineering, biology, genetic biology, chemistry, computer science, earthquakes, economics, ethics in science, meteorology, galactic and extragalactic astronomy, geography, geology, history and philosophy of science, nutrition, linguistics, marine chemistry, metallurgy, minority research, nuclear physics, science and technology to aid the handicapped, small-business research and development, sociology.

Rich Resources

The National Science Foundation funds research in all fields of science and engineering except for clinical research, by issuing grants and contracts. If you'd like information on how to apply for a grant, you can obtain the publication "Grants for Scientific and Engineering Research," which describes the guidelines for preparation of proposals, proposal processing and evaluation, and all other steps related to applying for NSF grants.

Contact: Public Affairs, National Science Foundation, Washington, DC 20550; 202-357-9498.

 National Transportation Safety Board

490 L'Enfant Plaza East
Washington, DC 20594
Main number: 202-382-6600
Public affairs: 202-382-6600

Scope Includes

Accident investigations involving aviation, railroads, highways, and hazardous materials.

Rich Resources

The National Transportation Safety Board conducts independent accident investigations and formulates safety improvement recommendations. The public can find out about these investigations by obtaining the board's "Accident Briefs" and "Accident Reports," which identify the circumstances and probable cause of the accident investigated. The reports are reasonably priced. To find out more, send for the board's publication "NTSB Documents and Information."

Contact: National Transportation Safety Board, Public Inquiries Section, 490 L'Enfant Plaza East, Washington, DC 20594; 202-382-6735.

NTSB's Safety Studies and Analysis Division will provide you with data regarding air accidents. For example, you can ask how many accidents occurred that involved a particular type of aircraft, or airline, during a specific year. There is no cost for the information.

Contact: National Transportation Safety Board, Safety Studies and Analysis Division, 490 L'Enfant Plaza East, Washington, DC 20594; 202-382-6536.

 Small Business Administration

409 Third Street SW
Washington, DC 20416
Main number: 202-606-4000
Public affairs: 202-205-6744
Toll-free help: 800-827-5722

Scope Includes

Women's business, veteran affairs, disaster assistance, financial assistance, management assistance, minority small businesses, statistical data, export advice.

Rich Resources

See chapter 4, "Business Information," for a description of the various kinds of business help available.

 U.S. International Trade Commission

500 E Street SW
Washington, DC 20436
Main number: 202-205-2000
Public affairs: 202-205-1819

Scope Includes

Agriculture, fisheries and forests, textiles, leather products and apparel, energy and chemicals, machinery and equipment, minerals and metals, instruments and precision manufacturers, automotive statistics.

Rich Resources

For a description of ITC's research reports, see chapter 4, "Business Information."

GUIDES TO GOVERNMENT INFORMATION

There are a number of excellent resources available to help you track down the precise bureau, division, or even person that can provide you with the information you need. These guides are published by both the government itself and commercial publishers. Here's the best of the bunch:

☑ Source: *United States Government Manual*

This comprehensive guide to the agencies and offices that make up the federal government is published by the office of the Federal Register, United States General Services Administration. All the departments are broken down into their various bureaus and offices, and key personnel within those offices are identified. The guide also includes information on quasi-governmental organizations like the Smithsonian Institution and multilateral organizations such as the Pan American Health Organization. Regional offices and Federal Information Centers—a specialized source of help described below—are also identified. Many libraries have this reasonably priced book, or you can order it from the Superintendent of Documents, U.S. Government Printing Office, Washington, DC 20402; 202-783-3238.

☑ Source: **Federal Information Centers**

These are clearinghouses set up by the United States for citizens who want to obtain information about the federal government. People who have questions about a government program or agency but are unsure about which office can help, may call or write to their nearest center. The FIC will either answer the question or locate an expert who can. Local numbers are listed in the *United States Government Manual* or check the "blue pages" governmental section of a nearby large city phone directory.

✔ Source: Internal Telephone Directories

The internal telephone directories of the federal departments are superb "insider's guides" to finding the person in the government who can help you. These directories provide the names, titles, and phone numbers of the individuals who work in specific divisions. Departments that make their directories available for the public's use include Defense, Energy, Health and Human Services, Labor, State, and Transportation. The directories are reasonably priced. To order, contact the Superintendent of Documents, U.S. Government Printing Office, Washington, DC 20402; 202-783-3238.

TIP: The Freedom of Information Act of 1966 requires federal agencies to provide the public with any identifiable records on request, unless the information falls into a special exempted category, such as classified national defense secrets or internal personnel data. If your request for some information is denied, you may seek assistance from the Freedom of Information Clearinghouse, Suite 700, 2000 P Street NW, P.O. Box 19367, Washington, DC 20036; 202-833-3000.

✔ Source: *Washington Information Directory*

Published by Congressional Quarterly, this is an excellent guide to information resources in Washington, D.C. The directory breaks down the various departments and agencies into their particular divisions, and it provides a one-paragraph description of the division's specialties and scope. A contact person and phone number for each division are also provided. This directory identifies sources of information within *not only federal agencies but also virtually any important organization—private or*

	Office Phone	Home Phone

STATE

Southern Africa Division (AA/S) Mary S Seasword 4635..........647-7163 362-7259

OFFICE OF ANALYSIS FOR INTER-AMERICAN REPUBLICS (INR/IAA)
Director John W DeWitt 7358..........647-2229 861-8314
Middle America-Caribbean Division (INR/IAA/MAC) Chief
  David Smith 7637..........647-4466 243-4278
South American Division (INR/IAA/SA) Chief
  James Buchanan 7534..........647-2251 971-6450

OFFICE OF ANALYSIS FOR EAST ASIA AND THE PACIFIC (INR/EAP)
Director John J Taylor 8840..........647-1338 241-3792
Deputy Director Louis G Sarris 8840..........647-1179 951-0064
China Division (INR/EAP/CH) (Vacant)..........647-1343
Northeast Asia Division (INR/EAP/NA) Chief
  Murray D Zinoman 8840..........647-2100 768-5370
Southeast Asia and Pacific Division (INR/EAP/SEA) Chief
  Allen Kitchens 8647..........647-2061 536-9310

OFFICE OF ANALYSIS FOR NEAR EAST AND SOUTH ASIA (INR/NESA)
Director George S Harris 4643..........647-8397 229-7175
Deputy Director Ronald D Lorton 4636..........647-2757
North Africa and Arabian Peninsula Division
  (NESA/NAP) Chief (Vacant)..........647-8403

Internal Telephone Directory: Department of State

FEDERAL AVIATION ADMINISTRATION

AIRWORTHINESS, OFFICE OF—Continued

	Exch.	Ext.
Technical Advisor Robert Allen rm 336B	426	8161
Policy and Procedures Branch John McGrath Manager rm 335C	426	8192
Technical Analysis Branch A C Caviness rm 337A	426	8200
Aircraft Manufacturing Division Sandy DeLucia Manager rm 333B	426	8361

AVIATION MEDICINE, OFFICE OF

	Exch.	Ext.
Federal Air Surgeon Frank H Austin Jr MD rm 300E	426	3535
Secretary Louise C Dille rm 300E	426	3535
Deputy Federal Air Surgeon Jon L Jordan MD rm 300E	426	3537
Secretary Monica Russell rm 300E	426	3537
Chief Psychiatrist Barton Pakull MD rm 327	472	5866
Aeromedical Standards Division William H Hark MD Manager rm 322	426	3802
Occupational Health Division Donald M Watkin MD Manager rm 327	426	3767
Computer Systems Analyst Carol A Thomas rm 329	426	3783
Industrial Hygiene Robert N Thompson PhD rm 327	426	3769
Biomedical and Behavioral Sciences Division Evan W Pickrel PhD Manager (Acting) rm 325	426	3433
Program Scientist—Accident Investigation Andrew F Horne MD rm 325	426	3434
Program Scientist—Human Resources Evan W. Pickrel PhD rm 325	426	3435
Program Scientist—Human Performance Alan H Diehl PhD rm 325	426	3433
Program Scientist—Protection & Survival William T Shepherd PhD rm 325	426	3436
Program Operations Division Virginia Meadows Manager rm 300E	426	3536
Administrative Officer Annette Lyles rm 321A	426	8326
Management Programs Leonard C Ryan rm 321B	426	8318
Program Evaluation Charles O Ensor rm 321D	426	8318

CIVIL AVIATION SECURITY, OFFICE OF

public—that operates out of Washington, D.C. These organizations deal with topics that range from health to the environment, labor, minorities, and much more. A subject index at the back of the book makes it easy to track down the particular information source that can best help you. The directory also lists the current top-level government personnel such as members of the cabinet, Senate, and House of Representatives. You'll find the *Washington Information Directory* in many libraries.

> **TIP:** I've found this guide—and Washington sources in general—especially helpful for answering consumer-oriented questions. For example, once I had to find out whether a certain energy-saving device really worked as claimed. The product was a device that fitted on top of a furnace's flue, and the vendor claimed it recirculated the hot air and thereby cut heating bills. I figured that the U.S. Department of Energy might have some kind of expert who could handle a question like this. The *Washington Information Directory* listed a Department of Energy division called Building Technologies, whose purpose is to keep up to date on technologies that may reduce building energy costs. Upon contacting the division, I discovered that, sure enough, there was a technical person in the division who was able to help. (Final verdict on the device: it *can* save some energy on older, inefficient furnaces, but not very much on newer ones.)

☑ **Source: *Federal Executive Directory***

Published by Carroll Publishing Company in Washington, D.C., this is another excellent guide to the federal government. Unlike the *Washington Information Directory*, it does not provide descriptive material on each agency and does not include a description of nongovernment organizations in Washington. However, it does provide a very detailed listing of federal personnel—their names, titles, and phone numbers. Using this guide enables you to zero in on the specific person who specializes in your subject of interest. A very handy subject index is provided at the back. This directory is available at most large libraries.

10804	Administrative Compliance Br	David T Head	301-443-3650
10805	Regulatory Affairs Div	Albert Rothschild	301-443-3640
10806	Deputy Director	Vacant	301-443-3640
10807	Product Information Coordination Staff		
		Ann Myers	301-443-4320
10808	Files and Reporting Sec	Ann Myers	301-443-4320
10809	Documents and Records Sec	Paul Chapman	301-443-5896

Drug Research and Review

10810
10811 *5600 Fishers Lane, Rockville, MD 20857*

10812	**Director**	Dr. Robert Temple	301-443-4330
10813	Program Management Dep Dir	Richard A Terselic	301-443-4330
10814	Medical Affairs Dep Dir	Paula Botstein (A)	301-443-4330
10815	Pharmacology Asst Dir	Dr. Vera C Glocklin	301-443-4330
10816	Chemistry Assistant Director	Dr .Charles Kumkumian	301-443-4330
10817	**DRUG BIOLOGY DIV**	Dr. Elwood O Titus	245-1118
10818	Deputy Director	Dr. Sidney Ellis	245-1118
10819	Technical and Animal Services Staff	Daniel Walker	472-5746
10820	Drug Bioanalysis Br	Dr. Joseph F Reilly	245-1400
10821	Drug Pharmacology Br	Elwood Titus (A)	245-1118
10822	Drug Toxicology Br	Dr. Tibor Balazs	245-1356
10823	Antimicrobial Drugs Br	Dr. Joseph H Graham	245-1034
10824	**CARDIO-RENAL DRUG PRODUCTS DIV**		
		Dr. Raymond J Lipicky (A)	301-443-4730
10825	Deputy Director	Stewart J Ehrreich	301-443-4730
10826	Project Management Staff	Natalia Morgenstern	301-443-4730
10827	**NEUROPHARMACOLOGICAL DRUG PRODUCTS DIV**		
		Dr. Paul D Leber	301-443-4020
10828	Project Management Staff	John S Purvis	301-443-3800
10829	Drug Abuse Staff	Edward C Tocus	301-443-3504
10830	**ONCOLOGY AND RADIOPHARMACEUTICAL DRUG PRODUCTS DIV**		
		Dr. John F Palmer	301-443-4250
10831	Deputy Director	Robert A Jerrusi	301-443-4250
10832	Project Management Staff	Robert G Scully	301-443-4250
10833	**SURGICAL- DENTAL DRUG PRODUCTS DIV**		
		Dr. Patricia Russell	301-443-3560
10834	Deputy Director	Philip G Walters	301-443-3560
10835	Project Management Staff	Gary H Boyer	301-443-3560
10836	Administrative Officer	Sandra Howard	301-443-2806

Center for Food Safety and Applied Nutrition

10837
10838 *200 C Street, SW, Washington, DC 20204*

10839	**Director**	Dr. Sanford A Miller	245-8850
10840	Deputy Director	Richard J Ronk	245-1057
10841	Scientific Advisor	Dr. William Horwitz	245-1057
10842	**PROGRAM OPERATIONS DIV**	Edward A Steele	245-2140
10843	Field Programs Br	Shane Carter	755-1606
10845	Center Programs Br	Dr. Ray L Russo	245-1564
10846	**INFORMATION RESOURCES MGT DIV**		
		Charles Exley	485-0010
10847	Administrative Ofcr	Thomas J Walsh	485-0009
10848	Automation Br	Dr. James Tucker	485-0018
10849	Computer Systems Br	George A Brindza	245-1233

Partial right-edge column (cut off):

10876	
10877	PC
10878	
10879	
10880	
10881	NUT
10882	Dep
10883	Med
10884	Staf
10885	Reg
10886	Con
10887	Nut
10888	D
10889	Cor
10890	N
10891	C
10892	E
10893	Mi
10894	
10895	
10896	
10897	1(
10898	F
10899	L
10900	10
10901	M
10902	Mi
10903	10
10904	Vii
10905	10
10906	Foc
10907	D
10908	F
10909	10
10910	F
10911	
10912	
10913	Fi
10914	C
10915	R
10916	C
10917	C
10918	Re
10919	
10920	
10921	
10922	Fc
10923	
10924	
10925	
10926	P
10927	D
10928	A
10929	A
10930	C

✔ **Source: *Info Power***

This book, published by Information U.S.A., provides more than a thousand pages of government information sources. Reading it is an excellent way to expand your mind and see what the government can really do for you. A detailed subject index makes it simple to find what you need. You'll find it in many bookstores.

The author of this book, Matthew Lesko, is a renowned expert in finding government information. His company, *Information U.S.A.*, publishes a monthly newsletter called *The Data Informer*, which identifies all sorts of federal and state sources of information. For more information contact Information U.S.A., P.O. Box 15700, Chevy Chase, MD 20815; 301-657-1200.

GOVERNMENT INFORMATION DATABASES

The U.S. federal government, over the past few years, has been making an effort to turn at least some of its massive information holdings into electronic databases. The following are two of the best sources for pinpointing which of these sources may cover a topic of interest to you:

✔ **Source: *SIGCAT CD-ROM Compendium***

This directory lists information on about 300 CD-ROM titles produced by the federal government, on topics ranging from acid rain to zip code display mapping. SIGCAT, which stands for the Special Interest Group on CD-ROM Applications and Technology, is an organization in the federal government made up of persons who have an interest in CD-ROM creation and distribution.

Contact: U.S. Government Printing Office, Superintendent of Documents, Washington, DC 20402; 202-783-3238. The stock number of this publication is 021-000-00-158-9.

☑ **Source: *Fedworld***

There are scores of federal government agency databases, and you can connect to over 100 of them by linking up with Fed-World, a one-stop electronic gateway, created by National Technical Information Service (NTIS). Among the services available are:

- National Agricultural Library
- Computer Security Bulletin Board
- Energy Information and Data
- FDA Information and Policies
- Department of Labor Information and Files
- Human Nutrition Information Service
- Health and AIDS Information and Reports
- Pollution Prevention
- Total Quality Management
- FCC Daily Digest, Statistics, Reports
- EPA Office of Research and Development
- Space Environment Information Service

While FedWorld is not free, it's quite inexpensive. It costs $35 per year to subscribe, which entitles you to four hours of online time. After that, the hourly charge ranges from $3 to $12, depending on the time of day.

FedWorld also offers its own files. For example, the Patent Licensing Bulletin Board allows for full-text searching of public inventions. An abstract describes the invention, and a complete copy of the patent application can be ordered from NTIS.

How to connect: To connect to FedWorld, set your communications software to dial 703-321-8020. Set parity to "none," data bits to eight, and stop bit to one. Terminal emulation should be set to ANSI or VT-100. If you have questions, you can call Bob Bunge at 703-487-4608.

Tip: It's important to remember that, while the NTIS gateway provides an extremely useful link-up to all kinds of federal agency data, it does not connect to *every* such service. For example, one not accessible through the NTIS gateway is the Environmental Protection Agency's Online Library System. This free system contains bibliographic citations to a wide variety of environmental information. (For information on signing up, call 919-541-1370.)

4

Business Information

A Sampling of Sources

(continued)

Many information searches involve the need to find business data of some sort. This chapter identifies some of the most popular and most available sources of quick information on six popular business topics: industries, companies, economic statistics, investments, starting a new business, and international business.

If you need to find business information, you should not only read about the specific business sources described in this chapter, but also note the broader information sources identified earlier in this book that include business within their scope (*Subject Guide to Books in Print*, periodical directories, trade associations, and so on). In addition, you should read about those business information sources found in the library, covered in chapter 1.

INDUSTRY INFORMATION

Do you want to find out all about the jewelry industry? Need to dig up some business growth projections on the restaurant business? Here are the places to turn to for information about industries:

First See

- The following indexes to find articles on industry news and trends:
  Wall Street Journal Index, p. 22
  Funk & Scott Index, p. 24
  Business Periodicals Index, p. 11
- Trade associations for free advice and information, p. 48
- Convention information for up-to-the-minute developments in an industry, p. 51

✔️ Source: Brokerage Houses

Let's say you need to find out the latest developments in the hotel industry, or discover what the experts think the chances are of a takeover of a television network. An excellent place to go is a brokerage house. Talking to stock analysts is one of the very best ways to obtain inside information about industries and about companies within an industry. Often, you'll see these analysts quoted in newspapers like the *Wall Street Journal*, giving an expert opinion about some industry development.

How do you find these analysts? The bible is probably a guide called **Nelson's Directory of Investment Research,** which provides the names, phone numbers, and areas of expertise of 4,500 security analysts whose expertise ranges from aerospace to waste disposal. The book is quite expensive, however, so try to locate it in a university business library or a corporate library. Or consider contacting the publisher and asking the editor to look up the name of the analysts for the industry you are interested in.

How to Find:

Contact W. R. Nelson & Company, 1 Gateway Plaza, Port Chester, NY 10573; 914-937-8400.

Another way to track down brokerage analysts is simply to call a very large brokerage firm like Merrill Lynch and ask to speak to an analyst who follows your industry of interest. (See chapters 6–10 for advice on interviewing experts for information.)

> **TIP:** Security analysts are very busy and often tough to reach on the phone. You might try asking to speak with the analyst's "associate" instead. Also, I've found that analysts located in the South or on the West Coast have more time and are more available to chat than those in the Northeast.

 Source: International Trade Administration

A superb—and free—source of information on specific industries can be found on the staff of the U.S. Department of Commerce's International Trade Administration. The ITA has 350 analysts who provide free information on industries such as automobiles, aerospace, capital goods, construction, electronics, services, textiles, and basic industries. The experts will give you up-to-date statistics, information on major U.S. and international markets, and more.

How to Find:

To find the expert you need, contact the U.S. Department of Commerce, International Trade Administration, Room 4805, Washington, DC 20230; 202-482-2000. The ITA will send you a photocopied list of their industry analysts from the *ITA Directory of Services and Employers* for seven cents per page. You can also order the entire directory of industry analysts and their phone numbers by calling ITA's publications department at 202-482-5494.

 Source: International Trade Commission

The International Trade Commission publishes free reports that cover various industries. Past reports include the monthly report on the steel industry, the world market for fresh-cut roses, generic pharmaceuticals from Canada, an annual report on selected economic indicators for rum, and studies of natural-bristle paint brushes from the People's Republic of China and cellular mobile telephones from Japan. These are the kinds of reports that, if prepared by a private research firm, could cost well into the hundreds or thousands of dollars.

INDUSTRY	CONTACT	PHONE 377-	ROOM	CLUSTER	INDUSTRY
A					
Abrasive Products	Presbury Graylin	5157	H4055	BI	Cement (Major Proj
Accounting	McAdam Milton B	0346	H4320	SERV	Ceramics
ADP Support (For Dir Invest in US)	Simon, Leslie B	3867	H2204	TIA	Ceramics (Advance)
ADP Support for Aerospace	Westover, Harion	2038	H3015	AERO	Cereals
Advertising	Nelson, Theodore	4581	H1122	SERV	Chemicals
Aerospace Financing Issues	Rand, Elizabeth	8228	H6881	AERO	Chemicals (Liaison
Aerospace Industry Analysis	Kingsbury, Gene	0678	H6733	AERO	Chemicals (Major
Aerospace Industry Analysis	Myers, Randolph Jr	0678	H6733	AERO	Chemicals & Allie
Aerospace Industry Data	Kingsbury, Gene	0678	H6733	AERO	Chinaware
Aerospace Industry Data	Myers, Randolph Jr	0678	H6733	AERO	Chloralkali
Aerospace Information & Analysis	Myers, Randolph Jr	0678	H6733	AERO	Coal Exports
Aerospace Market Development	Cohen, Richard E	8228	H6885	AERO	Coal Exports
Aerospace Market Promo	Sarsfield, Claudette	2835	H1012	AERO	Coal Exports
Aerospace Market Promo	Bevans, Samuel	2835	H1012	AERO	Cobalt
Aerospace Market Support	Bowie, David C	8228	H6883	AERO	Cocoa Products
Aerospace Marketing Assistance	Bowie, David C	8228	H6883	AERO	Coffee Products
Aerospace Military	Jackson, Jeff	8228	H6881	AERO	Coloring Extracts
Aerospace Policy & Analysis	Bath, Sally H	8228	H6887	AERO	Commercial Lighti
Aerospace Trade Issues	Jackson, Jeff	8228	H6733	AERO	Commercial/Indus
Aerospace Trade POLICY	Rand Elizabeth	8228	H6881	AERO	Commonline/Stan
Aerospace Trade Promo	Grafeld, George	3353	H1014	AERO	Components & Ec
Agribusiness (Major Proj)	Bell, Richard	1246	H2013	CGIC	Computer Progran
Agricultural Chemicals	Maxey, Francis P	0128	H4029A	BI	Computer Service
Air Conditioning Eqpmt	Shaw, Eugene	3494	H2100	CGIC	Computer Service
Air, Gas Compressors	McDonald, Edward	0680	H2128	CGIC	Computer Eqpmt
Air, Gas Compressors (Trade Promo)	Zanetakos, George	0552	H2126	CGIC	Computers
Air Pollution Control Eqpmt	Jonkers, Loretta	0564	H2811	CGIC	Computer Eqpmt
Aircraft & Aircraft Engines	Driscoll, George	8228	H6883	AERO	Computer & Busin
Aircraft & Aircraft Engines	Grafeld, George	3353	H1014	AERO	Computers (Trade
Aircraft Auxiliary Equipment	Driscoll, George	8228	H6883	AERO	Computers (Trade
Aircraft Equip	Grafeld, George	3353	H1014	AERO	Computers & Trad
Aircraft Parts	Driscoll, George	8228	H6883	AERO	Computers & Bu
Aircraft Parts/Aux Eqpmt	Grafeld, George	3353	H1014	AERO	Confectionery Pr
Airlines	Elliott, Frederick T	5071	H1122	SERV	Construction, De
Airports, Ports, Harbors (Major Proj)	Piggot, Deboorne	3352	H1012	CGIC	Construction M:
Alum Sheet, Plate/Foil	Cammarota, David	0575	H4059	BI	Construction M:
Alum Forgings, Electro	Cammarota, David	0575	H4059	BI	Construction Ma
Aluminum Extrud Alum Rolling	Cammarota, David	0575	H4059	BI	Consumer Electro
Ammunitions Ex Small Arms, Nec (Trade Promo)	Cummings, Charles	5361	H2126	CGIC	Consumer Goods
Ammunitions Ex Small Arms, Nec	Nordlie, Rolf	0305	H2124	CGIC	Contract Machini
Analytical Instrument (Export Promo)	Gwaltney, G.P	3090	H1108	S&E	Converted Paper I
Analytical Instruments	Donneliy, Margaret	5466	H1104	S&E	Conveyors/Conve
Asbestos Prod (Part)	Manion, James J	5157	H4055	BI	Conveyors/Conve
Audio Visual Equipment	Beckham, Reginald	0311	H4040	AACG	Copper Brass Wi
Auto Ind Affairs Parts/Supplies	Jerschkowsky, Oleg	1419	H1003	AACG	Copper
Auto Ind Affairs Parts/Supplies	Reck, Robert O	1419	H1003	AACG	Copper Products
Auto Ind Affairs Parts/Suppliers	Allison, Loretta M	1419	H1003	AACG	Cosmetics
Auto Ind Affairs Parts/Suppliers	Springmann, Michael J	1419	H1003	AACG	Costume Jewel
Auto Ind Affairs Parts Suppliers	Deborah Semb	1418	H1003	AACG	Current-Carryin
Auto Ind Affairs Parts, Suppliers	Heather Jones	1418	H1003	AACG	Cutlery
Auto Industry Affairs	Warner, Albert T	0669	H4039	AACG	
Automobile Dealers	Kostecka, Andrew	0342	H4316	SERV	

How to Find:

> Contact the International Trade Commission, Attention: Publications, 500 E Street SW, Washington, DC 20436; 202-205-1806, and ask for "Selected Publications of the United States International Trade Commission."

The Federal Trade Commission issues reports concerning industries as well; these are related to its activities in protecting consumers from deceptive advertising and marketing.

How to Find:

> Contact the Federal Trade Commission, Public Reference, Room 130, Washington, DC 20580; 202-326-2222.

✔ Source: Congressional Committee Hearings

Before final action is taken on a proposed piece of legislation, the Congress holds hearings. As part of these hearings, Congress often obtains testimony from various industry experts and notable persons. Transcripts of these hearings are ultimately created, and they are available to the public.

The following sample of standing committees and subcommittees in the House of Representatives should give you a feel for the scope of subject areas and industries that these hearings may cover:

- *Agriculture:* Subcommittees include: cotton, rice, and sugar; forests, family farms, and energy; livestock, dairy, and poultry; tobacco and peanuts; wheat, soybeans, and feed grains.

- *Energy and Commerce:* Subcommittees include: commerce, transportation, and tourism; energy conservation and power; fossil and synthetic fuels; health and the environment; telecommunications, consumer protection, and finance.

- *Public Works and Transportation:* Subcommittees include: aviation; public buildings and grounds; surface transportation.

- *Veterans Affairs:* Subcommittees include: hospitals and health care; housing; and memorial affairs.

- *Select Committees:* These include: aging; children, youth, and families; hunger; and narcotics abuse and control.

How to Find:

Here's how to track down transcripts of past hearings as well as find out what's currently happening in Congress. First, to find out if there are any *current* bills pending in the House or Senate on your subject of interest, call **Washington Legislative Information** at 202-225-1772. The person at that number will be able to tell you if there is such a bill and which committee is sponsoring it. The office can provide information as timely as one-day old and as far back as 1979. The office will also perform free keyword searches on its own database to locate legislative information and provide printouts from its legislative database for twenty cents per page ($5 minimum charge). To get the best results from this office you should try to be as specific as possible in your request; rather than asking for anything on "child care," narrow the topic down further to prevent being swamped with data. You can call the committee and ask to speak with an aide to the congressperson sponsoring the bill. He or she will be able to give you more details on the bill and tell you how to obtain copies of transcript hearings.

TIPS: Locating a Committee

▪ For a list of all the House's standing and select committees, contact the Office of the Clerk, House of Representatives, Room H, The Capitol, Washington, DC 20515; 202-225-7000. For Senate committees, contact the Office of the Secretary of the Senate, The Capitol, Room S-221, The Capitol, Washington, DC 20510; 202-224-2115.

▪ To find transcripts of past hearings, get hold of the Congressional Information Service's *CIS Index* or its *Index to Congressional Committee Hearings*. Both index hearings held prior to 1970, and the *CIS Index* also lists other committee reports and documents. These sources can be found in university or large public libraries. The actual transcripts themselves may be kept on microfilm at the library.

✔ **Source: United States Industrial Outlook**

The Department of Commerce publishes the *United States Industrial Outlook*, which provides projections on the economic outlook for over 350 manufacturing and service industries. Industries covered range from insurance to motion pictures. It's especially helpful for the nonexpert, as it provides a thumbnail sketch of critical factors like production, employment, prices, import competition, and projections. The guide is updated every December.

How to Find:

Order it from the Superintendent of Documents, U.S. Government Printing Office, Washington, DC 20402, 202-783-3238, or check a library for a copy.

☑ **Source: Market Research Studies**

How can you find out what studies have been privately conducted on, say, the cheese market, or the drug packaging industry? Check out a free publication, *The Information Catalog,* published by FIND/SVP. This catalog is published bimonthly and lists dozens of industry, market, and company studies. One problem, however, is that most of these studies are *very* expensive, ranging from hundreds of dollars to a couple of thousand. But you can use the "information interview" techniques outlined in chapters 6–10 to try to speak with the reports' authors.

TIP: Often, excerpts of these research reports are published in relevant trade publications. See page 16 for advice on identifying publications in your field of interest. Alternatively, you might identify a relevant trade association and check to see if their library will make a copy available.

How to Find:

Contact FIND/SVP, 625 Avenue of the Americas, New York, NY 10011; 800-346-3787 (in New York State, 212-645-4500).

When reading a study that purports to measure the size of a market, or forecast an industry or product's growth, it's wise to be a bit skeptical. Here are some guidelines for analyzing these types of reports:

▪ **Where did the data come from?** A seemingly obvious question, but Portia Isaacson, Ph.D., chairman of Channels Incorporated, Colorado Springs, Colorado, says published market numbers are derived from all manner of sources: complex and statistically valid measurement studies, informal questionnaires, someone's educated guess, or even "a remark overheard at a trade show." You need to pin down the provider of the data to explain specifically where the data came from.

▪ **How were the data collected?** Was it via personal interviews, phone calls, mail surveys, or a combination? If you can, it is desirable to get a copy of the actual questionnaire and examine it closely.

▪ **Who provided the data?** Wright notes that data that are "demand driven"—derived from users rather than manufacturers—are the most reliable. Reliability of data obtained from distributors or dealers sits between the two.

▪ **Does the study provide text?** Raw data alone are not enough. You need to be able to find out what the assumptions, reasoning, and logic were behind those numbers. Then you can determine for yourself whether the numbers derived from those assumptions are legitimate.

▪ **Can you speak with the researcher?** This is important to get your specific questions answered.

▪ **Does the firm have experience and credibility?** Is the specific subject of the report a field where the firm has credibility? If not, be sure to find out the analysts' and other principals' competencies in this field. Recent MBAs, says Wright, may someday be experts—but not right away. Sometimes you can find out a firm's track record by obtaining copies of their previous market reports and checking to see how accurate they were.

If the study is a forecast, it should try and take into account the various social, economic, and political events that may affect the phenomena being measured. Be wary of forecasts whose projections increase or decrease in a strict linear manner, because these calculations will not be taking into account real-world events that alter neat progressions.

How Is the Report Marketed? Beware of published data that appear more "sensational." In those cases, the need to market and sell the information can take precedence over the truth. Also be careful of slickly packaged market studies that scream of exploding markets and industries without providing convincing evidence. Some firms tend to be extremely optimistic in their

12 CONSUMER DURABLES

The Market for Rugs & Carpeting
Manufacturer & retailer profiles.

Their homes are their castles, and consumers are spending more than ever to furnish and decorate them. In this study—one of three available from FIND/SVP on segments of the home furnishings market—the market for residential rugs and carpeting is analyzed. Sales by type of rug, domestics versus imports, and by style are included. Competitor profiles of leading rug and carpeting manufacturers and retailers are provided.
AA210   June, 1989   119 pages $695

The Market for Lifestyle & Ready-to-Assemble Furniture
"Nesting" fuels growth for emerging market.

Typified by furniture sold in stores like Conran's and Pottery Barn, lifestyle and ready-to-assemble furniture represents a growing share of the overall residential furniture market. Baby boomers setting up new homes are the main force behind this dynamic, emerging market.

The study by FIND/SVP—one in a series of three on important segments of the home furnishings market—analyzes sales and growth for the category. It examines the role of offshore sourcing in the industry and profiles major retailers and manufacturers such as IKEA, Armstrong World, Bush, and Rospatch.
AA211   January, 1989   131 pages $695

The Market for Home Textiles
Stable, long-term growth; player profiles.

In the past three years, designers and manufacturers have turned home textiles—tablecloths, curtains, towels and linens—into upscale fashion, as trendy and appealing as apparel. Home textiles will increasingly become consumers' primary means of updating their homes without buying entire new rooms of expensive furniture—fueling the market and insuring stable, long-term growth.

The FIND/SVP study—one in a series of three studies on segments of the home furnishings market—examines the market for all types of home textiles, including sheets/pillowcases, towels, bedspreads/comforters, blankets, table linens, kitchen linens and curtains/drapery. Sales and growth, import data, and the growing trend toward designer fashions are included. Forecasts by segment and profiles of leading competitors are provided.
AA212   May, 1989   140 pages $695
AA213   Order any two reports & save $140 .... $1,250
AA214   Order all three reports & save $285 ...... $1,800

The Tabletop Market
Latest developments in this $3+ billion market.

The Packaged Facts study explores in depth the three major tabletop categories—dinnerware; glassware; and flatware. Products are analyzed according to type, style, pricing, distribution and import vs. domestic. Overall sales and growth are highlighted, and pinpointed are the significant growth factors. Sales statistics are given for the past five years, and projected to 1993. Also covered are advertising and promotion and the competition.
LA140   April, 1988   420 pages $1,250

Personal Care Appliances
New products spur sales in $1.5 billion market.

The comprehensive report from FIND/SVP examines forces shaping the $1.5 billion personal care appliance business. The study analyzes three segments in depth: cosmetic appliances, grooming appliances and health aids. Products covered include hair dryers, electric curlers, electric shavers, lighted mirrors, electric toothbrushes and digital scales. Consumer demographics are addressed. Major marketers are profiled.
AA187   July, 1988   c. 200 pages $995

The Greeting Card Market
Projections to 1995 for $4 billion retail market.

The Packaged Facts study analyzes the $4 billion retail market for greeting cards and pinpoints trends propelling the market into the 1990s. Discussion covers the continued growth of "alternative" cards, the increased emphasis on alternative line segmentation and marketer exploitation of new market niches.

The report offers sales projections to 1995. Current sales are broken out by type of card, distribution outlet, holiday and season. The competitive situation, involving leaders as well as the dozens of smaller players, is examined in detail. New product trends, advertising/promotion, the situtation at retail and consumer usage are also highlighted.
LA163   June, 1989   125+ pages $1,150

The Lawn & Garden Market
3 major components of the $14 billion market.

The comprehensive Packaged Facts study covers three major components of the $8 billion lawn and garden market: tools and equipment; supplies; and professional lawn care services. For each segment, it details the products involved, growth factors, projected sales, market composition, leading marketers, the competitive situation, new product development, advertising, promotion, distribution channels, retail outlets and consumer usage both of specific products and of gardening in general.
LA138   March, 1988   270 pages .... $1,3?

1988-1989 National Gardening Survey
Consumer trends & sales; 15 major segments.

This in-depth study by the National Gardening Association in arrangement with the Gallup Organization, provides marketing information and analysis and sales in 15 key areas: lawn care, flower gardening, houseplants, landscaping, ornamentals, vegetable gardening and more. The report includes consumer profiles, market size data, five-year market trends and a 1988-1989 Sales Index. New to this year is purchase trend information on more than 120 ~pecific types of lawn and garden products. Also included are cross-tabulation of all data.
NG04   July, 1989   370 pages $350

Large Kitchen Appliances
1989 international market; prospects to 1992.

This report from Euromonitor Publications covers the markets for large kitchen appliances in France, Italy, U.K., U.S. and West Germany in detail and provides summary coverage for other major international markets. Retail sales trends are examined for the 1983-1988 period. In-depth market studies—including market sizes, the latest brand shares and major company profiles—are offered for the five countries. Product categories include: laundry appliances; refrigeration equipment; cooking appliances (freestanding and built-in cookers, microwave ovens) and dishwashers. Forecasts are provided to 1992.
EP136   1989   225 pages .... $2,3?

Small Kitchen Appliances
International analysis: 1982-1988 & 1992 forecast.

The Euromonitor Publications report analyzes dynamics driving the market for drinks makers, food processors, deep-fat fryers, kettles, toasters and electric carving knives in the following countries: U.S., U.K., France, Italy and West Germany. Trends in retail sales and manufacturers' brand shares, sales breakdown by subsector, retail distribution trends, advertising expenditures, demographics and purchasing patterns are analyzed for the 1982-1988 period. Forecasts are available to 1992.
EP106   1989   130 pages $2,395

 FIND/SVP, 625 Avenue of the Americas, New York, NY 10011

projections, because a soaring new market will mean more buyers of their reports and consulting services. Similarly, beware of very positive projections where the issuer has something to gain. For example, city chamber of commerce studies nearly always show growth and positive trends for their region.

Experts in this field advise users of market studies not to rely on a single study, but to try to find as many studies as possible and compare the findings. Plot low and high points and look for consensus. When in doubt, go with the most conservative numbers—and assume that even those numbers may be optimistic. Even more to the point, never use published market data alone as the basis for making a major decision. Instead, get input from many different sources—talking to vendors, attending trade shows, talking to customers, and doing your own research.

COMPANY INFORMATION

If you're trying to get information on a particular company, there are several avenues to try, ranging from the company itself to the U.S. government.

First See:

The following indexes, to dig up published articles about a company:

- *Wall Street Journal Index,* p. 22
- *Funk & Scott Index,* p. 24
- *Business Periodicals Index,* p. 11

These directories to find financial data and information on company officers:

- *Standard & Poor's Register,* p. 25
- Dun & Bradstreet *Million Dollar Directory,* p. 25

Strategies for finding information on large companies and corporations are somewhat different than for small firms. Let's look at both cases.

Large Firms

A good place to start digging out information is the company itself. Call the public affairs or public relations office and ask for a copy of the company's **annual report,** issued by any publicly held corporation. The annual report will give you a very broad overview of the company's goals and operations, including an opening letter from the chief executive, results of continuing operations, market segment information, new product plans, subsidiary activities, research and development activities for future programs, information on the highest officers, an evaluation of performance over the last year, and a detailed financial statement. Getting the annual report is a good first step, but the financial tables are difficult to understand for most people.

TIP: If you do not know how to read financial tables, send for Merrill Lynch's excellent free publication "How to Read a Financial Report." Contact Merrill Lynch, Market Communications, P.O. Box 9019, Princeton, NJ 08543; 1-800-Merrill. Another superb guide, which concentrates on how to analyze business rations, is Dun & Bradstreet's *Understanding Financial Statements: A Guide for Non-Financial Professionals.* Contact Dun & Bradstreet, One Diamond Hill Road, Murray Hill, NJ 07974; 800-255-1033.

If the firm is not publicly held, and does not issue an annual report, it may produce a "company fact book" that serves a similar purpose. You can ask for it from the public affairs or public relations office.

Another source of information on large firms is the government. Here's where to go:

 Source: Securities and Exchange Commission

The SEC keeps information on corporations with publicly traded stock. All publicly held corporations and investment companies must file certain documents with the SEC, which are then made available to the public at no charge.

The following types of document are among those available from the SEC:

- *Annual Report:* See page 135 for a description.

- *Prospectus:* This is the basic business and financial information on the issuer. Investors use it to help appraise the merits of the offering.

- *10K Report:* This important document identifies the company's principal products and services, tells where properties are located, describes any legal proceedings pending, identifies owners of 10 percent or more of the stock, provides data on the background and salaries of the officers, and gives extensive financial information.

- *8Q Report:* This is a quarterly report that provides more timely data than the 10K.

- *8K Report:* The 8K Report must be filed within fifteen days of certain specified significant developments; these include filing for bankruptcy, a major acquisition, or a change in control.

How To Find:

You can obtain the documents you need by visiting or writing the SEC offices. Public reference rooms are maintained in New York, Chicago, and the Washington, D.C., headquarters. During normal business hours, individuals are permitted to review and photocopy all public findings. Or you can ask for request forms; contact SEC Public Reference Branch, Stop 1-2, 450 5th Street NW, Washington, DC 20549; 202-272-3607. The SEC charges twenty-two cents per page to photocopy and sends you any requested reports. Turnaround time is three to four weeks.

The SEC has the capability to perform computer searching of certain files. A free booklet, "A User's Guide to the Facilities of the Public Reference Room," explains all the information and services available and how to make the best use of them.

> **TIP:** A company called the Washington Service Bureau has established a library of SEC filings and documents. The firm can send you the materials you need for forty cents per page. The Washington Service Bureau can also obtain other federal documents for you, such as FCC rulings, Supreme Court opinions, and patent searches, at varying rates. Contact them at 655 15th Street NW, Washington, D.C. 20005, 202-508-0600. Another firm that offers the same service is called Disclosure. Their toll-free number is 800-638-8241. Disclosure offers two excellent free brochures: "A Guide to SEC Corporate Filings" and "Contents of SEC Filings." Disclosure also produces CD-ROMs containing data filed with the S.E.C. by over 11,000 public companies. Many larger libraries (especially business-oriented ones) offer these.

> **TIP:** Brokerage houses, discussed previously with regard to finding information on industries, can also provide information about large companies that operate in industries they follow. See page 126 for more details.

Small Companies

Finding information on small companies is harder, but there are still some avenues worth trying.

 Chambers of Commerce

Local chambers of commerce keep certain information on companies operating within their town or city, for example, the number of years a firm has been conducting business and whether any problems have been reported, such as customer complaints.

 Better Business Bureaus

BBBs keep reports on the performance records of companies based on their files and investigations. To find a local BBB office, check your phone book's white pages. (Also note that the

12

Quick Reference Chart to Contents of SEC Filings

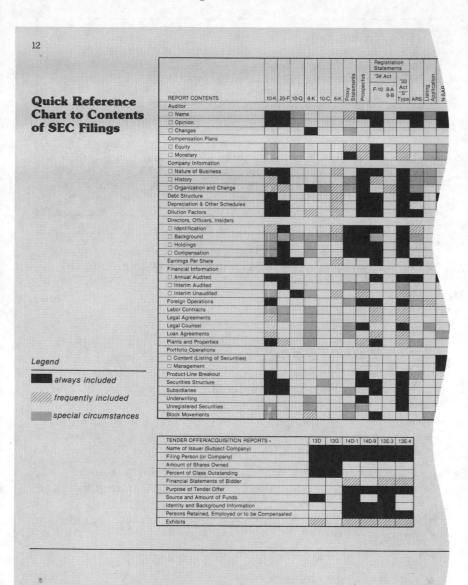

REPORT CONTENTS	10-K	20-F	10-Q	8-K	10-C	6-K	Proxy Statements	Prospectus	'34 Act F-10 8-A 8-B	'33 Act "S" Type	ARS	Listing Application	N-SAR
Auditor													
☐ Name													
☐ Opinion													
☐ Changes													
Compensation Plans													
☐ Equity													
☐ Monetary													
Company Information													
☐ Nature of Business													
☐ History													
☐ Organization and Change													
Debt Structure													
Depreciation & Other Schedules													
Dilution Factors													
Directors, Officers, Insiders													
☐ Identification													
☐ Background													
☐ Holdings													
☐ Compensation													
Earnings Per Share													
Financial Information													
☐ Annual Audited													
☐ Interim Audited													
☐ Interim Unaudited													
Foreign Operations													
Labor Contracts													
Legal Agreements													
Legal Counsel													
Loan Agreements													
Plants and Properties													
Portfolio Operations													
☐ Content (Listing of Securities)													
☐ Management													
Product-Line Breakout													
Securities Structure													
Subsidiaries													
Underwriting													
Unregistered Securities													
Block Movements													

Legend

■ always included

▨ frequently included

▩ special circumstances

TENDER OFFER/ACQUISITION REPORTS	13D	13G	14D-1	14D-9	13E-3	13E-4
Name of Issuer (Subject Company)						
Filing Person (or Company)						
Amount of Shares Owned						
Percent of Class Outstanding						
Financial Statements of Bidder						
Purpose of Tender Offer						
Source and Amount of Funds						
Identity and Background Information						
Persons Retained, Employed or to be Compensated						
Exhibits						

Council of Better Business Bureaus, 4200 Wilson Boulevard, Arlington, VA 22209, 703-276-0100, publishes inexpensive consumer advisory materials, such as "Tips on Buying a Home Computer" and "Tips on Car Repair.")

✔ Local Government

According to Washington Researcher's *How to Find Information About Companies,* City Hall may have certain records on file that you could find useful. For example, the county or city clerk could tell you the buyer and seller and description of a parcel of land, the tax assessor could tell you the property value and tax, the planning department may be able to provide you with information on building permits, environmental impact statements, and other data; and the building department could give you information on permit records and the building itself, such as its size and type of construction.

If you need assistance in searching local government records, you should request a catalog from a publisher called BRB. That firm has produced six inexpensive volumes providing sources and strategies for searching public records. These include: *County Court Records, Public Record Providers, Asset/Lien Searching,* and more. Contact BRB Publications, 1200 Lincoln, #306, Denver, CO 80203; 800-929-4981.

✔ Source: Local Media

Editors of local business journals and business editors of the local dailies can be excellent sources of information on firms operating within their community. These people are generally very easy to speak with and don't mind spending a few minutes telling you what they know.

Detective Work. You may need to do some detective work to unearth the information you need. Here are some hints on how to do the digging:

- Call the company itself. You might be surprised how much help you receive.

- Talk to customers. To find customers, send for company literature, which often provides names or just call the company and ask for references; once you've contacted the customers, ask them if they know of others who are also customers; this way you'll get to speak to people who were not directly named by the company.

- Talk to competitors. Check the yellow pages to find them.

- Talk to businesses that operate in the same building or are nearby neighbors.

- Talk to suppliers. See who makes deliveries.

- Talk to employees.

Digging up information on companies is a recognized discipline called "Competitive Intelligence." See page 257 for ethical guidelines and considerations when undertaking this type of research.

TIP: If you need to find information on a nonprofit organization—a charity, religious organization, professional association, and so on—you are legally permitted to examine a copy of that organization's tax return (form 990). Contact the IRS: Freedom of Information Reading Room, Internal Revenue Service, U.S. Department of the Treasury, P.O. Box 388, Ben Franklin Station, Washington, DC 20044; 202-662-5164.

ECONOMIC STATISTICS

Statistics are a typical component of many business information searches. Here are some good places to check:

First See

Statistical Abstract of the United States, p. 61

U.S. Bureau of the Census, p. 59

 Source: Bureau of Economic Analysis

This bureau within the Department of Commerce measures and analyzes U.S. economic activity and provides information on issues such as economic growth, inflation, regional development, and the nation's role in the world economy. Two excellent periodicals issued by the bureau are *Survey of Current Business* and *Business Conditions Digest.* The former provides estimates and analyses of U.S. economic activity and includes a review of current economic developments and quarterly national income and product account tables. The latter provides tables and charts for 300 economic series, featuring the composite indexes of leading coincident and lagging indicators. The bureau also publishes various economic papers, such as "Selected Data on U.S. Direct Investment Abroad 1950–1976" and "New Foreign Securities Offered in the United States 1952–1964."

How To Find:

Contact the Bureau of Economic Analysis, U.S. Department of Commerce, Washington, DC 20230; 202-606-9900. A helpful document is "A User's Guide to BEA Information."

TIP: Economic Statistics by Computer
- If you have a computer, you can obtain economic statistics inexpensively by tapping into the Department of Commerce's database "The Economic Bulletin Board." For more information, see page 191.

 Source: Bureau of Labor Statistics

The Department of Labor publishes statistical data on employment, prices, wages, living conditions, and productivity. Other specialties include state economic statistics, industry statistics, consumer expenditures, economic growth projections, and occupational outlooks. The BLS publishes a special directory called "Telephone Contacts for Data Users," which identifies the bureau's experts and specialists with their phone numbers. A periodical titled *Bureau of Labor Statistics News* is free.

How to Find:

Contact the U.S. Department of Labor, Bureau of Labor Statistics, Division of Information Services, Washington, DC 20212; 202-606-5902.

Federal Reserve Board Publications

The Federal Reserve Board publishes statistical data on banking and monetary interest rates, subjects like flow of funds and savings, business conditions, wages, prices, and productivity.

How to Find:

Contact the Board of Governors of the Federal Reserve System, Washington, DC 20551; 202-452-3245. Ask for the guide "Federal Reserve Board Publications."

 Source: Bureau of the Census

The Census Bureau makes available data about employment, unemployment, housing starts, wholesale and retail trade, manufacturers' shipments, inventories and orders, and exports and imports, as well as other business and economic statistics.

Two helpful guides published by the Bureau are designed specifically to assist businesspersons who want to understand various economic reports and series. ***Introduction to the Economic Censuses*** is a short pamphlet that identifies the different economic censuses and advises businesses how to use data appropriately; ***Census ABCs*** explains more broadly how the Census collects its data, and how to choose the right type of data depending on a business' particular needs.

How to Find:

Contact the Bureau of the Census, Customer Services Division, Washington, DC 20233; 301-763-4100.

One particularly useful series is "County Business Patterns." These are employment and payroll statistics in each county in the United States, broken down by SIC code. For each SIC classification, information is provided on number of people employed, payroll figures, and other data. (Be careful in using this source, sometimes the information is old.)

How to Find:

Contact the Superintendent of Documents, U.S. Government Printing Office, Washington, DC 20402; 202-783-3238. For more details on census information sources, see page 59

Source: IRS Statistics of Income Division

This division can provide you with various financial statistics drawn from past tax returns. Statistics are broken down into various filing categories—corporation income tax returns, industry statistics, investment tax credit statistics, estate tax returns, foreign income and taxes, partnership returns, the underground economy, and so forth. The statistics are published in the *Statistics of Income Bulletin*, which includes both statistics and summaries that explain and interpret the data. Many statistics are not published in the bulletin, but are available if you write to the division directly.

How to Find:

The bulletin is available from the U.S. Government Printing Office. To contact the division itself, write: Internal Revenue Service, Statistics of Income Division, 500 North Capitol Street NW, Washington, DC 20224; 202-874-0700.

 United Nations

Annual publications issued by the United Nations are a good source of facts and statistics on international business. Samples include "Agricultural Trends in Europe," "International Trade Statistics: Concepts and Definitions," "Statistics of World Trade in Steel," and "World Economic Survey." Some UN publications are expensive, but many are reasonably priced.

How to Find:

Contact United Nations Publications, Room DC2-0840, United Nations, New York, NY 10017; 212-963-8325/8302.

INVESTMENT INFORMATION

Here are a few places you can go to get some readily available and inexpensive help on learning the basics about investments:

Source: Standard & Poor's *The Outlook* **(McGraw-Hill)**

This is a leading source designed to provide some general investment-type information for nonexperts. *The Outlook* is a weekly bulletin that analyzes and projects business and market trends. It analyzes changes in the stock market, discusses firms currently in the limelight, and evaluates the worthiness of buying or selling particular stocks. The graphics are pleasing and it is overall very easy to use and read. It can be found in most large public libraries or in nearly all business libraries.

 Source: New York Stock Exchange

The NYSE publishes a very inexpensive "Investor's Investment Kit." The kit consists of four guides that provide a detailed description of how the market and various investments work, definition of accounting and financial terms, and descriptions of the advantages and disadvantages of various types of investment. The four guides are a "glossary," "Understanding Stocks and Bonds," "Getting Help When You Invest," and "Understanding Financial Statements."

How to Find:

Contact the New York Stock Exchange, Inc., Publications Division, 11 Wall Street, New York, NY 10005; 212-656-2089.

 Source: National Association of Securities Dealers

This is the self-regulating organization of the securities industry. Its members represent virtually all the broker-dealers in the nation doing a securities business with the public. The association publishes two free useful guides: "Guide to Information and Services," which lists various specialists within the association, and the "NASDAQ Fact Book," which provides various data and summaries of stock prices and volume of the NASDAQ (National Association of Securities Dealers Automated Quotation System) securities. The association can also help you if you have a complaint against a broker or are looking for market statistics.

How to Find:

Contact the National Association of Securities Dealers Inc., 1735 K Street NW, Washington, DC 20006; 202-728-6900.

✔ **Source: Investment Company Institute**

This national association of mutual funds publishes various inexpensive brochures on mutual funds, for example, "What is a mutual fund?" and "Gift to Minors Laws." It also publishes a directory of about 2,000 funds, their investment objectives, address, and phone number.

How to Find:

Contact the Investment Company Institute, 1600 M Street NW, Washington, DC 20036; 202-293-7700.

Finally, the **Securities and Exchange Commission** publishes free advice on investing—their booklet is titled "What Every Investor Should Know." Call 202-272-7460 for more details.

HELP IN RUNNING OR STARTING A BUSINESS

One of the most sought-after types of business information is that which will assist in operating a current business or in the start-up of a new one. Here are some of the best places to turn for help.

✔ **Source: Small Business Administration**

Among the services and resources offered by the SBA are: business loans; assisting small high-technology firms; special programs for veterans, minority, and women-owned small businesses; encouraging international trade by educational, outreach, and trade programs; assistance in procuring federal contracts; counseling and training in developing new business; and other programs.

Various books and pamphlets to help people in business are

published by the SBA. Materials include general advisory publications that would be of interest to all beginning businesspersons like "Going into Business," "Business Plan for Home-Based Businesses," "Researching Your Market," and "Outwitting Bad Check Passers," as well as publications about starting a business in one particular field, such as "Starting Out in Cosmetology." The booklets are all free or very inexpensive.

Unfortunately, the SBA's services and publications have been drastically cut back from what they once were. However, the agency can still provide useful materials and services.

How to Find:

A useful free brochure outlining the various programs available is titled, *Your Business and the SBA*, Office of Public Communications, Small Business Administration, 409 Third Street SW, Washington, DC 20416. For a free catalog of publications, contact SBA Publications, P.O. Box 15434, Forth Worth, TX 76119. You can also call a toll-free "answer desk" at 800-827-5722, but the advice given over this hotline is so simple that it is virtually useless.

 Source: National Technical Information Service

You can obtain a very useful publication that lists more than 180 federal and 500 state business assistance programs. This directory provides information on finding funding, obtaining mailing lists of prospects, how to find free management consulting, and more—it's called *The Directory of Federal & State Business Assistance.*

How to Find:

Write the National Technical Information Service, U.S. Department of Commerce, Springfield, VA 22161; 703-487-4650.

 Source: NTIS Center for Utilization of Federal Technology

You can locate government inventions with specific commercial value, obtain relevant technical information, and then negotiate a license by contacting the National Technical Information Service's Center for the Utilization of Federal Technology (CUFT). Inventions have been developed at various federal laboratories associated with NASA, the U.S. Army, the Department of Energy, and other government agencies. Those that have been made available free to the public to develop and market have included a low-cost humidity sensor, a braille reading system, a book-retrieving device for use by handicapped people in libraries, and thousands of other devices and ideas.

The CUFT also publishes the *Directory of Federal Laboratory and Technology Resources*, which is a guide to more than 800 government sources of state-of-the-art research and development expertise, laboratory facilities, and technology information centers. These federal agencies and laboratories are willing to share expertise, equipment, and sometimes even their facilities. Technologies covered include environmental science, medicine and health, transportation, engineering, and computer technology. You look up your subject of interest in the directory, and it refers you to the resources available.

How to Find:

Contact the National Technical Information Service, Center for the Utilization of Federal Technology, U.S. Department of Commerce, P.O. Box 1423, Springfield, VA 22151; 703-487-4838. To find out about NASA's inventions and apply for licenses, subscribe to a free publication called *NASA Tech Briefs,* available from Associated Business Publications Inc., 11 East 42nd Street, New York, NY 10017; 212-490-3999. NASA will provide you with back-up data on any of its inventions that you express an interest in developing commercially.

✔ **Source: Wisconsin Innovation Service Center**

If you already have an idea for an invention, but aren't sure how good it is or how it stacks up against the competition, here's a place to turn for help. The Wisconsin Innovation Service Center, which is associated with the University of Wisconsin, will provide you with a comprehensive and *confidential* evaluation at a relatively low cost. You submit your idea, and the center consults with university and private experts to form an evaluation. You are sent the full evaluation report, which includes the center's verdict on a variety of criteria, such as legality, safety, environmental impact, profitability, and competition. The report tells you the center's conclusions on your idea's strong points, and provides an overall evaluation of its chances for success in the commercial market.

How to Find:

Contact the Program Manager, WISC, 402 McCutcham Hall, University of Wisconsin, Whitewater, WI 53190; 414-472-1365.

 Source: Patent and Trademark Office

If you want to find out whether your idea for a new product has already been registered for a patent, or find out about the use of a trademark, contact the U.S. Patent Office. The office registers and grants patents and trademarks, and it provides information on them to the public. You can obtain an index of patents and order printed copies of patents for $1.50 each. There are also many depository libraries around the United States where you can go and inspect copies of patents.

How to Find:

Contact the Patent and Trademark Office, Washington, DC 20231; 703-557-3158 (General Information); 703-557-4636.

> **TIP:** You can find out about patent depository libraries located nearer to you—request a copy of Basic Facts about Patents, available from the office.

 Source: Mailing List Brokers

Here's a good way of finding the type of person or organization who might be most interested in buying your product or using your service. Mailing list brokers can provide you with thousands of names and addresses of people in specific professions —say, rabbis or biologists—and types of business and organization—pet shops, funeral homes, and so on. You can order the names and addresses on pressure-sensitive labels, so you can stick them on envelopes and mail your promotional flyer or other information. Prices for the names are less than what you may think—typically running about $45 to $100 per thousand labels.

How to Find:

Look in the yellow pages under "Mailing Lists" to find a firm.

TIP: Free tax advice
- Free tax-planning booklets are available from most local offices of "Big 6" accounting firms, such as Peat Marwick, Ernst & Young, and Price Waterhouse.

✔ **Source: *Deciding to Go Public***

A free 140-page booklet *Deciding to Go Public: Understanding the Process and Alternatives* is offered by the national accounting firm Ernst & Young. Among the subjects discussed in the book are the benefits and drawbacks of going public, selecting an underwriter, use of an accountant, and alternatives to going public.

How to Find:

Contact Herbert S. Braun, Ernst & Young, 2000 National City Center, Cleveland, OH 44114, 216-861-5000, or a local branch office.

TIP: Marketing information
- The previously mentioned "County Business Patterns" (page 142), published by the Bureau of the Census, can be used as a marketing tool to find out what kinds of establishments exist in a particular region of the country. For example, according to the Census Bureau, an East Coast department store chain considered opening a new store in an established shopping mall when store planners used census data to find the numbers and types of retail outlet in the area. From this information, they established business growth in the area and potential sales in the new store.

TIP: Consumer Demographic & Opinion Sources
* Here are four handy sources for finding out about characteristics, opinions, and other data on potential customers:

The Insider's Guide to Demographic Know-How (American Demographics, Ithaca, New York) provides a "do-it-yourself" approach to analyzing demographic data (e.g., analyzing characteristics of certain targeted populations by key variables such as sex, age, and income) and lists 600 federal, state, local, and private sources of demographic information.

Almanac of Consumer Markets: Also published by American Demographics, this invaluable sourcebook is a compilation of data on consumer demographics and behaviors for hundreds of cross-categories: age, income, marital status, race, education, labor force, health, expenditures, and more. The book isn't an inexpensive purchase, but could well be worth it if you need this kind of data. American Demographics has a toll-free phone number: 800-828-1133.

Population Reference Bureau: This organization is a private, scientific and educational organization established to gather, interpret, and disseminate facts and implications of population trends. It covers almost all areas in the field, such as, income statistics, elderly in America, the world labor market, international demographics, and much more. Most of the Bureau's reports and publications are very inexpensive. Contact: Population Reference Bureau, 777 14th St, Washington, DC 20005; 202-639-9040.

The Roper Center for Public Opinion Research, located at the University of Connecticut in Storres, has a database of over 7,000 "opinions" of the public on subjects ranging from views on AIDS to supermarket buying habits. You can find out answers to questions such as how many people own home computers or whether consumers are willing to pay more for a brand name. (This source is more expensive than others listed in this book; it costs $50 for the center to do a typical search.) Contact the Roper Center at 203-486-4440.

☑ **Source: *Small Business Sourcebook* (Gale Research Company)**

An extremely comprehensive yet easy-to-use directory for finding all sorts of sources of information and assistance for the small business. The book not only identifies where to find general business help, but also includes special sections covering 250 specific types of small business and where to find advice and assistance. Some of those industries include: antique shops, art galleries, bed and breakfasts, bookstores, gourmet food stores, consumer electronic stores, day-care centers, ice cream shops, magazine publishing, pet shops, pizzerias, software publishing, and videocassette stores. Overall, the guide is an excellent place to begin digging out information on starting a new business.

How to Find:

Check large libraries, university business school libraries, or contact Gale Research Company directly at 800-877-4253. The book is expensive, however.

REACHING FOREIGN MARKETS

If you want to know how to reach foreign markets for your product, the government can be a great place to turn for assistance.

☑ **Source: Export Promotion Service**

The mission of the U.S. International Trade Administration's Export Promotion Service is to 1) increase awareness and provide counseling to U.S. businesses to initiate and increase export activities; 2) provide information on overseas trade opportunities; 3) offer guidance on the use of market identification, market assessment, and contact information; and 4) provide related statistics, regulations, and other data.

The following programs and services are all available for a modest cost:

- Market sector analyses for 173 countries
- Access to a National Trade Databank—a comprehensive source of information and statistics on international trade
- Comparison Shopping Services to locate agents/distributors in host countries, D&B-type credit evaluations of agents, and competitive assessments of a product's market potential.

How to Find:

Contact the U.S. Department of Commerce, Export Promotion Service, Office of Information Product Development and Distribution,

Cheese/Wine/Gourmet Food Shop

Start-up Information

2681
"Cheese and Wine Shop" in *Small Businesses That Grow and Grow and Grow (pp. 206-207)*
Betterway Publications, Inc.
White Hall, VA 22987
Phone: (804)823-5661
Woy, Patricia A. 1984. $7.95 (paper). A chapter about establishing a cheese and wine shop.

2682
Gourmet Wine and Cheese Shop Start-up Manual
American Entrepreneurs Association (AEA)
2311 Pontius Ave.
Los Angeles, CA 90064
Phone: (800)421-2300
$59.50 ($54.50 for AEA members). Contains step-by-step instructions on how to start a cheese, wine, and gourmet food store. Includes information on profits and costs, location, market potential, financing, advertising and promotion, customers, and related data. **Toll-free/Additional Phone Number:** 800-352-7449 (in California).

Primary Associations

2683
American Cheese Society (ACS)
Main St.
P.O. Box 97
Ashfield, MA 01330
Phone: (201)236-2990
Purpose: To provide a network for members who seek solutions to problems regarding cheesemaking processes or related regulations. Activities include cheese tastings, gourmet cooking demonstrations, and cheese making demonstrations. **Membership:** Primarily small-scale cheese producers; also includes retailers and wholesalers.

2684
International Dairy-Deli Association (IDDA)
313 Price Pl., Suite 202
P.O. Box 5528
Madison, WI 53705
Phone: (608)238-7908
Purpose: Promotes professional development and the exchange of information and ideas among members. Bestows awards for outstanding achievement. Holds annual seminar and exposition. **Membership:** Companies and organizations engaged in the production, processing, packaging, marketing, promotion, and/or selling of cheese, bakery, or delicatessen-related products. **Publications:** 1) *Dairy-Deli Digest* (monthly); 2) *Dairy-Deli Wrap-Up* (quarterly); 3) *Who's Who in Deli*Dairy*Bakery* (semiannual); 4) *Annual Seminar Proceedings*. Also publishes research reports and produces educational slide-tape programs.

2685
National Association for the Specialty Food Trade (NASFT)
215 Park Ave., S., Suite 1606
New York, NY 10003
Phone: (212)505-177
Purpose: To promote the specialty food industry. Sponsors competitions, bestows awards. Holds annual trade show. **Membership:** Manufacturers, processors, importers, and brokers of specialty and gourmet foods. **Publications:** 1) *NASFT Showcase* (semimonthly); 2) *RD Trends* (bimonthly).

Other Organizations of Interest

2686
International Federation of Wine and Spirits (IFWS)
103 Blvd. Haussmann
F-75008 Paris, France
Phone: 1 265
Purpose: To protect the industry at all levels of comm **Membership:** Industrialists and wholesalers of wine, spirits, br and liqueurs. **Publications:** 1) *Bulletin* (5/year); 2) *Newsletter* (5/;

2687
National Association of Specialty Food and Confection Broker (NASFCB)
Burgess, Bradstreet, and Associates
14229 Bessemer St.
Van Nuys, CA 91401
Phone: (818)997-056
Membership: Professional food brokers who supply department stores, gourmet shops, grocery chains, health food trades, and other companies with quality products for retail purposes. **Publications:** 1) *Newsletter* (quarterly); 2) *Directory of Members* (annual).

Educational Programs

2688
International Dairy-Deli Association (IDDA)
313 Price Pl., Suite 202
P.O. Box 5528
Madison, WI 53705
Phone: (608)238-79
Provides slide-tape programs on merchandising, sales, emplo motivation and training, customer satisfaction, and research in cheese and deli industry.Offers home-study courses, cosponsore the Cornell University Food Industry Management Program.

Reference Works

2689
The Cheese Handbook: A Guide to the World's Best Cheeses
Dover Publications, Inc.
31 E. Second St.
Mineola, NY 11501
Phone: (516)294-7000
Layton, T. A. Revised edition, 1973. $3.50 (paper).

P.O. Box 14207, Washington, DC 20044; 202-482-6220 or 202-482-2867.

 Source: Flash Fax Service

A number of U.S. agencies have recently begun a "Fax on Demand" information service. This is a system that uses voice mail technology and presents callers with a menu of items that can be selected via a touch tone phone. After making selections, the caller taps in his or her fax number before hanging up. The system then automatically faxes the desired materials, often in a matter of just a few minutes. One of the biggest users of this technology is the U.S. Department of Commerce. The following is a listing of offices currently offering free reports and documents on international market via its "Flash Fax" service. Users may request up to five documents per call.

- Eastern Europe Business Information Center.
  (202) 482-5745

- Office of the Pacific Basin
  (202) 482-3875 and (202) 482-3646

- Business Information Service for the Newly Independent States
  (202) 482-3145

- Offices of Africa, Near East, and South Asia
  (202) 482-1064

- Office of Mexico
  (202) 482-4464

Among the type of information available are export financing sources, investment opportunities, upcoming trade shows, permits and customs, statistics and demographics, country profiles, investment opportunities, and publications.

 Source: Eastern Europe Business Information Center

Recently established by the U.S. Department of Commerce, the EEBIC is designed to be a "first-stop"-type clearinghouse for companies interested in doing business in Eastern Europe.

One of the specialties of the EEBIC is assisting businesses in analyzing a country's overall climate for doing business. For example, the Center will advise whether a country's phone systems are workable. Also available is the Eastern Europe Looks for Partners service, whereby Eastern European firms send in requests for U.S. partners, and the "Bulletin," a monthly newsletter profiling countries, industry sectors, and trade opportunities. For more information, contact the EEBIC at: Room 6043, U.S. Department of Commerce, 14th & Constitution Avenue NW, Washington, DC 20230; 202-482-2645.

✔ **Source:** *Overseas Business Report*

Another good, moderately priced publication put out by the Department of Commerce's International Trade Administration is its *Overseas Business Report*. Each issue covers a different country and provides detailed information on trade and investment conditions and marketing opportunities. Information is provided on trade patterns, industry trends, natural resources, population, trade regulations, market prospects, and more.

How to Find:

Contact the Superintendent of Documents, U.S. Government Printing Office, Washington, DC 20402; 202-783-3238.

✔ **Source: Export Counseling Center**

If you've decided you'd like to give selling overseas a try, you can obtain free help from the International Trade Administration's Export Counseling Center. The center publishes a variety of helpful publications, such as "How to Get the Most from Overseas Exhibitions," "A Guide to Financing Exports," and a regular bulletin, which is a weekly publication on export opportunities for U.S. firms. The bulletin includes direct sales leads from overseas buyers, foreign government bid invitations, notification of foreign buyer visits to the United States, and more. Lots of other help is available too, including a mailing list of foreign business contacts—agents, distributors, retailers, wholesalers, manufacturers, and exporters for virtually any industry in 116 countries.

How to Find:

Contact the Trade Information Center, U.S. Department of Commerce, International Trade Administration, USSCS, HCHB-7424, Washington, DC 20230; 800-872-8723.

✔ **Source: Country Desk Officers**

Other good sources of help in finding out about foreign markets are the International Trade Administration's Country Desk Officers—about 200 government staff members who are true experts on a particular country's economic and commercial situation. These officers may also have some expertise in a country's political situation, because they keep in touch with the U.S. State Department's desk officers.

How to Find:

To find the expert you need, contact the U.S. Department of Commerce, International Trade Administration, Washington, DC 20230; 202-482-2867. The ITA will send you a photocopied list of their Country Desk Offices from the *ITA Directory of Services and Employees* for seven cents per page.

✔ **Source: Country Consulates and Embassies**

Finally, you can obtain help on questions you have about a particular market in a country by contacting its consulate office. Check the white pages of a major city phone book to find the consulate you seek. Or you can try the country's embassy in Washington, D.C. The State Department publishes a "Diplomatic List," which gives the names and addresses of embassy personnel. You can obtain this list from the Superintendent of Documents, U.S. Government Printing Office, Washington, DC 20402; 202-783-3238.

The United Nations also publishes a list called "UN Services and Embassies." This is a listing of the addresses and phone numbers of consulate and embassy locations. Contact the U.N. Public Inquiries Unit, Department of Public Information, United Nations, Room 6A57, New York, NY 10013; 212-963-1234.

Source: *Exporters Guide to Federal Resources for Small Business*

This handbook is an exception to the generally poor quality of recent publications being issued by the now pared-down Small Business Administration. This is a very useful and well-organized guide that identifies key contact points throughout the federal government designated to help small businesses reach markets in other countries. The book describes the various programs and services, provides full contact names and phone numbers, and includes an appendix that lists further sources of information. It is very inexpensive.

How to Find:

Contact: Department 36-XK, Superintendent of Documents, Washington, DC 20402-9325; 202-783-3238. The stock number is 045-000-00250-1.

INTERNATIONAL INFORMATION SOURCES

As discussed earlier, because today we live in a global marketplace, it is critical to be aware not only of sources of information about U.S. businesses and industries, but of foreign ones as well. The following is a selection of some of the most useful and timely sources.

 Source: *Information Gathering on Japan*

This book is designed to offer business researchers resources for finding leads on information on Japan. Among the resources listed in this directory are: U.S. government agencies, research and academic organizations, publications, on-line databases, trade associations, consultants, translators, and more. The author, Mindy Kotler, is one of the leading experts on finding Japanese business information.

How to Find:

Contact: Japan Information Access Project, 1706 R Street NW, Washington, DC 20009; 802-660-9636. This book costs $50.

COUNTRY	DESK OFFICER	AREA	PHONE 377-	ROOM	CABLE CODE	COUNTRY
A						
Afghanistan	Stan Bilinski	ANESA/OSA	2954	2029B	4530	Germany (West)
Albania	James Ellis	EUR/EE	2645	3419	4232	Ghana
Algeria	Jeffrey Johnson	ANESA/ONE	4652	2039	4520	Greece
Angola	Simon Bensimon	ANESA/OA	0357	3317	4510	Grenada
Argentina	Mark Siegelman	WH/OSA/BRP	5427	3021	4332	Guadeloupe
ASEAN	George Paine	EAP/OPB/SA	3875	2332	4430	Guatemala
Australia	Tony Costanzo/					Guinea
	Gary Bouck	EAP/OPB	3646	2010	4430	Guinea-Bissau
Austria	Philip Combs	EUR/WE/NE	2434	3411	4212	Guyana
B						**H**
Bahamas	Libby Roper	WH/CB	2527	3029A	4322	Haiti
Bahrain	Claude Clement	ANESA/ONE	5545	2039	4520	Honduras
Bangladesh	Christine Coady	ANESA/OSA	2954	2029B	4530	Hong Kong
Barbados	Vacant	WH/CB	2527	3029A	4322	Hungary
Belgium	Boyce Fitzpatrick	EUR/WE/NE	2920	3415	4212	
Belize	Robert Dormitzer	WH/CB	2527	3029A	4322	
Benin	James Robb	ANESA/OA	4564	3317	4510	**I**
Bermuda	Libby Roper	WH/CB	2527	3029A	4322	Iceland
Bhutan	Richard Harding/					India
	Christine Coady/					
	Renee Hancher	ANESA/OSA	2954	2029B	4530	
Bolivia	Roger Turner	WH/OSA/AD	4302	3314	4331	Indonesia
Botswana	Reginald Biddle	ANEAS/OA	5148	3317	4510	
Brazil	Robert Bateman/					Iran
	Roger Turner/					Iraq
	Patricia Hanigan	WH/OSA/BRP	3871	3017	4332	Ireland
Brunei	Gary Bouck	EAP/PB/SA	3875	2310	4430	Israel
Bulgaria	James Ellis	EUR/EE	2645	3419	4232	Italy
Burkina Faso	John Crown	ANESA/OA	4564	3317	4510	Ivory Coast
Burma	Kyaw Win	EAP/PB/SA	5334	3820	4430	
Burundi	Simon Bensimon	ANESA/OA	0357	3318	4510	**J**
						Jamaica
C						Japan
Cambodia	JeNelle Matheson	EAP/PRC&HK	4681	2323	4420	Jordan
Cameroon	Philip Michelini	ANESA/OA	0357	3317	4510	
Canada	Joseph Payne/					**K**
	Kenneth Fernandez/					Kampuchea
	Caratina Alston	WH/OC	0849	3643	4310	Kenya
Cape Verde	Renee Hancher	ANESA/OA	4564	3317	4510	Korea
Caymans	Libby Roper	WH/CB	2527	3029A	4322	Kuwait
Central African Rep.	Philip Michelini	ANESA/OA	0357	3317	4510	
Chad	Fred Stokelin	ANESA/OA	4564	3317	4510	**L**
Chile	Herbert Lindow	WH/OSA/BRP	4302	3027	4332	Laos
Colombia	Richard Muenzer	WH/OSA/AD	4302	3027	4331	Lebanon
Comoros	Fred Stokelin	ANESA/OA	4564	3317	4510	Lesotho
Congo	Philip Michelini	ANESA/OA	0357	3317	4510	Liberia
Costa Rica	Fred Tower	WH/CB	2527	3029A	4322	Libya
Cuba	Ted Johnson	WH/CB	2527	3029A	4322	Luxembourg
Cyprus	Ann Corro	EUR/WE/SE	3945	3044	4220	
Czechoslovakia	James Ellis	EUR/EE	2645	3419	4232	

Country Desk Officers

Source: *Japan's High Technology*

This directory lists descriptive data for over 500 of "the best" English-language sources of information on Japanese science, technology, and related business topics. Among the types of sources listed: conference reports, industry reports, online databases, patent literature, directories, periodicals, translation guides, and more.

How to find:

Contact: Oryx, 4041 North Central at Indian School, Phoenix, AZ 85012; 602-265-2651.

 Source: Association for Asian Studies

The Association for Asian Studies is a scholarly, nonpolitical, nonprofit professional association that facilitates contact and exchange of information among scholars, students, businesspersons, journalists, and others for an increased understanding of Asia. It publishes a directory titled *Directory of Japan Specialists and Japanese Studies Institutions in the United States and Canada*, which provides information on nearly 1,500 Japan specialists, along with their research interests, areas of specialization, academic affiliations, and more.

How to Find:

Contact: Association for Asian Studies, One Lane Hall, University of Michigan, Ann Arbor, MI 48109; 313-764-1817.

 Source: The Office of Japan, Department of Commerce

This office assists U.S. firms needing information about Japan. A key service that the office may be able to provide is a list of contact names. Building contacts is critical for doing business in Japan.

How to Find:

Contact: Deputy Assistant Secretary Marjory Searing, Department of Commerce, International Trade Administration, Office of Japan,

14th Street and Constitution Avenue NW, Room H-2318, Washington, DC 20230; 202-482-4527.

 Source: *International Business Handbook: Republic of Korea*

This is a 311-page book that guides the reader to over 1,000 information sources on Korea. This book can be used for attracting Korean investors, finding office space in that country, meeting Korean product standards, locating Korean bankers or lawyers, obtaining corporate strategies of major Korean firms and much more. It looks like an indispensable handbook for any organization planning to do business in Korea.

How to Find:

Contact Global Quest Inc., 2713 S. Lang Street, Arlington, VA 22206; 703-683-4485. The book costs $135.

 Source: *China Trade Directory*

Published by the Embassy of the People's Republic of China, this directory is a 50-page white paper that provides basic facts about China, an overview of foreign trade statistics and events, a description and analysis of China's foreign trade system, export and import licensing, tariffs, business practices and customs, and documentation. A chart lists China's major imports and exports, by country. At the end of the directory, there is a listing of key government offices with names of officials, titles, and contact information. The directory is free.

How to find:

Contact: Guang Ming Song, Commercial Attache, Embassy of the People's Republic of China, 2300 Connecticut Avenue NW, Washington, DC 20008; 202-328-2520.

Source: Single Internal Market: 1992 Information Service

The U.S. Department of Commerce is making a major effort to provide advice and assistance to businesses about the single European market. This special office will provide, for free, copies of the single internal market regulations, background information on the European Community, and assistance regarding specific opportunities or potential problems.

How to Find:

Contact: Single Internal Market, U.S. Department of Commerce, Office of European Community Affairs, Room 3036, 14th Street and Constitution Avenue NW, Washington, DC 20230; 202-482-2645. (Also see the desk officers described on page 155 for information about doing business in specific countries.)

 Source: *Latecomer's Guide to the New Europe*

A nice, readable, and inexpensive 95-page pamphlet designed for firms interested in expanding their market into Europe, but need some basic advice. Easy to read, but filled with valuable information on developing a marketing strategy for the European Commission.

How to find:

Contact: American Management Association, Publications Division, 135 W. 50th Street, New York, NY 10020; 212-903-8270.

TIP: If you need to gather facts, statistics, and analyses of European countries and markets, request a catalog from a United Kingdom firm called Euromonitor. This company produces some of the most comprehensive and detailed reference directories on European business issues. Note, though, that most are quite expensive, so your best bet may be looking for these guides in a university business library and/or one whose scope includes international trade. You can reach the firm at: Euromonitor, 87-88 Turnmill Street, London EC1M 5QU, U.K. Phone (from U.S.) 011-44-71-251-8024.

Source: NAFTA and Doing Business in Mexico

One of the best places to turn for information on NAFTA and trade with Mexico are Chambers of Commerce. The following two can be of assistance:

- American Chamber of Commerce of Mexico
  Among its publications are: ***Business Mexico, Directory of American***

Company Operations in Mexico, Maquiladora Handbook, Maquiladora Newsletter, Mexican Export Manual, Mexican Import Manual.

How to find:

Contact: American Chamber of Commerce of Mexico, Lucerna 78, Co. Juarez, 06600 Mexico City, Mexico; phone: 011-525-705-0995; fax: 011-525-705-3908.

- U.S. Mexico Chamber of Commerce
Promotes private sector trade, conducts seminars, publishes a newsletter, bulletin, and various booklets.

How to find:

Contact: U.S. Mexico Chamber of Commerce, 1211 Connecticut Avenue NW, Suite 510, Washington, DC 20036; (202) 296-5198.

BUSINESS SUPERSOURCES

The following sources are so comprehensive that they do not fit into any of the previous business information categories; each can provide many different types of business information—statistics, industry or company data, and more.

☑ **Source: *The Dow Jones—Irwin Business and Investment Almanac***

This almanac, published yearly, is a comprehensive source of business and investment information. Each edition typically includes the following information: a month-by-month business review of the past year; industry surveys—financial data, trends, and projections; financial statement ratios by industry; general business and economic indicators—GNP, corporate profits, CPI, national income, and largest company data—rankings, assets, net income, stockholder equity, and employees; top growth companies; capital sources for start-up companies and small businesses; bonds and money market investment data; tax shelters; investment in gold, diamonds, and collectibles—what to look for, terms to know; investing in real estate; on-line business databases; and a directory of other business sources.

The almanac is especially abundant in stock information—

returns on stocks, bonds, and bills; major market averages; and guides to SEC filings, mutual funds, investment, and financial terms.

How to Find:

You can find this book in many bookstores. Or you can contact the publisher: Dow Jones—Irwin, 1818 Ridge Road, Homewood, IL 60430; 800-634-3961. (Dow Jones has a free catalog that describes many other business books too. One interesting-sounding one is *The Dow Jones—Irwin Guide to Using the* Wall Street Journal.)

 Source: UNIPUB

An excellent source for finding a variety of publications from international organizations is through a publisher called UNIPUB. UNIPUB is a distributor for the United Nations, The European Communities, The Food & Agriculture Organization (FAO), The World Bank, International Monetary Fund (IMF), General Agreement on Tariffs and Trade (GATT), the official British government publisher HMSO, Organization for Economic Cooperation and Development (OECD), the International Labor Organization (ILO), and other well-known international and non-U.S.–based institutions.

How to find:

Contact: UNIPUB, 4611-F Assembly Drive, Lanham, MD 20706-4391; 800-274-4888.

 Source: Brooklyn, New York Business Library

Whether you need industry statistics, company financial data, or stock information, or have an inquiry on virtually any other business-related subject, the Brooklyn, New York Business Library may be able to help you. It's one of the leading, if not *the* leading, business library in the country. It takes phone inquiries and tries to answer any financial, economic, or industry-oriented question that can be answered with a fact or referral.

How to Find:

Call the library's reference desk at 718-722-3333.

✔ Source: State Government

Lots of buried business-related information is available from state governments. The best department to contact is the state's department of commerce, department of economic development, or a similar-sounding bureau. Just as an example, here is what I uncovered by contacting the Arizona Department of Commerce:

Arizona's business and trade division of its department of commerce publishes a number of free guides packed with business-related information. For example, it collects state export statistics and publishes an international trade directory that lists companies in Arizona that do exporting, and it publishes a guide to establishing a business in Arizona—licenses required, regulations, and so forth. The office prepares an economic profile of the state that gives data on areas like population, labor, and financing programs. Special research reports are issued too. Past subjects have included a review of high-tech companies in Arizona and a study of the aerospace industry and its suppliers. The directory of high-tech companies listed the firms' names, addresses, current products, SIC codes, numbers of employees, and other data. All of these are made available free to the public.

Another division of the Arizona Department of Commerce is devoted to "policy and research." That division publishes a book, *Arizona's Changing Economy: Trends and Projections*, that lists data on trends in land, population, and different manufacturing and service economies.

Other departments that looked promising were the Arizona Department of Economic Security, for free employment and job search information; the Department of Revenue, for licensing information; and the Department of Tourism, for information on expenditures made by out-of-state visitors.

How to Find:

Check your phone book for a listing, or consult the *State Executive Directory* in a library (p. 64). Or you can simply call directory assistance in your state's capital.

✔ Source: On-Line Databases

Be sure to read the information in chapter 5 about on-line databases. As explained in detail in that chapter, a database is simply a collection of related information, and "on-line" databases are those made available over a computer. Here's a tiny sample of the kind of business information you can tap into by using this technology:

- Summaries of articles from top business and management journals
- Company directory listings from Dun & Bradstreet
- Indexes to articles from economic journals and books
- Text of the *Harvard Business Review*
- The full text of the *Wall Street Journal*
- Summaries of published industry forecasts and historical data
- Late-breaking financial news on U.S. public corporations from Standard & Poor's
- Management summaries from Arthur D. Little's market research reports
- Detailed financial report listings from the SEC
- A nationwide electronic yellow pages, with over 9 million listings
- Descriptions of sources of financial and marketing data in major industries worldwide
- Highlights of business and management topics from business journals and proceedings
- Information on product introductions, market shares, strategic planning
- Trade opportunity information based on purchase requests by the international market for U.S. goods and services

Again, this list doesn't even scratch the surface. For much more information on the subject, see chapter 5.

Although there are thousands of databases in existence, and the proper selection of a database is not always a simple task, I have a few specific "favorites." The following is a list of the databases I use most often and have had the most success with when performing business research on the Dialog system (see chapter 5 for more information):

When looking for	Try these databases
Precise information or statistics about industries, products, market shares	Predicasts (PTS) Promt; Trade & Industry ASAP
Management techniques, general business trends, and developments	ABI Inform
Inside look at operations and executives of smaller, private firms	Business Dateline
Expert analysts' views on companies' outlooks, strengths, and weaknesses	Investext
Basic data on companies (e.g., size, number of employees, and sales)	D & B Market Identifiers

---

TIP: Two Last Potential Sources
- Two other places you might look for all types of business information are universities and banks.
- State university business schools often publish data and studies and make them available to the public.
- Some large banks publish results of their own research too. For example, the Valley National Bank of Arizona publishes the *Arizona Statistical Review,* which provides statistics on construction, employment, housing, income, manufacturing, real estate, retail trade, taxes, tourism, and other areas.

The subject of business information is a book in itself. In fact, an excellent one is *Business Information Sources*, by Lorna Daniells, published by the University of California Press. If it's business information you need, this is the place to turn to find out where to get it.

5

Computer Searches
Facts at Your Fingertips

**QUICK PREVIEW:
COMPUTER SEARCHES**

- Using computers to find information offers certain advantages over using traditional sources. Benefits include the huge scope of data available, timeliness, speed, and the capability to combine keywords to isolate the precise information you need.

- Finding information through a computer involves searching on-line databases. A "database" is simply a collection of related information. An "on-line" database is one available for rapid browsing and searching via a computer. "On-line vendors" sell access to these databases.

- To actually perform the computer search, you can go to a library that offers the service, or you can obtain your own computer, software, and modem and do the searches on your own.

- Factors to examine when selecting an on-line vendor include the extent of the firm's coverage of your subjects of interest, cost, ease of use, timeliness, sophistication of search techniques, and special features offered.

- Among the consumer online services, CompuServe offers by far the most comprehensive research databases, such as IQuest and Knowledge Index; GEnie has fewer but offers a gateway to profes-

(continued)

sional systems; Delphi offers full Internet access; America Online is the fastest growing and offers the best graphics and several electronic journals; and Prodigy contains the fewest research databases.

- A computer search is typically performed by selecting an appropriate database to search and then identifying keywords that best describe the desired information. Then, the computer searches the database for instances of articles or reports that contain those keywords and provides you with an abstract or the full text of items located. To obtain optimum results, it's important to learn how to perform an efficient search.

- Costs to consider when performing a computer search include the hardware and software, as well as the on-line vendor's search fees. These may include a start-up fee, annual subscription fee, hourly connect-time fee, database surcharges, printout charges, and telephone charges.

- You can keep costs down by becoming as familiar as possible with how the on-line vendor's service works, buying a fast modem, selecting an easy-to-use communications package, using vendors that offer reduced "off-peak" rates, and reducing the time you spend on-line.

- Computer searches are not a panacea. There are drawbacks: you must be skilled in performing efficient searches, databases may not contain the information you need, short "abstracts" may not be sufficient in some cases, and costs can get out of hand. It's important to know when it *does* make sense to use the computer to find information, and when it *does not*.

- Data received via computer are not necessarily any more accurate than any other source of information. Users need to take specific steps to ensure the data received are reliable—this includes becoming extra proficient with a few databases, confirming findings, checking the age of the data, and double-checking against other resources.

- The hottest electronic information resource is the Internet: a web of networks linking 120,000 sites in over 60 countries with over

(continued)

20 million users. You can use the Internet to send and retrieve electronic mail throughout the world, search databases, join electronic discussion groups, and search library card catalogs. The Internet is difficult to use, but new software and services are making it easier to navigate.

- Another type of electronic databases are CD-ROMs: laser discs that store over 250,000 pages that you use with your own computer. Types of CD-ROMs include encyclopedias, journal collections, government statistics, national phone directories, health information, and much more. The newest CD-ROMs are "multimedia." These offer not just text, but audio, photographs, and sometimes video and animation. When buying CD-ROMs, you need to check compatibility, data quality, search power, ease of use, warranty, and price.

- "Information brokers" are firms that perform computer search services—and often other research services—for a fee. These firms are especially useful if you have only very occasional information needs.

WHAT IS A COMPUTER INFORMATION SEARCH?

Do you want to find out about developments in artificial intelligence in West Germany? Are you trying to find articles about Albania published prior to 1960? How about forecasts on the growth of the health care industry? How dangerous a certain chemical is? What writers conferences, if any, are coming up in California? Where to find educational material for gifted children? Market intelligence on the alcoholic beverage industry? What Japanese patents on computers were registered in the last year? What publications provide investment advice on precious metals? Journal articles about juvenile delinquents among wealthy French families?

That's a minuscule sample of the kinds of questions that can be answered by using a computer—your own or a library's—to tap into on-line databases. Until around 1980, the ability to search databases was available mainly only to professional researchers like librarians, scientists, or company information specialists. But these days the power of the computer is accessible to the public. Today anybody can use a computer to tap into vast amounts of data covering a huge variety of subjects.

A few definitions: A "database" is simply a collection of information that's related in some way, e.g., electronic parts manufacturers, biographies of prominent people, news about the chemical industry, recent journal articles on pollution, books currently in print, company annual reports. A database is, in fact, nothing more than what you commonly encounter all the time in "hard copy," or published form. For example, the white pages of your phone book represent a database of the names, addresses, and phone numbers of people who live in a particular city or region. The main difference between a database such as that one and the databases we will be talking about in this chapter is that the latter are "on-line," which means available for rapid browsing and searching through a computer.

There currently exist about 5,000 databases, and this number is growing rapidly. There are databases to track stocks, get the latest world news, find the lowest airline rates, obtain industry and company financial reports, get sports results, find obscure information, tap into a national "electronic yellow pages," find patent information, and much more. Some databases attract a very narrow clientele—say, articles published in a magazine like *Toxic Material News*—while other databases appeal to a much broader group of people, such as a database of articles published in the *New York Times* or that of a popular encyclopedia.

Where do these databases come from? A variety of sources, including associations, government agencies, private publishers, and other organizations. In fact, many sources already mentioned in this book, including the Wilson Subject Indexes, *Books in Print*, brokerage reports, and government documents, are made available on-line by the organizations that created those original "hard copy" sources.[1]

The way you actually tap into these databases is by subscribing to an "on-line database vendor." A database vendor sells

[1] Special thanks to the following people for their assistance with this chapter: Tim Miller, New York City; Marven Weinberger, Telebase Systems, Bryn Mawr, Pennsylvania; Ann Cain, Pasadena, California, Public Library. Also thanks to PIN Services Inc., New York, for permission to reprint certain material previously written by the author and published in *Online Databases, 1986*.

access to databases, providing users with the ability to search them for information.

THE BENEFITS OF USING A COMPUTER

Using computers to find information offers certain inherent advantages over using traditional information sources like books or library indexes. The following are some of the biggest benefits:

Vast Scope. An on-line information vendor can provide you with access to an enormous amount of information—hundreds of magazines, dozens of directories, scores of technical reports. It would be impossible to actually read through all of these documents to try to locate the information you need. And many of the information sources—especially the obscure ones— would not be accessible, even at the largest of libraries. But it's all made available to you through the computer.

Timeliness. By using the computer, you may be able to locate information that's just been released and not yet bound in published indexes. For example, if you wanted to see whether the *New York Times* or the *Wall Street Journal* had recently published any articles about a particular company, you would be able to use the computer to search for articles published during the last few days. The library index for those newspapers would not have been updated quickly enough to contain references to these most recent issues. Similarly, you can use the computer to obtain up-to-the-minute stock quotes and newswire information— data that won't even be published until the next day.

Speed/convenience. Instead of spending a day at the library to look for information, you can spend a few minutes sitting at a computer. And if you wish, you can obtain an immediate printout of the information you've located. With many on-line vendors, you can do this searching virtually around the clock.

Specificity. One of the biggest benefits of computer searches is the capability to create and manipulate "keywords" to zero in on precisely the kind of information you seek. For example, let's say that you are trying to find out if there are any published reports that discuss links between migraine headaches and food allergies. You could instruct the computer to examine thousands of articles published in medical journals and directories to search for text in which the keywords *migraine* and *food allergy* appear close to each other.

HOW TO GET GOING

How does one actually conduct an on-line information search? The first step is to have access to the necessary computer equipment. If you do not own a personal computer or terminal, you can have a computer search performed for you at a library.

More and more libraries are acquiring computers, subscribing to one or more database vendors, and making computer searching services available to patrons. Doing computer searches at a library is a particularly good option for people who think they will want to make searches only very occasionally and don't want to invest in a personal computer or subscribe to an on-line vendor themselves.

To find a library that offers on-line searching, contact the largest public library or university library in your area. Or you can examine a copy of the reference book *Online Database Search Services Directory,* published by Gale Research Company. This directory identifies libraries and organizations that perform computer searches and lists information about each. Look in a large library's reference department for a copy.

Doing searches at a library provides certain advantages. For one, libraries normally charge a modest fee, usually only enough to cover their own out-of-pocket expenses. Another advantage of a library search is that the procedure is normally performed by the librarian, who is experienced in doing the work and can do it efficiently and quickly.

The other option is to obtain your own equipment. What

you'll need is a terminal or personal *computer* (e.g., IBM PC, Macintosh); *communications software*, which allows your computer to communicate with the on-line vendor's "host" computer; a *telephone;* and a *modem.* A modem is a device that transforms the digital signals used in computers to analog tone signals used on phone lines, and then back again into signals understood by the computer.

Once you have the necessary equipment, the next step is to select a database vendor.

SELECTING AN ONLINE VENDOR

Okay, you're convinced that you want to try your hand at some online searching. Great! Now you just need to decide *which* of the several major services to sign up with.

This is not an insignificant decision. Your choice will directly determine the kinds of information available to you, as well as greatly impact matters such as ease of use and costs.

The first thing to know is that while there are thousands of different databases, there are only a handful or two of major online vendors; these are the firms that provide access to dozens or even hundreds of individual databases. You also need to know that there are basically two different kinds of online vendors: consumer-oriented systems and professional-level systems.

The differences between the two are fairly self-explanatory. Consumer-oriented systems are geared for non-experts, who are usually searching out of their home. These services typically offer not only databases, but features such as games, clubs, chat lines, shopping, and so on. The largest consumer online services today include America Online, CompuServe, Delphi, GEnie, and Prodigy. (A somewhat more specialized consumer-oriented system is Ziffnet, devoted mostly to computer-related issues.)

In contrast, professional systems are used mainly by serious researchers such as librarians, market research professionals, scientists, corporate information specialists, writers, and others who need the most powerful and in-depth data available—and can afford to pay for it! Major systems in this category include Data-Star, Dialog, Dow Jones News/Retrieval, Nexis/Lexis, and NewsNet.

Since this book is written for the non-expert researcher, this section will concentrate on examining the consumer-oriented services. However, don't feel constrained to necessarily limit yourself to those services. If you have the need for the highest level online searching available and want to learn more about searching professional databases, check the end of this chapter and the Appendix of this book for references to additional sources.

Now let's take a thumbnail profile of each of those consumer services. For each, I'll describe what I feel to be its most valuable online reference and research offerings.

Compuserve

CompuServe, owned by H&R Block, currently boasts nearly 1.5 million users. Of all the consumer online services, Compu-Serve has the most to offer, and will often prove to be the best choice for the serious researcher.

Here's a list of some of the most valuable and useful research-oriented databases on CompuServe:

- *Grolier's Academic American Encyclopedia:* An online encyclopedia equivalent to the 21-volume, 33,000-article print version.

- *Consumer Reports:* An electronic equivalent to the popular magazine.

- *Healthnet:*An encyclopedic-type database of consumer-oriented medical and health-related information.

- *Consumer Reports Drug Reference:* Facts on prescription and over-the-counter drugs.

- *NewsGrid:* Up-to-the-minute headlines of the latest national and international news.

- *A.P. Online:* Up-to-the-minute news as filed by reporters working for the Associated Press.

- *UK News Clips/UK Sports Clips:* The latest news and sports results from the United Kingdom and Europe

- *Peterson's College Database:* A searchable electronic version of the popular hard copy guide to U.S. colleges.

- *Ziff Files:* The Ziff files are a series of superbly designed full-text databases, created with outstanding search capabilities. They are a great bargain in the online world.

- Business Database+ (the fulltext of 500 business journals and 550 newsletters)

- Computer Database+ (the fulltext of 230 computer magazines)

- Health Database+ (100,000 articles drawn from major health and consumer-oriented publications)

- Magazine Database+ (the full text of 130 popular periodicals).

- *Executive News Service:* This is an interesting customizable electronic "news clipping" service that monitors the Associated Press (AP), U.P.I., Reuters, and *The Washington Post.* To use it, you input key words and concepts that you want the service to track. The service continually checks the wires for matches and daily provides you with a list of relevant headlines. You scan the headlines and determine which, if any, you want to read in full.

- *IQuest Service:* An electronic "gateway" linking Compu-Serve users to over 850 top-notch professional databases, drawn from services such as Dialog, Data-Star, NewsNet, and selected European online vendors. A few examples of the kinds of high-level databases available through IQuest are:

- Dun's Electronic Business Directory (data on over 8.5 million U.S. public and private companies)

- Corporate Affiliations (detailed relationships between parent and subsidiary companies)

- Thomas Register (names and contacts for who manufactures what type of product around the United States)

- Newspaper Library (the fulltext of 48 major city newspapers from around the United States)

- Investext (in-depth company and industry analyses written by experts at Wall Street brokerage houses and research firms)

- Phonefile (names, addresses, and phone numbers for 75 million individuals around the United States)

- Disclosure (detailed financial data on public companies, derived from documents filed with the U.S. Securities and Exchange Commission)

- TRW Business Profiles (credit and payment history data for both public and private firms).

Other IQuest databases include a patent research center, demographic data, government publications, international company directories, and much, much more.

One particularly useful feature is IQuest's "S.O.S." feature: if you're in the middle of conducting a search and are having some problems or need help, just type "S.O.S." Your message is then received almost instantaneously by an expert searcher at IQuest's headquarters. That expert sends you an electronic reply directly to your computer, and asks what you need. You then can have an electronic "real-time" dialog with that expert until you feel you have enough information to go forward yourself. It's an ideal solution to addressing search problems (though the service is only available on weekdays).

One caution. IQuest can be *very* expensive. However, IQuest does do a very good job of explaining its pricing for each of its databases, so do be sure you read it all before you decide to make a search. A single search can easily cost $15, $25, or a whole lot more depending on the file you've selected. Be careful!

- *Knowledge Index:* Knowledge Index is probably the best deal around in the online world. It's a selection of about 100 of Dialog's 400+ top-notch professional-level databases, but at a cut-rate price. Instead of paying the normal $60–$130 per hour or so, you pay just $24 per hour. And, unlike through the regular Dialog service, there's no additional per item "print" charges either!

There is one, rather small catch, though. You can only use Knowledge Index at night or on the weekends. And you're not allowed to use it for any kind of profit-making resale work, such as "information brokering." If you can live with these restrictions, you should definitely give "K.I." a try. Here's just a sampling of the subject areas covered in Knowledge Index databases:

- Agriculture
- Arts

176

- Biology
- Books
- Business
- Chemistry
- Computers and electronic
- Environment
- Food
- Government
- History
- Law
- Literature and Language
- Magazines
- Mathematics
- Medicine
- Newspapers
- Psychology
- Reference
- Religion
- Social Science

What's also nice about Knowledge Index is that you have a choice of two ways to perform your search: by menu or by command. The menu version helps you determine step by step which database is most likely to contain the information you seek, and is useful for novice searchers. Command-based searching gives you more flexibility and power, and is quicker for the more experienced searcher. Commands also let you use advanced "Boolean" logic searching (using the words "AND," "OR," "NOT") to make for much more powerful searching.

Keep in mind, though, that as highly as I recommended Knowledge Index, you may still want to use Dialog directly, depending on your needs. There you have access to the full 400+ databases, can search more than one database simultaneously, and can perform more advanced sorting and ranking functions. But you'll pay a lot more for those privileges.

In summary, CompuServe offers a huge amount of information. Far and away, it's the best choice for the serious researcher who needs access to lots of data, and doesn't want to sign up with a more expensive professional system.

GEnie Information Services

GEnie is another major consumer online service, and is also owned by a well-known corporation: General Electric. Here are some of its best offerings:

- *Grolier's Academic American Encyclopedia:* This is the same electronic source mentioned on the CompuServe service.

- *NewsBytes:* The best source for locating breaking stories and finding expert analysis of news from and impacting the computer industry.

- *Reuters Newswires:* GEnie breaks the Reuters wires into two sections: a "world report," covering the latest global news, and the "business report," with breaking international business news.

- *The Sports Network:* The latest standings, schedules, results, and summaries in the world of sports.

- *CASHE:* Assists students in searching over 14,000 sources of financial aid to determine potential matches.

- *Gateways:* GEnie offers electronic gateways to two major professional services, Dialog and Dow Jones News/Retrieval. For access to Dialog, GEnie uses a gateway provider called Advanced Retrieval Technologies (ART) and organizes the Dialog databases into larger groups. Users of this service are charged a premium. The Dow Jones databases, which concentrate on financial and business areas, are linked directly without a gateway "middleman"; this makes it important that you first learn how to search the Dow Jones databases before connecting to them.

Delphi

Delphi is the smallest of the major consumer online services, with less than 100,000 users. But in 1993 it was purchased by the international media conglomerate, News Corporation, and is likely to grow quickly.

Delphi's biggest claim to fame is that, as of this writing, it is the only major online service—consumer or professional—to offer **full** access to the global Internet service. The Internet (described in full later in this chapter) is an international "network of networks" encompassing 12,000 computer networks in over 60 countries, and has been growing at an absolutely phenomenal rate during the last few years. And while other online services offer some limited Internet access, such as e-mail capabilities, only Delphi offers a means to tap into all of the Internet resources and capabilities.

Not only does Delphi allow its users to fully interact with the Internet, but it goes even further by making the complex and decidedly un-user friendly Internet world a lot easier to manage. It does so by offering users loads of help screens, advisories, simple explanations, and a series of "auto-connect" menus that automatically perform some of the more complicated logging on and searching functions.

Delphi's offerings, of course, go beyond just Internet access. Here is a listing of some databases that you may find of particular interest:

- *Grolier's Academic American Encyclopedia:* The same set offered on CompuServe and GEnie.

- *CAIN—California Aids Information Network:* A superb and professional-level information database covering all aspects of the AIDS disease. Highly recommended.

- *PR Newswire/BusinessWire:* Very useful database consisting of press and news releases issued by corporations and organizations around the United States.

- *UPI Headline News:* A handy way to track the day's breaking news stories.

- *Worldline Country Search:* Travel information for more than 200 countries.

- *ParentNet:* An encylopedic-type volume covering various issues and concerns of parents.

In summary, while Delphi does not offer anywhere the breadth of databases as CompuServe, or even GEnie, it does have some unique offerings, and its access to Internet remains the best around.

America Online

With 500,000 users, America Online is not one of the biggest consumer online services—but it may be the most innovative, and is the fastest growing. America Online was the first to offer a full graphical interface, and today still probably has the finest one around. Searching this service is, indeed, a pleasure. The graphics are attractive, clean, logically ordered, and eminently easy to work with. The company is attempting, and in many ways succeeding, to be at the forefront in providing leading-edge interactive information services in as easy to use format as possible.

However, when it comes to powerful databases, America Online falls rather short. It's nowhere near CompuServe in terms of the amount or breadth of its services, and does not offer gateways to more powerful vendors (as GEnie does). And, in fact, many of America Online's databases suffer from an overly short "backfile" (the extent of coverage of past articles and news) and inadequate search capabilities. Still, there are several useful files that could be of interest to the researcher. These include:

- *Compton's Encyclopedia:* While not as comprehensive as the Grolier's electronic version, it is quite convenient to have an encyclopedia available online.

- *News Search:* An easy-to-use, basic news headline and article reporting service.

- *Microsoft Small Business Center:* While not fully searchable, this "center" contains various reports and advice of interest to those looking to learn about small business.

- *Newsbytes:* The premiere computer newswire. However, on GEnie Newsbytes has a much longer backfile and superior search capabilities.

- *Network Earth:* Information relating to environmental issues.

- *College Board:* An electronic equivalent to the Board's 2,000-page book describing U.S. colleges and universities.

- *Winebase:* An unusual and fun database of wines. You can get descriptions of specific types of wines based on various criteria that you input.

In addition to offering these databases, America Online has been making an effort to add electronic versions of a select group of popular magazines. Currently available are: *The Atlantic, MacWorld, Worth, New Republic, Wired,* and *Time.*

Prodigy

Last—and, I'm afraid least—is the Prodigy service. Prodigy, a joint venture of IBM and Sears, claims more members than any other consumer online service—about 1.7 million—though this number has been disputed. In any case, it is a popular mass-market online service, which certainly has a number of nice features and services, but is unlikely to be of great interest to serious researchers.

First, let's look at the positive side of Prodigy. It is easy to use; simple in fact. The system employs graphics to display some pretty pictures while you are online. And, it can be quite convenient for doing some simple financial-and investment-type tracking. In addition, Prodigy contains the following databases, which I find to be the best of their offerings:

- *Grolier Academic American Encyclopedia:* Again, the same version as found on CompuServe, GEnie, and Delphi.

- *Consumer Reports:* An online version of the popular magazine.

- *Business News:* Quite a handy source of up-to-the-minute news from the business world, supplied to Prodigy by Dow Jones Inc.

- *Magill's Movie Guide:* A neat little searchable database filled with reviews of popular and classic movies.

- *Software Guide:* Useful evaluations and reviews of various computer software products, as written by the editors of *Home Office Computing* magazine.

- *Zagat Restaurant Survey:* Ratings and reviews of major restaurants in large cities around the United States. Corresponds to the well-known print version of the same

But that's really about it for searchable research-oriented databases. Again, you may find it a fun service, and there are some nice investment-and stock-tracking services; but there are few powerful information databases, and no gateways to larger systems. And then there are Prodigy's ubiquitous advertisements, popping up all over your screen, unannounced, uninvited, and, for many people, unwanted.

So there you have it. To reiterate, if you're looking for a powerful consumer online service, you don't need to look any further than CompuServe. However, all of the other services offer at least something unique that could also be of interest to those of you with special or unique information needs.

Of course, the other factor that will likely determine your choice is cost. Pricing varies widely among these services, and it seems that the vendors introduce completely new pricing plans every few months. Most offer more than one type of pricing plan at any given time. Study the plans carefully and try to select the one that's going to make the most sense for you. Obvious advice, right? But after you've chosen a service and been using it for a few months, take another look at your choice to make sure that your initial selection is still working the best for you. If not, you can always switch to another price plan. What about the professional-level services? As mentioned earlier, I'm not going to spend much time on them in this book. However, here is a thumbnail sketch of how they differ, and their special characteristics.

- *DataStar:* A highly-respected Swiss-based vendor (now owned by Dialog; see below), with a particular niche in covering European issues, companies, and news.
- *Dialog:* Offers more databases (400+) than any other online vendor, and its scope of coverage—from aerospace to zoology—is unsurpassed.
- *Dow Jones News/Retrieval:* As one might expect, Dow Jones' online service specializes in financial, company, and business information (in addition to national and international news).
- *Nexis:* A product of Mead Data Central, Nexis, along with its legal counterpart, Lexis, is a powerful and sophisticated service, and is often the system of choice for professional information searchers and librarians.
- *NewsNet:* Smaller than the previous four, but noteworthy and well respected for its database of full-text articles from hundreds of special-

ized industry and trade "insider"-type newsletters. These publications are typically very expensive in print form.

For more information on these professional services, I'd (highly, of course!) recommend my other book *Find it Online* (Windcrest/McGraw-Hill, 1994) or check out the other online books listed at the end of this chapter (recommended *nearly* as highly).

TIP: Finding Magazines On-line
- If you know of a trade magazine that covers your subject well, you may want to find out if that publication is made available on-line anywhere. If so, you will be able to search through scores of issues to zero in on precisely the type of articles you want. Call the publication directly and ask if they are "on-line" with any service, and if so, which ones. Then you can contact that service directly to find out about signing up for a search.

Here are some other differences between database vendors that should be examined:

Costs. Costs vary quite a bit between vendors. Find out if there is a start-up fee and/or an annual subscription fee. Is there a monthly minimum? What are the hourly connect-time rates? Is there an evening discount? If you know that you'll be searching a particular database frequently, find out what, if any, surcharges exist to use it, and compare that cost among vendors. See "Tips on Cutting Costs" on page 188 for more information on costs.

Ease of Use. Some services are simpler to use than others. If you are a beginner, you will find it easier to use a vendor that allows you to instruct the computer via "menus" (a list of tasks written in plain English that the computer can perform; you select the particular task you want done) instead of asking you to memorize "commands." (The disadvantage of menus, however, is that they can become cumbersome after you become proficient with a system. Having the capability of bypassing menus is desirable.) Some vendors make searching easier by offering special services that select the proper database and assist the user in making a search.

Sophistication of Search Techniques. Database vendors vary in the sophistication of their search capabilities. Does the system provide flexibility with regard to how far apart one key word must be from another? Say you are looking for journal articles about food in the Soviet Union. One system may be able to identify articles that contain the keywords *food* and *Soviet Union* only if the words appear next to each other in the text. Another system would allow you to locate articles in which the two terms appear within a few words of each other. The more flexibility the system provides, the more you will get out of the procedure.

Special Features. What, if any, additional services and features does the vendor provide? Is there a toll-free hot line that users can call to obtain assistance? Is there a regular publication that provides searching tips?

PERFORMING THE SEARCH

How does one actually perform an information search? Most advanced databases are searched in a similar fashion—through the use of keywords. The user identifies certain words that best describe the kind of information he or she is looking for, and combines these words with Boolean logic connectors—"AND," "OR," and "NOT"—to zero in on the precise information desired.

Here's a very simplified example. Say you need to find information about injuries caused by toys or dolls in the state of California. The first step would be to select an appropriate database to search. This might be a general one like the *New York Times,* or it could be a more specific one such as a database of reports published by the U.S. Consumer Product Safety Commission or a trade newsletter covering the toy industry. The next step would be to type in instructions. You might tell the

DIALOG® Databases by Subject Category
Database Name (File number[s])

Agriculture and Nutrition
AGRIBUSINESS U.S.A.℠ (581)
AGRICOLA (10, 110)
AGRIS INTERNATIONAL (203)
CAB ABSTRACTS (50, 53)
CRIS/USDA (60)
FOOD SCIENCE AND TECHNOLOGY
   ABSTRACTS (51)
FOODS ADLIBRA™ (79)

Books and Monographs
BOOK REVIEW INDEX (137)
BOOKS IN PRINT (470)
BRITISH BOOKS IN PRINT (430)
DIALOG® PUBLICATIONS (200)
LC MARC – BOOKS (426)
REMARC (421-425)

Business Information

Public Companies
DISCLOSURE® DATABASE (100)
DISCLOSURE®/SPECTRUM OWNERSHIP (540)
INSIDER TRADING MONITOR (549)
INVESTEXT® (545)
MEDIA GENERAL PLUS (546)
MOODY'S® CORPORATE PROFILES (555)
PTS ANNUAL REPORTS ABSTRACTS™ (17)
STANDARD & POOR'S CORPORATE
   DESCRIPTIONS (133)

Corporate Directories
COMPANY INTELLIGENCE™ (479)
CORPORATE AFFILIATIONS (513)
D&B – DUN'S ELECTRONIC YELLOW PAGES (515)
D&B – DUNS FINANCIAL RECORDS PLUS™ (519)
D&B – DUN'S MARKET IDENTIFIERS® (516)
D&B – MILLION DOLLAR DIRECTORY® (517)
STANDARD & POOR'S REGISTER –
   BIOGRAPHICAL (526)
STANDARD & POOR'S REGISTER – CORPORATE
   (527)
TRINET COMPANY DATABASE (532)
TRINET U.S. BUSINESSES (531)

International Companies
CANCORP CANADIAN CORPORATIONS (491)
D&B – CANADIAN DUN'S MARKET IDENTIFIERS®
   (520)
D&B – EUROPEAN DUN'S MARKET IDENTIFIERS®
   (521)
D&B – INTERNATIONAL DUN'S MARKET
   IDENTIFIERS® (518)
*EXTEL CARDS (500)
HOPPENSTEDT DIRECTORY OF GERMAN
   COMPANIES (529)
ICC BRITISH COMPANY DIRECTORY (561)
ICC BRITISH COMPANY FINANCIAL
   DATASHEETS (562)
ICC INTERNATIONAL BUSINESS RESEARCH
   (563)
INFOMAT INTERNATIONAL BUSINESS (583)
KOMPASS EUROPE (590)
KOMPASS UK (591)
MOODY'S® CORPORATE NEWS –
   INTERNATIONAL (557)

Economic Data
CENDATA™ (580)
ECONBASE: TIME SERIES AND FORECASTS
   (565)
D&B – DONNELLEY DEMOGRAPHICS (575)
PTS INTERNATIONAL FORECASTS™ (83)
PTS U.S. FORECASTS™ (81)
PTS U.S TIME SERIES™ (82)

Financial News
AMERICAN BANKER FULL TEXT (625)
AMERICAN BANKER NEWS (BANKNEWS)
BOND BUYER FULL TEXT (626)
*DIALOG/MONEYCENTER (MONEYCENTER)
DIALOG® QUOTES AND TRADING (QUOTES)
FINANCIAL TIMES COMPANY ABSTRACTS (560)
KNIGHT-RIDDER FINANCIAL NEWS (609)
MOODY'S® CORPORATE NEWS – U.S. (555)
STANDARD & POOR'S NEWS (132, 134)

Markets, Products, Technologies
ARTHUR D. LITTLE/ONLINE (192)
FINDEX (196)
HEALTH DEVICES SOURCEBOOK® (188)
INDUSTRY DATA SOURCES™ (189)
McGRAW-HILL PUBLICATIONS ONLINE (624)
PTS F&S INDEX™ (18, 98)
PTS NEW PRODUCT ANNOUNCEMENTS/PLUS™
   (621)
PTS PROMT™ (16)

Industries
BIOBUSINESS® (285)
BIOCOMMERCE ABSTRACTS AND DIRECTORY
   (286)
CHEMICAL BUSINESS NEWSBASE (319)
CHEMICAL INDUSTRY NOTES (19)
COFFEELINE® (164)
FINIS: FINANCIAL INDUSTRY INFORMATION
   SERVICE (268)
PTS MARKETING & ADVERTISING REFERENCE
   SERVICE (MARS)™ (570)

Product Listings & Announcements
PTS NEW PRODUCT ANNOUNCEMENTS/PLUS™
   (621)
THOMAS NEW INDUSTRIAL PRODUCTS™ (536)
THOMAS REGISTER ONLINE® (535)

General Business Information
ABI/INFORM® (15)
ECONOMIC LITERATURE INDEX (139)
FOREIGN TRADE & ECON ABSTRACTS (90)
HARVARD BUSINESS REVIEW (122)
MANAGEMENT CONTENTS® (75)

Business News
BUSINESS DATELINE® (635)
BUSINESSWIRE (610)
FINANCIAL TIMES FULLTEXT (622)
IDD M&A TRANSACTIONS (550)
M&A FILINGS (548)
McGRAW-HILL NEWS (600)
MERGERS (MERGERS)
MHNEWS (MHNEWS)
NEWSWIRE ASAP™ (649)
PR NEWSWIRE (613)
PTS NEWSLETTER DATABASE™ (636)
PTS NEWSLETTER DATABASE™ (PTSNL)
TRADE & INDUSTRY ASAP™ (648)
TRADE & INDUSTRY INDEX™ (148)

International Business Information
ARAB INFORMATION BANK (465)
ASIA-PACIFIC (30)
CANADIAN BUSINESS AND CURRENT AFFAIRS
   (262)
JAPAN ECONOMIC NEWSWIRE™ PLUS (612)

Travel
OAG ELECTRONIC EDITION® – Travel Service
   (OAG)

Chemistry
AGROCHEMICALS HANDBOOK (306)
ANALYTICAL ABSTRACTS (305)
BEILSTEIN ONLINE (390)
CA SEARCH (399, 308, 309, 310, 311, 312)
CHEM-INTELL (318)
CHEMICAL ENGINEERING ABSTRACTS (315)
CHEMICAL EXPOSURE (138)
CHEMICAL REGULATIONS AND GUIDELINES
   SYSTEM (174)
CHEMICAL SAFETY NEWSBASE (317)
CHEMNAME® (301)
CHEMSEARCH™ (398)
CLAIMS™ COMPOUND REGISTRY (242)
EUROPEAN DIRECTORY OF AGROCHEM
   PRODUCTS (316)
HEILBRON (303)
KIRK-OTHMER ONLINE (302)
PAPERCHEM (240, 840)
POLYMER ONLINE (322)
REGISTRY OF TOXIC EFFECTS OF CHE
   SUBSTANCES (RTECS) (336)
RINGDOC (911, 912, 913)
TSCA CHEMICAL SUBSTANCE INVENTO

Computer Technology
BUSINESS SOFTWARE DATABASE™ (256)
BUYER'S GUIDE TO MICRO SOFTWARE (5
   (237)
COMPUTER ASAP™ (675)
COMPUTER DATABASE™ (275)
MICROCOMPUTER INDEX™ (233)
MICROCOMPUTER SOFTWARE GUIDE (278)
THE SOFTWARE DIRECTORY (263)

Energy and Environment
AQUACULTURE (112)
AQUATIC SCIENCES AND FISHERIES
   ABSTRACTS (44)
DOE ENERGY (103, 104)
ELECTRIC POWER DATABASE (241)
ENERGYLINE® (69)
ENVIROLINE® (40)
ENVIRONMENTAL BIBLIOGRAPHY (68)
NUCLEAR SCIENCE ABSTRACTS (109)
OCEANIC ABSTRACTS (28)
P/E NEWS (257, 897)
PETROLEUM EXPLORATION & PRODUCT
   (987)
POLLUTION ABSTRACTS (41)
WATER RESOURCES ABSTRACTS (117)
WATERNET™ (245)

Law and Government
ASI (102)
BRITISH OFFICIAL PUBLICATIONS (228)
CIS (101)
COMMERCE BUSINESS DAILY (194, 195)
CONGRESSIONAL RECORD ABSTRACTS (13)
CRIMINAL JUSTICE PERIODICAL INDEX (171)
EBIS™ – EMPLOYEE BENEFITS INFOSOURCE
   (22)
FEDERAL INDEX (20)
FEDERAL REGISTER (669)
FEDERAL REGISTER ABSTRACTS (136)
GPO MONTHLY CATALOG (66)
GPO PUBLICATIONS REFERENCE FILE (166)
INSURANCE ABSTRACTS (168)
INSURANCE PERIODICALS INDEX (169)
LABORLAW I (244)
LABORLAW II (243)
LEGAL RESOURCE INDEX™ (150)
NCJRS (21)
TAX NOTES TODAY (650)
TAX NOTES TODAY (TNT)
WASHINGTON PRESSTEXT™ (145)

Dialog Database Listing

185

DIALOG® Databases by Subject Category
Database Name (File number[s])

Medicine and Biosciences

*AGELINE (163)
AIDSLINE (157)
BIOSIS PREVIEWS® (5, 55)
BIOTECHNOLOGY ABSTRACTS (357)
CANCERLIT† (159)
CHEMICAL EXPOSURE (138)
CLINICAL ABSTRACTS (219)
CURRENT BIOTECHNOLOGY ABSTRACTS (358)
DE HAEN'S DRUG DATA (267)
DIOGENES† (158)
DRUG INFORMATION FULLTEXT (229)
EMBASE (72, 172, 173)
F-D-C REPORTS (187)
HEALTH DEVICES ALERTS® (198)
HEALTH DEVICES SOURCEBOOK† (188)
HEALTH PERIODICALS DATABASE™ (149)
HEALTH PLANNING AND ADMINISTRATION® (151)
INTERNATIONAL PHARMACEUTICAL ABSTRACTS (74)
LIFE SCIENCES COLLECTION (76)
MARTINDALE ONLINE (141)
MEDLINE† (152, 153, 154, 155)
MENTAL HEALTH ABSTRACTS (86)
THE MERCK INDEX ONLINE™ (304)
NURSING & ALLIED HEALTH (CINAHL) (218)
OCCUPATIONAL SAFETY AND HEALTH (NIOSH) (161)
PHARMACEUTICAL NEWS INDEX (PNI®) (42)
SEDBASE (70)
SMOKING AND HEALTH (160)
SPORT (48)
ZOOLOGICAL RECORD ONLINE† (185)

News

AP NEWS (258, 259)
CHICAGO TRIBUNE (632)
COURIER PLUS™ (484)
CURRENT DIGEST OF THE SOVIET PRESS (645)
DIALOG† CHRONOLOG† NEWSLETTER (410)
FACTS ON FILE† (264)
LOS ANGELES TIMES (630)
MIDDLE EAST: ABSTRACTS & INDEX (248)
MIDEAST FILE (249)
NATIONAL NEWSPAPER INDEX™ (111)
NEWSEARCH™ (211)
NEWSPAPER ABSTRACTS (603)
ONLINE CHRONICLE (170)
PAIS INTERNATIONAL (49)
PAPERS (PAPERS)
PHILADELPHIA INQUIRER (633)
REUTERS (611)
SAN JOSE MERCURY NEWS (634)
UPI NEWS (260, 261)
USA TODAY DECISIONLINE (644)
USATODAY (USATODAY)
WASHINGTON POST ONLINE (146)
WORLD AFFAIRS REPORT (167)

Online Training and Practice

DIALOG† HOMEBASE™ (HOME)
ONTAP℠ ABI/INFORM® (215)
ONTAP℠ AEROSPACE (282)
ONTAP℠ AGRICOLA (210)
ONTAP℠ ANALYTICAL ABSTRACTS (385)
ONTAP℠ ART LITERATURE INDEX (RILA)(176)
ONTAP℠ ARTS & HUMANITIES SEARCH™ (255)
ONTAP℠ BEILSTEIN ONLINE (389)
ONTAP℠ BIOSIS PREVIEWS® (205)
ONTAP℠ CA SEARCH (204)
ONTAP℠ CAB ABSTRACTS (250)
ONTAP℠ CHEMNAME† (231)
ONTAP℠ CLAIMS™ (279)
ONTAP℠ COMPENDEX® PLUS (208)

ONTAP℠ COMPUTER DATABASE™ (805)
ONTAP℠ D&B – DUN'S MARKET IDENTIFIERS® (276)
ONTAP℠ DIALINDEX℠ (290)
ONTAP℠ DMS CONTRACT AWARDS (289)
ONTAP℠ DOE ENERGY (803)
ONTAP℠ EMBASE (272)
ONTAP℠ ERIC (201)
ONTAP℠ FOOD SCIENCE AND TECHNOLOGY ABSTRACTS (251)
ONTAP℠ INPADOC (253)
ONTAP℠ INSPEC (213)
ONTAP℠ INVESTEXT® (277)
ONTAP℠ KIRK-OTHMER ONLINE (386)
ONTAP℠ MAGAZINE INDEX™ (247)
ONTAP℠ MEDLINE® (254)
ONTAP℠ NTIS (206)
ONTAP℠ PsycINFO® (212)
ONTAP℠ PTS MARKETING & REFERENCE SERVICE (MARS)™ (281)
ONTAP℠ PTS PROMT™ (216)
ONTAP℠ SCISEARCH® (207)
ONTAP℠ SOCIAL SCISEARCH® (207)
ONTAP℠ SOCIOLOGICAL ABSTRACTS (177)
ONTAP℠ TAX NOTES TODAY (199)
ONTAP℠ TRADEMARKSCAN® – FEDERAL (296)
ONTAP℠ WORLD PATENTS INDEX (280)

Patents and Trademarks

CHINESE PATENT ABSTRACTS IN ENGLISH (344)
CLAIMS™/CITATION (220, 221, 222)
CLAIMS™/REASSIGNMENT & REEXAMINATION (123)
CLAIMS™/REFERENCE (124)
CLAIMS™/U.S. PATENT ABSTRACTS (23, 24, 25, 340)
CLAIMS™/U.S. PATENT ABSTRACTS WEEKLY (125)
CLAIMS™/UNITERM (223, 224, 225, 341)
INPADOC/FAMILY AND LEGAL STATUS (345)
TRADEMARKSCAN® – FEDERAL (226)
TRADEMARKSCAN® – STATE (246)
WORLD PATENTS INDEX (350)
WORLD PATENTS INDEX LATEST (351)

Popular Information

CONSUMER DRUG INFORMATION FULLTEXT (271)
CONSUMER REPORTS (646)
MAGAZINE ASAP™ (647)
MAGAZINE INDEX™ (47)
MAGILL'S SURVEY OF CINEMA (299)

Reference

ACADEMIC AMERICAN ENCYCLOPEDIA (180)
AMERICAN LIBRARY DIRECTORY (460)
AMERICAN MEN AND WOMEN OF SCIENCE (236)
BIOGRAPHY MASTER INDEX (287, 288)
CAREER PLACEMENT REGISTRY (162)
COMPUTER-READABLE DATABASES (230)
ENCYCLOPEDIA OF ASSOCIATIONS (114)
EVERYMAN'S ENCYCLOPAEDIA (182)
EXPERTNET® (183)
FOUNDATION DIRECTORY (26)
FOUNDATION GRANTS INDEX (27)
GRADLINE (273)
GRANTS (85)
MARQUIS WHO'S WHO (234)
PETERSON'S COLLEGE DATABASE (214)
PUBLISHERS, DISTRIBUTORS, AND WHOLESALERS (450)
ULRICH'S INTERNATIONAL PERIODICALS DIRECTORY (480)

Science and Technology

(see also CHEMISTRY)
(see also PATENTS)
AEROSPACE DATABASE (108)
CERAMIC ABSTRACTS (335)
COMPENDEX® PLUS (8)
CURRENT TECHNOLOGY INDEX (142)
DMS CONTRACT AWARDS (588)
DMS CONTRACTORS (984)
DMS MARKET INTELLIGENCE REPORTS® (988)
ENGINEERED MATERIALS ABSTRACTS™ (293)
FEDERAL RESEARCH IN PROGRESS (265, 26
FLUIDEX (96)
GEOARCHIVE (58)
GEOBASE™ (292)
GEOREF (89)
IHS INTERNATIONAL STANDARDS AND SPECIFICATIONS (92)
INSPEC (12, 13)
ISMEC (14)
JANE'S DEFENSE & AEROSPACE NEWS/ANALYSIS (587)
MATERIALS BUSINESS FILE (269)
MATHSCI® (239)
METADEX (32)
METEOROLOGICAL AND GEOASTROPHYS ABSTRACTS (29)
NONFERROUS METALS ABSTRACTS (118)
NTIS (6)
PACKAGING SCIENCE AND TECHNOLOGY ABSTRACTS (252)
PASCAL (144)
PTS AEROSPACE/DEFENSE MARKETS & TECHNOLOGY™ (80)
SCISEARCH† (34, 432, 433, 434)
SOVIET SCIENCE AND TECHNOLOGY (270)
SPIN® (62)
SSIE CURRENT RESEARCH (65)
STANDARDS AND SPECIFICATIONS (113)
SUPERTECH (238)
TEXTILE TECHNOLOGY DIGEST (119)
TRIS (63)
WORLD ALUMINUM ABSTRACTS (33)
WORLD TEXTILES (67)

Social Sciences and Humanities

ACADEMIC INDEX™ (88)
AIM/ARM (9)
A-V ONLINE (46)
AMERICA: HISTORY AND LIFE (38)
ARCHITECTURE DATABASE (179)
ART LITERATURE INTERNATIONAL (RILA) (19
ARTBIBLIOGRAPHIES MODERN (56)
ARTS & HUMANITIES SEARCH® (439)
AVERY ARCHITECTURE INDEX (187)
BIBLE (KING JAMES VERSION) (297)
BRITISH EDUCATION INDEX (121)
CHILD ABUSE AND NEGLECT (64)
CONFERENCE PAPERS INDEX (77)
CURRENT CONTENTS SEARCH™ (440)
DIALOG† BLUESHEETS™ (415)
DISSERTATION ABSTRACTS ONLINE (35)
THE EDUCATIONAL DIRECTORY (511)
ERIC (1)
EXCEPTIONAL CHILD EDUCATION RESOURCI (54)
FAMILY RESOURCES (291)
HISTORICAL ABSTRACTS (39)
INFORMATION SCIENCE ABSTRACTS (202)
LINGUISTICS AND LANGUAGE BEHAVIOR ABSTRACTS (36)
LISA (61)
MLA BIBLIOGRAPHY (71)
MUSIC LITERATURE INTERNATIONAL (RILM) (97)
PHILOSOPHER'S INDEX (57)
POPULATION BIBLIOGRAPHY (91)
PsycINFO® (11)
RELIGION INDEX (190)
SOCIAL SCISEARCH® (7)
SOCIOLOGICAL ABSTRACTS (37)
U.S. POLITICAL SCIENCE DOCUMENTS (93)
WORLD TRANSLATIONS INDEX (295)

Dialog Database Listing

	You select desired database
	TYPE IN LABEL FOR DATABASE DESIRED: • ————————
	XX--> *info*
	WOULD YOU LIKE INSTRUCTIONAL PROMPTS? PLEASE TYPE
	YES OR NO: *y*
	WOULD YOU LIKE A DESCRIPTION OF THE DATABASE? (YES
	OR NO):
	XX-->
System describes selected database.	ABI/INFORM, PRODUCED BY DATA COURIER, INC., CONSISTS OF 200-WORD ABSTRACTS OR SUMMARIES OF THE PRINCIPAL ARTICLES APPEARING IN MORE THAN 600 BUSINESS AND MANAGEMENT PERIODICALS WORLDWIDE MORE THAN 140 OF THESE ARE NON-U.S. PUBLICATIONS. VIRTUALLY EVERY ASPECT OF BUSINESS IS COVERED IN THE FILE, WITH PARTICULAR EMPHASIS ON ACCOUNTING, BANKING, DATA PROCESSING, FINANCE, INSURANCE, MARKETING . . .
	BRS/INFO 1971 - JAN 1985
System requests your instruction	TYPE IN SEARCH TERMS, OR ENTER COMMAND: M TO RETURN TO MASTER MENU, D TO CHOOSE NEW DATABASE. OR O TO SIGN OFF.
System asks for your first inquiry (S1); answers with the number of items found (A1).	S1--> *office administration and telecommunications*
	A1 35 DOCUMENTS FOUND
System requests your instruction.	TYPE IN SEARCH TERMS, OR ENTER COMMAND: P TO PRINT DOCUMENTS FOUND, R TO REVIEW SEARCH QUESTIONS, M TO RETURN TO MASTER MENU, D TO CHOOSE NEW DATABASE OR O TO SIGN OFF.
	S2--> *p;1;l;3* • ———————— You ask to print from (S1) the long format of the 3rd document.
	3
1st Item: Author Title Source.	AU Cowan-William-M.
	TI Mailroom Equipment: Increasingly Efficient and Productive.
	SO Office Administration & Automation. Vol: V45N11. Pag: 37-43, 98-100. 6 Pages. Nov 1984.
Descriptors.	DE Mailrooms. Mail. Handling. Equipment. Manyproducts. Manycompanies.
Abstract.	AB New advances in mailrooms systems and equipment are accelerating as a result of higher postage costs and the ever increasing quantities of incoming, interoffice, and outgoing mail. Mailroom equipment must become more productive and efficient in order to handle the volumes of hard-copy communications that telecommunications and electronic mail systems cannot route. Pitney Bowes is constantly improving its . . .
	END OF DOCUMENT. HIT ENTER TO SEE NEXT DOCUMENT, OR TYPE ANOTHER DOCUMENT NUMBER, OR TYPE S TO CONTINUE SEARCHING, P TO PRINT DOCUMENTS FOUND, R TO REVIEW SEARCH QUESTIONS, M TO RETURN TO MASTER MENU, D TO CHOOSE NEW DATABASE, OR O TO SIGN OFF.
	XX--> *o* • ———————— You sign off.

Annotated sample of typical database search of major on-line vendor computer to search the selected database for articles that contain the words "Toys OR Dolls AND injuries AND California." (The exact wording and order would depend on the specific protocol of the database selected.) The computer would then scan the database and search for text or index terms that contain those terms. Then the computer would alert you to what it discovered.

Typically, the way the computer alerts you is by telling you how many successful "hits" (articles, reports, citations, etc.) it came up with based on the keywords you entered. In this example, it may tell you that "eight articles were located that contain the words Toys OR Dolls AND California." You are then given the option to look at those articles in more depth, alter your search strategy, or quit your search.

If you choose to examine the articles, the system then typically provides you with an abstract of each. Some databases will automatically provide you with the full text instead. The abstract is usually a few lines or a couple of paragraphs that capture the essence of the full article. In addition, the abstract provides full bibliographic data on the original source itself.

Often, the information you obtain from the abstract is enough to answer your question. However, sometimes you'll want to obtain the full document. There are a few ways to get it. Some databases allow you to see the full text on the screen, which you can then read, store for later reading, or print out. Some on-line vendors offer a "document delivery" service—they will mail you a printed copy for an extra fee. You can also go to a library to try to find the source, or write to the original publisher.

The computer search won't always come up with a nice number of hits like eight. Sometimes you won't uncover any information at all; other times you may be overwhelmed with hundreds of hits. It's important to know how to perform a good search to avoid getting too many hits or none at all. You'd be buried with references if you did a search that was too broad, e.g., all news articles in which the words Clinton and *White House* occurred. Conversely, if a search is too narrow, you won't come up with anything at all.

Here are some tips on how to conduct a good search:
- Plan a search strategy beforehand. Map out on paper what

you are looking for and think of keywords that best pinpoint your topic.

- Think of synonyms and alternative words to describe your topic. Use a thesaurus to help you. Be prepared to try using these words if your initial keywords don't get you what you want.
- Start your search narrowly, and then broaden it if necessary. This way you can first try to get the most precise information you need, but if you don't have luck, you can start broadening. Say you want to find out where in 1983 there were instances of asbestos contamination in schools—especially in junior-high-school buildings—that caused the school to shut down. You might choose a database like *HazardLine* (which obtains information from the U.S. Environmental Protection Agency and other health-and safety-related agencies). Then you could start your search with keywords like "1983 AND Asbestos AND Junior High School AND Close OR Closing." If your search did not turn anything up, you might consider substituting broader terms, such as "School" instead of "Junior High School," or you could eliminate a term, such as the words *close* or *closing*, to try to get more, although probably less specific, information. (Similarly, if you get too many hits, you can add more terms or make them more specific to *reduce* the number of sources located.)

TIP: When you need assistance in creating a search, it is almost always better to call the *provider* (creator) of the database, rather than the database *host* (reseller). The provider is normally the true expert in the subject matter and may sometimes even be able to tell you where to find other sources of information on the topic.

TIPS ON CUTTING COSTS

If you plan to do computer searches on your own equipment, there are a number of cost factors that need to be examined:

Hardware and Software. As mentioned earlier, you will need to acquire the basic setup of a personal computer or terminal, communications software, modem, and telephone.

Vendor Fees. After you have your equipment, the next step is to sign up with a database vendor. There are many different costs to consider when you subscribe. These are:

- Start-up fee: Some vendors have a one-time start-up fee.
- Annual subscription fee: A few vendors also have a monthly or yearly charge.
- Hourly connect-time fee: Most vendors charge a specified rate for each minute that the user is connected to the system. The fee is charged to the subscriber *whenever* he or she is officially linked up—it doesn't matter if the computer is waiting for a command, searching its databases for information, or displaying data on the screen. As long as the connection is made, the minutes tick off and the charges accumulate. This fee can grow rapidly if the subscriber is not careful. Connect-time charges vary quite a bit among vendors but typically run from $3–$12 + on the consumer-oriented services, and $45–$150 per hour on the professional systems. On some services, during off-peak times, normally evenings and weekends, the cost can be *less than half* the peak-hour rates.
- Database surcharges: Depending on *which* database you want to search, some vendors charge an extra hourly fee in addition to the standard connect-time fee. This surcharge can be as high as $180 per hour but typically ranges from $15 to $70. Vendors that do not charge this fee outright often have already built the fee into their hourly connect-time rate.
- Printout charges: There may be an extra fee charged for each item you want to view or print out (25¢–$2).
- Telephone charges: For most services, unless you live in a very remote location, you do not have to make a long-distance phone call to hook up with the vendor's computer. Instead, you can dial a local phone number to reach a national communications service that can access the vendor's computer. However, there are still phone charges to consider, and these range from about $3 to $10 per hour. The vendor normally adds these charges directly to your bill.

Because connect-time rates can build so rapidly, it's easy to underestimate how much money can be spent doing computer searches. Be especially careful about controlling costs during your first month of use, because you may not realize just how quickly those minutes add up. Otherwise your first bill may come as an unpleasant surprise.

It would be a good idea to try to figure out just how much you may be paying the vendor over the long haul. Try making a budget by estimating the number of searches you think you'll be making each week, multiply it by the connect fee prorated to ten minutes, and add other charges. Because actual search time can vary considerably, this will be a very rough estimate. But it will at least give you a feel for how much you will spend if you keep time spent on the computer to the amount you have budgeted.

If you'll be doing searches on your own computer, here are some tips for keeping costs down:

- Become as familiar as you possibly can with the particular service that you have selected. If you aren't comfortable with the system, you'll spend time on the computer trying to figure out how to use it—an expensive way to learn as the minutes tick away and costs add up. Read the instruction manual carefully, sign up for courses and seminars offered by the vendor, and become as knowledgeable as you can about doing searches.

- Buy the fastest modem that you can afford. Modem speed is measured in "baud," and typical speeds are 2400 and 9600 baud. When you use a high-speed modem, you are able to retrieve or "download" information faster and thus get more information for the money. Some vendors charge a premium to subscribers who use the higher-speed modems, but usually the extra charge will not be high enough to fully eliminate the user's advantage.

- Buy a communications software package that's easy to use. This will make it quick and easy to sign on (or "logon") to the databases. Before you select a particular piece of communications software, have the vendor let you try out a few so that you can determine which is easiest to use.

- Consider signing up with a vendor that offers reduced rates for using the service at night or on weekends. These rates may be half of what they are during weekday "prime-time" hours.

- Reduce the amount of time you spend on-line—and lower your connect-time charges—by trying the following techniques:

191

Write up your "search strategy" (the creation of keywords and alternatives) *before* you logon. Many vendors provide toll-free numbers users can call to get free advice on how to make a good search. The more of this preplanning you do, the better, because you'll avoid spending expensive minutes on-line while figuring out what to do next.

Find out when the vendor's response time (that is, the time it takes the computer to respond to your commands) is at its fastest (often this is during evening and nighttime hours). If you do your searching during these times, you will obtain information quicker and spend fewer minutes on-line.

Avoid, if possible, spending time reading full texts of documents displayed on the screen while you are on-line. Instead, you should copy the data onto your diskette for later reading at your leisure. Or, if the service is offered, order the document directly from the vendor. Another approach is to jot down the citations (name of source, volume, date, page, etc.) and then go to a nearby library to locate a print copy (this approach is best suited for print sources commonly available at the library, such as the *Wall Street Journal*, well-known magazines, and standard reference books). Finally, you can contact the original producer of the source directly to find out how to order it or where you can find copies.

TIP: Finding Free and Inexpensive Databases
- Some organizations, especially government agencies, make databases available for free or cheap. For example, for a $25 fee, the Department of Commerce's Office of Business Analysis and Economic Affairs offers the *Economic Bulletin Board*, which gives users access to the latest releases from the Bureau of Economic Analysis, the Bureau of Labor Statistics, and other federal agencies. Data are provided on topics such as the GNP, employment, personal income, consumer price indexes, and foreign trade. For more information, contact the Department of Commerce, Office of Business Analysis, Room H4887, 14th Street and Constitution Avenue NW, Washington, DC 20230; 202-482-1405 for direct on-line connections. You can obtain more information on free government databases by checking a library copy of *The Federal Database Finder,* published by Information USA (Potomac, Maryland).

ARE THERE DRAWBACKS
TO COMPUTER SEARCHING?

While on-line searches can be a very productive way to find information, some vendors oversell their capabilities. You might be told that electronic databases are the answer to all of your information problems and be warned that those who don't sign up will be left in the dark ages. This is simply not true. On-line database searching is simply an excellent tool. And as with any tool, sometimes it makes sense to use it, and other times it makes sense to use something else.

First it should be pointed out that there are a couple of inherent disadvantages to on-line searching. Conducting efficient searches is an art. If a user is not skilled in proper search techniques, the computer will be unable to do a good job and the user will end up with too much, too little, or irrelevant information. Another potential drawback is that sometimes the database one selects simply does not contain the desired information. As vast a scope as databases cover today, they still do not contain all types of information and in general are stronger in science, business, and news than they are in "softer" subjects like the humanities and social sciences. Finally, some databases provide the user with the full text of the document identified, but most provide only abstracts, or even just a bibliography. This is fine for most users, especially because the user is also given the necessary information to track down the full original source, but it may be insufficient for others.

Some words need to be said about the topic of database accuracy too. Unfortunately, information retrieved the high-tech way—from a computer terminal—need not be any more accurate than information obtained the old-fashioned low-tech ways from books, magazines, and so forth. In fact, there are various steps in the process of creating a database that could result in the creation of additional errors. For example, there is the possibility of transcription errors from the original source, inconsistent index terms, inaccurate or misleading coverage of sources, and plain old typos.

Some of the larger and more sophisticated database vendors

employ various automated checking routines and other methods to reduce errors, but no system is perfect. Remember also that just because the information comes off a computer—a fallible human being like you or me wrote and compiled the original information, so you need to be just as concerned about the reliability of that *original source* as you would when obtaining information from any other noncomputer source, like a newspaper article or published report.

Here are some assorted strategies and tips for making more sure that the information you retrieve on-line will be reliable:

▪ Get proficient at knowing the ins and outs of just a few databases versus having just passing knowledge of many. By becoming intimately familiar with a database, you not only become a better searcher, but are more likely to be able to spot errors.

▪ Always confirm findings by using two or three different sources, and more than one database—especially if the data are going to be utilized for any major decisions.

▪ Statistics and numerical data are sometimes best viewed not as precise measurements, but as rough indicators.

▪ Be sure you know when the database producer most recently *updated* its data.

Don't assume an on-line database—even the largest and most popular ones—will include *all* the information you need. Check other sources too—hard copy reference books, microfiche listings, and directories.

TIP: Sometimes the most valuable function of searching a database is not in the reading of the abstracts but for finding *leads*. In other words, don't think of the items you retrieve from the database as necessarily the "answers" but as a means to identify knowledgeable persons such as journalists, editors, and other experts cited in the abstracts to track down and interview to get all of your questions answered.

Also as mentioned earlier, users often spend a lot more money than they think they will doing searches. Using databases is a bit addictive. It can be a lot of fun to sit in front of a screen, type in a few words, and almost magically see the answers to your questions appear before your eyes. But when the bill appears, the magic can wear off quickly.

The trick is to know when it makes sense to use the computer to find information and when it is better to consider a less-expensive source like a library index.

Use the Computer When . . .

. . . you use the power of the keyword system to identify information virtually impossible to locate via conventional sources. For example, Tim Miller, a free-lance writer, used this power to its maximum advantage when researching a biography of Geraldine Ferraro. Miller wanted to locate prominent class-mates of hers from law school to interview them for recollec-tions. He knew that Ferraro graduated from Fordham Law School in 1960, but, unfortunately, names of classmates were not available from the school itself. Therefore, Miller decided to do a computer search of a database of *Who's Who in America*. He instructed the computer to give him the name of any person listed in the books whose name occurred near the keywords "1960, J.D.," and "Fordham." The result was a list of people who graduated Fordham with a J.D. degree in 1960. If Miller had attempted to read through the entire Who's Who volumes himself to try to find that information, he would have faced a nearly impossible task.

. . . the information you seek is so obscure that you need to search enormous amounts of data in the hopes of finding out whether anything at all is "out there."

. . . speed is of the essence, and you need information within minutes.

. . . timeliness is critical, and you want up-to-the-minute in-formation—possibly even before it's published anywhere.

. . . the information you seek is simply not available in any published source.

Think Twice About Using the Computer When . . .

. . . the information you seek is easily available. For example, if you want to know the length of the world's longest river, or some other simple fact, why not look it up in an encyclopedia? If you're looking for an article published in last year's *New York Times*, how about going to the library?

. . . the information you seek is available from another source for free. For example, you can spend $75 an hour or more to search a database that provides the same information that's available free from the U.S. Census Bureau. Some vendors charge $75 an hour to search indexes of trade publications when a professional association might provide the same data for much less or for free.

. . . the subject you need information on is too broad. For example, if you asked a business-information database for references on "marketing" or "management," you'd be buried with information. You'd be better off learning about these subjects from a few good books until you can narrow your topic down.

Before deciding that a computer search is the only answer to your information needs, check out other information sources like professional associations, libraries, business contacts, government sources, and other resources described in this book.

THE INTERNET

If you're interested in learning about the on-line world, you'd better get accustomed to hearing about, and being able to discuss, its hottest aspect: the Internet or, to those in-the-internet-know, simply, "the Net." These days an on-line searcher who doesn't know something about the Internet, would be looked upon about as favorably as a doctor who never heard of a cat-scan.

Alright then, exactly what is the Internet? The simple answer is that it's a computer network. It's a series of separate computers linked electronically, so as to allow anyone on one computer to communicate with and access data on the others. Something akin to the network your office may recently have been setting up.

Yeah, right. The Internet is "just" a computer network. Just like Microsoft is just another firm pushing software. This particular computer network currently links up about **120,000** different sites in **60 countries,** and is currently "populated" by roughly 20 million people! And since about 1990, these numbers have been soaring at a phenomenal rate. By the time you're reading this, these figures will surely have increased. Also, to be more precise, the Internet is not technically just a network, but a "network of networks" or, as it is commonly termed, a massive "web" of computer networks: comprising, at last count, about 12,000 or so networks.

Who exactly "populates" this supernetwork? What are all these computers linked up to? Universities, government agencies, libraries, database vendors, non-profit organizations—and ordinary PC users like you and me—are all "citizens" of this new type of community. And it's this incredibly diverse population that makes using the Internet's resources so exciting, and rewarding.

There is a mind-boggling number of things that you can do, find, and learn on the Internet. Since entire books are written on this subject, let's just mention a handful here:

▪ Send and receive electronic mail, not just to someone in another state, but to persons who live in far off countries;
▪ Search on-line databases for facts and information;
▪ Read "electronic" versions of magazines and journals;
▪ Join electronic discussion groups (called "usenet" and "listserv" groups) to debate, analyze, and hear opinions on hundreds of different topics;
▪ Tap into libraries from around the world and search their card catalogs.

It's really impossible, though, to illustrate in a short section of a single book chapter anywhere near the level of what it is possible to do on the Internet. The possibilities are almost limitless. Think about it. To exchange professional views on a new theory with a colleague in Switzerland; search Great Britain's national Library catalog for a rare Egyptian document; participate in a global give and take on the ethics of cloning; download the latest U.S. Supreme Court decisions; get up-to-the-minute meteorological reports on distant regions; and so on, and so on, and so on! One of the neat things about communicating via the Internet is that you can't be judged by your looks —only by what you "say." Your age, sex, race, and physical characteristics are invisible. A great cartoon published in the *New Yorker* captured this point nicely: a dog sits in front of his owner's computer and cheerfully explains to his canine friend sitting nearby that, "On the Internet, no one knows you're a dog."

Now, you might want to know, exactly where can you find a listing of all of this incredible "stuff" on the Internet? Are you sitting down? Why don't you pour yourself a little drink? I hate to be the one to tell you—but as they say, in front of every silver lining, there's always a cloud. And this one's a nasty one. There is no comprehensive list. And not only is there no list, there's nobody to "complain" to, since nobody really "runs" the Internet!

We had better take a short detour here, and explain how this all came to be. The Internet was originally founded by the Department of Defense as a government-sponsored research network. Eventually, it expanded to a broader based government network, and then into academia as a way scientists could exchange technical information. As the Internet grew, though, and its power began attracting more users, a few applications that were not purely technical and research-oriented were allowed, usage increased, more applications were developed, and so on. But during this time, the Net was still run as a self-regulating community, though with some general oversight from the U.S. National Science Foundation (NSF). So, the history of this unusual "nation" is akin to a pure democracy or, probably more accurately, anarchy. In any event, there is no "City Hall" to help organize the community.

Luckily, some inroads have been made, both by enlightened cyberspace citizens and by a few corporate members who do a little volunteer work and contribute to the community.

One particularly valuable and longstanding effort is a selective listing of Internet resources called the "Yanoff" list, which was created by Internet good-citizen Scott Yanoff. His list, updated regularly, contains names, descriptions, and the location ("address") of hundreds of some of the "best" of the Internet, organized by subject. Another recently developed guide is a white- and yellow-page-like on-line directory. This directory was created by AT&T as part of a cooperative Internet information service provider organization called InterNIC, which was funded by the National Science Foundation. Another very hot product catching on is called *Mosaic*, available free on the Internet and developed by the National Center for Supercomputing Applications in Champaign-Urbana, Illinois. With this software program, users can point and click through the Internet using hypertext links between words and documents.

In addition to the difficulties of finding what you need, the other major hurdle in using the Internet is that it's hard to use. Unlike the major consumer on-line services, who work diligently to create friendly graphics, plain English searching, and consistent interfaces to make use as easy as possible, the Internet makes no such concessions. In this new frontier, you can't give up too easily, and only the strongest survive. It takes a lot of practice to feel comfortable in getting around the Net, finding what you need, and logging on and off all the various computers —each of which uses their own methods and sports their own interface.

How do you sign on to the Internet and get going? There are a few options. If you are associated with a university or research institute of some kind, there is a good chance that that organization already is on the Net, and all you need to do is find out how to get a password. If you don't have any such affiliation, you need to sign up with one of the many Internet service providers that offer access for a fee. As of this writing, of the major consumer on-line services, only Delphi offers full Internet access. You can sign up with that firm, or with one of a number of other providers located around the country. For a list of providers, I'd recommend either checking the appendix of **The Internet Companion** (Addison-Wesley, 1993) or reading **Connecting to**

The Internet: A Buyer's Guide (Wiley, 1993). Keep in mind that access rates vary widely, and it's worth doing a fair bit of comparison shopping before choosing one.

Once you sign on to the Internet, you'll naturally need to know the key commands for getting around and finding what you need. This is a critical area, and it cannot be treated with any justice in this small section. Briefly, though, the two most critical are "Telnet," for logging onto remote computers, and "FTP," for downloading information. In addition, you'll need to understand the following Internet commands (or information finding utilities) in order to best search the Net for information and resources:

- *Gopher*: for creating a menuized list of options
- *Veronica*: for searching Gopher menus by keywords
- *Archie:* for locating files by name
- *WAIS:* for performing key word searches on databases
- *WWW* (World Wide Web): for finding related documents using "hypertext."

To get a full explanation and description of these critical functions, you should obtain one of the Internet books listed in the Appendix.

Where does the Internet stand today? As of this writing, the Internet continues to grow at a fantastic rate. More and more commercial services, including traditional on-line databases, are being added, creating even more resources. Concerns over the complexity of using the Net are spawning innovations and products to make access easier. And the major media and telecommunication giants are rapidly establishing links and various relationships with the Internet. This development is causing debate and concern in the Internet community over who, ultimately, will be in control and in charge of what has been, up until very recently, a thriving and vibrant, if rather messy, type of electronic utopia.

BUYING CD-ROMs

Up until now, this chapter has discussed one type of electronic databases: "on-line" ones. These are databases stored somewhere else and only available **remotely** through your modem. In a sense, searching an **on-line** database is like "renting" access to data since you don't "own" the database. (And your rent is based on how much information you want and/or how much time you spend looking for it.) But, as the real estate ads proclaim: why rent, when you can own? And you can, if you buy a "CD-ROM" database.

If you don't know what a CD-ROM is, refer to pages 40–46 in Chapter 1, where we discussed CD-ROMs in libraries. In essence, these discs are similar to the popular audio CDs, except that when attached to a CD-ROM reader on your PC, these discs "play" information (and sometimes sound, too). CD-ROMs can store a huge amount of data—550 MB or about 250,000 pages of information. In addition, many can display high-quality graphics and pictures.

Up until around 1990 or so, few consumers bought CD-ROMs for their computers. They were very expensive, as were the CD-ROM readers that were needed to use them. But since that time, prices have dropped dramatically, and today sales of both CD-ROM players and discs have soared. Some of the most interesting and successful CD-ROM titles have been electronic encyclopedias. Two leading products are Grolier Inc.'s *New Grolier Multimedia Encyclopedia* and *Compton's Multimedia Encyclopedia*. Today, though, there are thousands of CD-ROM database titles; here are several examples:

- African American Experience (Quanta)
  A history of African-Americans from their homeland.

- ASIST (U.S. Patent and Trademark Office)
  Data on U.S. patents: patent number and assignee name for all patents issued from 1977.

- Baseball's Greatest Hits (Voyager)
  Statistics on famous baseball players, and movie images of 65 memorable moments.

- Career Opportunities (Quanta)
  Data on careers, derived from the U.S. Department of Commerce.

- CIA World Factbook (Quanta)
  Facts on 249 countries.

- Cinemania (Microsoft)
  Movie reviewer Leonard Maltin's movie reviews on disc.

- Complete Works of Shakespeare (Creative Multimedia Corporation)
  Just like the title says.

- Consumer Reports (Dialog)
  Current and past issues of **Consumer Reports** magazine.

- The College Handbook (Macmillan New Media)
  Information on 2,700 colleges and universities.

- Darwin (Lightbinders)
  The collected works of Charles Darwin; includes illustrations.

- The Family Doctor (Creative Multimedia)
  Home medical guide, written for consumers.

- Food/Analyst (Hopkins)
  Nutritional information for over 4,800 foods.

- MicroSoft Bookshelf (Microsoft)
  A selection of reference sources: dictionary, almanac, quotation book, style manual, thesaurus, zip code directory, business information sourcebook, and more.

- MicroSoft Musical Instruments (Microsoft)
  Information on over 200 musical instruments, including photos and sounds.

- Multimedia Encyclopedia of Mammalian Biology (McGraw-Hill)
  Over 3,500 full-color images and nearly 500 maps, sound and video.

- The New Bible Library (Ellis Enterprises, Inc.)
  Contains more than 80 volumes and features 16 Bibles and 25 reference works.

- Newsbytes, Volume 2 (Wayzata)
  The latest news on the computer industry.

- ProPhone (ProCD)
  70 million residential listings and 7 million business listings.

- USA Wars—Civil War (Quanta)
  Chronologies, battles, biographies, campaigns, and other information.

- U.S. Government Manual on CD-ROM (Updata)
  Phone numbers, missions, etc., of U.S. government departments and agencies.

- U.S. History on CD-ROM (Bureau of Electronic Publishing) Political, military, and social history. Includes over 1,000 photographs, maps, and illustrations.

The following is a list of the names and addresses of the vendors of those CD-ROMs listed above:

- Bureau of Electronic Publishing, 141 New Road, Parsippany, NJ 07054; 201-808-2700.

- Creative Multimedia Corp., 514 NW 11th Avenue, Suite 203, Portland, OR 97209; 800-262-7668.

- Dialog, 3460 Hillview Avenue, Palo Alto, CA 94304; 800-334-2564.

- Ellis Enterprises, 4205 McAuley Boulevard, Suite 385, Oklahoma City, OK 73120; 800-729-9500.

- Hopkins, 421 Hazel Lane, Hopkins, MN 55343; 612-931-9376.

- Lightbinders, 2325 3rd Street, Suite 320, San Francisco, CA 94107; 415-621-5746.

- Macmillan New Media, 124 Mount Auburn Street, Cambridge, MA 02138; 617-661-2955.

- McGraw-Hill, 11 West 19th Street, New York, NY 10011; 800-262-4729.

- Microsoft, One Microsoft Way, Redmond, WA 98052; 800-426-9400.

- ProCD, 8 Doaks Lane, Marblehead, MA 01945; 617-631-9299.

- Quanta, 1313 5th Street SE, Suite 223A, Minneapolis, MN 55414; 612-379-3956.

- Updata, 1736 Westwood Boulevard, Los Angeles, CA 90024; 213-474-5900.

- U.S. Patent and Trademark Office, Office of Electronic Information Products and Services, Crystal Plaza 2, 9D30, Washington, DC 20231; 703-308-0322.

- Voyager, 1351 Pacific Coast Highway, Santa Monica, CA 90401; 800-446-2001.

- Wayzata Technology, PO Box 807, Grand Rapids, MI 55744; 800-735-7321.

Did you notice the word "multimedia" in the titles of many of these discs? "Multimedia" CD-ROMs provide not just text, but photographs, sound, and sometimes video. Some products offer one or two of these extra features, while others offer all of them.

Multimedia CD-ROMs have been making quite a splash in the electronic information world over the last few years. Some of these products are truly technologically dazzling. But you need to be careful that their shine does not blind you to carefully examining their substance.

Whether a CD-ROM is an ordinary text-only product, or a fully featured text/audio/photo/video multimedia product, the substantive evaluation criteria is mainly the same. As with any consumer item, you need to have a certain set of standards. In the case of CD-ROMs, you should check for the following:

Compatibility

Obviously, the CD-ROM you buy must be compatible with your CD-ROM drive and computer. With text-only CD-ROMs, this is not normally a problem. However, multimedia discs (including those formatted with the enhanced audio "XA" standard) will not play on all drives, and you need to check for compatibility.

Data Quality

Another obviously critical area, but one not quite as easy to assess, is quality. To evaluate, think about questions such as:

▪ Where did the information originally come from? A well-known reputable publisher or expert organization, or some unknown entity?

▪ When was the product released? How timely is the information? Can you receive updates on a regular basis?

▪ How comprehensive is the information? If, for example, the CD-ROM is a database of popular magazine articles, how many years back does it cover? Does it include every article from the magazines it lists, or just provide selective coverage?

- Is there a "controlled" index? These are specific terms pre-established by the vendor, used to consistently link items in the database on similar subjects with the same terms. Using these terms can greatly assist you in creating more precise searches.

Search Power

CD-ROMs vary greatly in the power and flexibility of their search software. Some critical questions to keep in mind:

- Is the database key word searchable?
- Can you use Boolean AND, OR, and NOT operators?
- Can you use advanced Boolean "proximity" operators (to specify how far key words must be from each other) and "truncation" (to search for variations of word stems)?
- Can you "browse" an index to look for already existing indexing terms? Can you highlight or mark relevant ones easily?

Ease of Use

This is also extremely important; unfortunately, you may not have the opportunity to make this evaluation until you have already bought the product. However, if you do get the opportunity to "test drive" a disk before purchase, note how easy it is to use. Are you led, logically and clearly, from one step to the next? Are the instructions easy to follow? Do you get "lost" somewhere in the middle of a search, and find it hard to "return" to where you left off? The best products make everything seem as easy as possible (even the powerful ones). Inferior products make you think that you are doing something wrong, when the real problem is a poorly designed system.

Warranty and Price

Of course, you'll want to find out about warranty and price. Regarding the latter, prices can vary quite a bit among vendors for the same product, so be sure to shop around and compare.

ANOTHER OPTION:
THE INFORMATION BROKER

What is an "information broker"? It is a firm that offers computer search services and/or other research services for a fee. Such a firm accepts inquiries from users and then tries to come up with the answers by searching on-line databases and, sometimes, by tapping into other information sources like associations and library resources.

A benefit of an information broker is that you are able to tap into the power of a computer search without needing access to a computer yourself. However, because it may be cheaper to do the searches on your own, using these firms is probably most appropriate for people who have only a one-shot information request or for those who need to make inquiries only very occasionally.

Information brokers vary enormously with regard to their staff size, research capabilities, and fees. Some brokers are simply individuals who own a personal computer and subscribe to an on-line database vendor. These people often get their customers by placing ads offering computer search services at low cost. Other information brokers are large corporations with extensive staffs and resources. These firms may charge well into the thousands of dollars for their services. Some information brokers specialize in a particular type of information search, while others handle any topic or search request.

Because the capabilities and resources of information brokers vary so widely, it's important that you select carefully. Before deciding which one to use, compare brokers using the following criteria:

- What databases does the broker have access to? Do they cover the subjects you are interested in?
- What is the broker's experience in performing information searches? How long has the searcher been doing this kind of work? (You don't want someone to be practicing at your expense.)
- What credentials does the information broker have? A degree in library science? Has the broker worked as an information specialist in some

capacity for another firm? Does he or she belong to the national trade association, the Association of Independent Information Professionals (AIIP)?

Another important factor is the amount of time and attention a broker pays to discussing your information project. A good information broker will try to learn as much as possible about your needs. The person who will actually be doing the search should discuss with you the details of what you need to find out, where you've already looked, why you're trying to find this information, what you're planning to do with it, and other details.

You can find information brokers by checking a variety of places. Some are listed in the yellow pages under the heading "Information" or "Research." Check writers' magazines (e.g., *Writers Digest*) and look for advertisements under "Professional Services" or a similar heading.

You can also check the *Burwell Directory of Information Brokers*. This handbook lists hundreds of firms around the country —and around the globe—that will do research for a fee. The directory includes helpful information such as subject specialties, specific services provided, as well as full contact information. You can order a copy from Burwell Enterprises, 3724 FM 1960 West, Suite 214, Houston, TX 77068; 713-537-9051. And if you yourself are interested in *becoming* an information broker, I recommend getting *The Information Broker's Handbook* (TAB McGraw-Hill) or get hold of *The Information Broker's Resource Kit*, available from the Rugge Group.

Also, sometimes nearby university libraries will offer on-line search services. Fees may be less than private firms, but the extent of services available is also likely to be more limited.

FUTURE DEVELOPMENTS

What kinds of changes might you see down the road with electronic databases? It's expected that the number of on-line databases, especially the "full-text" ones, will continue to grow. A good deal of attention is now being given to making access to all of this information easier and less threatening. Consumer on-line services (and some professional ones as well) have been working hard to create friendly and attractive graphical front ends, and do away with the old-fashioned and boring "ascii" text interface. Professional-level systems are also experimenting with new and potentially more powerful "relevance" based searching that may replace or at least supplement the traditional Boolean approach. With this search method, databases rank each item's "relevance" based on factors like placement of the key term in the story, and frequency. Another area professional services are experimenting with is replacing the cumbersome "ticking clock" method of pricing with less intimidating and more straightforward flat-fee plans.

The number of CD-ROMs is expcted to continue increasing rapidly too, especially the multimedia products. The latest CD-ROM technology are what's called "full image" discs: those that don't just contain the text of an original article, report, or item, but actually reproduce a duplicate of the original page, including elements like headlines, boxes, charts and graphics, etc. CD-ROMs with this kind of capability are much more pleasant to read. However, as of this writing, only a few very products offer this capability; they are generally quite expensive and can be found in libraries. Like most technological developments in this fast-moving field, though, this is likely to change quickly. There is still a lot more to come.

Not everything on the electronic information horizon is positive. One of the fastest growing areas of concern is personal privacy. With companies collecting and disseminating more and more information, many people and several civil liberty organizations are worried that citizens are unwittingly revealing personal information that could be utilized in undesirable or harmful ways. Other matters of concern include security (especially on the Internet) and dealing with novel ethical issues that have emerged from the communication of information through electronic networks.

WHERE TO GO FOR MORE INFORMATION

If you're intrigued by the idea of using computers to find information, here are some good places to learn more:

In bookstores, you may want to examine a copy of another book of mine called *Find it Online* (Windcrest/McGraw-Hill), which is devoted solely to the topic of finding information through electronic databases.

In libraries, look for any of the following guides to on-line databases. They list thousands of databases and provide various information on each, including the name, producer, frequency of updates, time span covered, and a short summary of its subject matter and scope. A subject index will tell you whether there are any databases available on your subject of interest.

- *Gale Directory of Databases* (Gale Research Inc.): A leading guide, it provides information on over 5,000 on-line databases and over 1,400 CD-ROMs and is updated semi-annually.

- *The CD-ROM Finder* (Learned Information)

These are not the only database directories in existence. The library you visit may have similar guides created by other publishers.

ON-LINE VENDORS

The following are the addresses and telephone numbers of some of the more popular consumer and professional on-line vendors:

America Online
8619 Westwood Center Drive
Vienna, VA 22182
703-448-8700

CompuServe
CompuServe Information Service
P.O. Box 20212
Columbus, OH 43220
800-848-8990

Dow Jones News/Retrieval
Dow Jones and Company
P.O. Box 300
Princeton, NJ 08543
800-522-3567

GEnie
P.O. Box 6403
Rockville, MO 20850
800-638-9636

Data-Star
D-S Marketing
Suite 1110
485 Devon Park Drive
Wayne, PA 19087
800-221-7754

Delphi
1030 Massachusetts Avenue
Cambridge, MA 02138
617-491-3393

Dialog Information Services Inc.
3460 Hillview Avenue
Palo Alto, CA 94304
800-334-2564

NewsNet
945 Haverford Road
Bryn Mawr, PA 19010
800-345-1301

Nexis Mead Data Central
9443 Springboro Pike
Dayton, OH 45401
513-865-6800

Prodigy
P.O. Box 791
White Plains, NY 10601
914-993-8000

TIP: Financial Information Searches by Telephone
▪ A different approach to conducting an information search is the "DowPhone," a service available from Dow Jones in New York. All that's needed to access this information service is a telephone. Users punch codes on their push-button phone to "search" for the information they need, and they hear voice reports of specified financial news and data. The information available includes stock market updates, company and industry news, late-breaking economic reports, and business indexes. Dow Jones charges a modest fee, which is based on the number of minutes spent on the phone. Call 800-345-6397 to find out more.

PART II

Experts Are Everywhere

6

Identifying Experts
Who They Are, Where to Find Them

**QUICK PREVIEW:
IDENTIFYING EXPERTS**

An expert is simply a person with in-depth knowledge about a subject or activity. For most information-finding projects, there are nine types of experts worth tracking down and contacting:

- **Book authors** are solid sources, but be sure those you speak with have stayed up to date with their subject.

- **Periodical staff writers and editors** can be excellent information sources. Technical and trade publication staffers are typically more knowledgeable in a specific field than are journalists who work on popular interest newspapers and publications.

- **Experts cited in periodical articles** make excellent information sources.

- **Convention speakers** are another potential top information source.

- **Federal government personnel** may take time to track down, but once you do, you'll find them to be surprisingly helpful.

- **Association staffers** are superb information sources—knowledgeable, helpful, and very easy to reach.

(continued)

- **Experts at private companies** are often valuable sources, but they may be hard to find and reluctant to reveal their knowledge.
- **Consultants,** although often very knowledgeable, typically are not fruitful resources for the researcher, because they normally charge a fee for sharing their knowledge.
- **A "hands-on" expert** actually performs the activity you need to find out about.

Identifying and using written source materials is only the first step of the information-finding process. The next step is to locate and talk to the experts behind the sources. Here's why:

- Reading written information means wading through piles of published materials to try to isolate the information you need. But talking to an expert gives you the opportunity to pose questions and zero in on specific issues that concern *you*. In essence, the information you receive from the expert is "custom designed" to meet your needs.

- If an expert makes a point that's confusing, you can ask a question to clear it up—not so easy to do with a magazine article or book!

- When you talk to an expert, you receive the timeliest information possible. You can find out what has happened in the last couple of days—or couple of hours.

- Talking to an expert is simply more interesting and fun. You get the kind of live opinions and candid remarks not ordinarily found in published materials.

But before you begin, you need to learn the best techniques for getting to the "best" experts.

LOCATING THE EXPERTS

Experts are everywhere. An expert is anybody who has in-depth knowledge about a particular subject or activity. A few of these experts are famous—someone like a Benjamin Spock or Julia Child—but the overwhelming majority are not. The experts that you'll be talking to are most likely to be businesspersons, government workers, technical writers, shop foremen, teachers, and other ordinary persons with special know-how, skills, or background.

Here is a quick overview of eight of the best types of expert to track down and talk to. The pros and cons of each type are examined; and strategies are provided on how best to make contact.

✔ Book Authors

PRO: Book authors typically have a solid and in-depth understanding of their subject. They possess a broad view of their field and can provide excellent background information.

CON: A book author may no longer be up to date on his or her subject. This can be especially true in fields that change very rapidly (such as computer technology). Book authors can also be hard to find.

HOW TO REACH: The standard approach for contacting an author is to send a letter in care of the book's publisher. The publisher is then supposed to forward your letter to the author. This can be a slow and unreliable approach to making contact: it's possible that your letter will sit for days, weeks, or even months at the publishing house before it's mailed out—especially if the book is an old one. It's better to call the publisher and talk to the book's editor to find out where *you* can contact the author.

TIP: Tracking Down a Book Author
- You can often find the editor's name mentioned in the "acknowledgments" section in the front of the book. If you don't find it there, you can call the editorial department of the publisher and ask for the editor's name. Just be sure to make it easy for the publisher to help you. This means providing complete information on the book —title, author, and date of publication. (If you cannot reach the editor, the next best person to speak with is probably someone in the publicity department.)

Will the publisher give you the author's address and phone number? Although many publishers have house rules prohibiting the release of this information, these rules are flexible. One key to getting the information is to make it easy for the editor or other staffer to help you: again, be sure you have as much information about the book as possible. An editor at a major publishing house told me that her decision on whether to release information about an author often depends on *why* someone wants it. So think a little beforehand about whether your reasons for wanting to contact the author sound legitimate and important.

If you are trying to find the author of a paperback book, first check the book's copyright page to see if a different publisher put out a hardcover edition. If so, it's best to contact that publisher instead.

 Periodical Staff Writers and Editors

PRO: Staff writers and editors of magazines and journals are typically nontechnical types who are easy to get hold of, easy to talk to, and very helpful. They usually keep up with developments in their field and are good at pointing out other places and people to contact for information.

CON: While an editor or staff writer for a *technical or trade* publication may be quite knowledgeable about a field (such people have often covered a specific field for so long that they become experts themselves), newspaper journalists or writers or editors of publications geared for the general public (*Time, Good Housekeeping,* etc.) may not be. They may indeed write an article on a technical topic, but their knowledge of the field can still be somewhat sketchy, because they are usually journalists first and subject experts only through their contacts and interviews. But they can still be helpful sources. For example, I recently contacted a popular magazine's staff writer about an article he wrote regarding the overnight delivery services industry. Although the staffer had a good working knowledge of the field, the real value of speaking with him was getting his referrals to the true experts in the industry that he spoke with when researching the piece.

HOW TO REACH: When you read an article that's of interest to you, look for the writer's byline at the beginning or end of the piece. Then turn to the periodical's masthead (normally found in the first five pages of the magazine) and search for the writer's name. Contact the publication and ask to speak with that person. If the person is not on the masthead, he or she is probably a free-lance writer. The editorial department of the magazine will be able to tell you how to make contact.

Another way to utilize magazine staff members as experts is to look at the masthead of a publication devoted to your subject of interest and try to zero in on a specific department editor (e.g., "technology editor" or "new products editor") who sounds as though he or she covers the kind of information you need. If you can't pick out a specific department editor but want to speak with someone on the magazine, ask to speak with the editor or the managing editor. If you are a subscriber, or at least a regular reader, it will help your cause to say so.

TIPS: Zero in on The Best Expert

▪ Take special care to note those articles that are written concisely and clearly enough to be easily understandable for the nonspecialist (i.e., you!). Chances are that the writer of these articles will be equally clear and enlightening to talk to.

▪ An excellent source of experts on lesser-known and privately held companies are editors and reporters of regional business publications. You can get a free listing of these publications by contacting the Association of Area Business Publications, 202 Legion Avenue, Annapolis, MD 21401; 410-269-0332. Ask for a free copy of its *Directory of Members.*

✔ Experts Cited in Periodical Articles

PRO: Virtually all periodical articles quote experts when examining an issue. For example, an article about a decline in the public's attendance of movie theaters, published in *Theatre Industry News*, quotes an industry expert on why moviegoing is declining, what can be done about it, what may happen in the future, and so forth. This makes your job of finding a knowledgeable source easy. The magazine has already done the necessary research to find an expert and bring his or her opinions and expertise to its readers. All you need to do is make contact. Such people are typically leaders in their field and can be extremely valuable sources. They can provide you with a wealth of information and are one of my favorite types of expert.

CON: Occasionally, you might run into a very knowledgeable source who is not so adept at communicating his or her expertise. This can make for a confusing information interview. If you encounter a confusing source, try to get the person to define any buzzwords or jargon.

HOW TO REACH: When an article quotes an expert, the piece normally provides the reader with his or her name and place and city of work. It is then a simple task to call up directory assistance in that city and obtain the phone number of the organization. (You can get the area code of any city by calling the operator.) If the article does not provide the expert's place of work or the city, call the publication directly to ask for it.

✔ Convention Speakers

PRO: People who are invited to present technical sessions at professional conventions are often real leaders and innovators in their field. They should be intimately informed about the topic of their presentation.

CON: Again, you may encounter a top-notch authority who is not as talented at communicating his or her expertise. Otherwise, there is no real drawback with this sort of expert.

HOW TO REACH: You can find out where conventions are being held on your subject by checking a library copy of the *Directory of Conventions* or by scanning an "upcoming events" column in a relevant trade publication. (See page 51 for more information on conventions.)

✔ Federal Government Personnel

PRO: Many experts in government view sharing information with the public as an important part of their job. What is surprising to many is that government experts are sometimes the most helpful of all sources. In fact, there is actually a law requiring government personnel to be helpful to the public!

CON: If you don't have an expert's name, it can be time-consuming and frustrating to track down the person you need. If you do telephone, be prepared to be transferred around a bit.

HOW TO REACH: See pages 113, 114, 117, and 119 on finding your way around Washington, and chapter 3 for an overview of obtaining information from the government.

✔ Association Staffers

PRO: As explained earlier in this book, people who work at professional associations are one of the very best sources of information. They are normally very knowledgeable, helpful, and easy to reach.

CON: An association executive might slant his or her remarks to advance the association's particular industry or cause. In addition, some association personnel are true experts in their field, while others are more oriented toward administrative or public relations work. Be sure you dig for the real experts. (Sometimes the true experts do not work in the association office itself, but work in private industry while maintaining a position with the association. It's fine to contact these people at their regular place of work.)

HOW TO REACH: Simply look up your subject in a library copy of the *Encyclopedia of Associations*. Call the association and ask your question.

✔ Company Personnel

PRO: Whether it's the person who buys tomatoes for Ragú, or the employee in charge of computer keyboard quality control at Texas Instruments, sometimes the "inside" information you need can be provided only by a specific person at a particular firm. If you're researching a type of *product*, a good place to start getting information is a company that makes it. I've found that salespeople for manufacturers are more than happy to educate interested people about their product, and they don't mind if your questions are elementary.

CON: It can be hard to identify the precise people you need to reach at a company, and if you do find them they may be reluctant to reveal what you want to know. (See page 257 on obtaining "sensitive" information.) When interviewing company personnel, you also have to be on guard against receiving information that's biased toward promoting their firm.

HOW TO REACH: To find the names, addresses, and phone numbers of companies, consult Dun & Bradstreet's *Million Dollar Directory*, or Standard & Poor's *Register*, found in the library. Once you have a company's address and phone number, you can try to get the information you need by calling its public affairs or public relations office; if the people there don't have the answer, they should be able to connect you with someone who does.

✔ Consultants

PRO: Some consultants are outstanding experts in their field, and can provide a great deal of inside information, advice, and in-depth knowledge.

CON: There are a number of disadvantages in using a consultant in a research project. First, it can be difficult to determine how good a particular consultant truly is (however, see chapter 9 for tips on evaluating a source's expertise). An even bigger drawback is that unlike the other types of expert described in this chapter, most consultants will want to charge a fee for sharing their knowledge. This is understandable because a consultant's livelihood is based on selling access to his or her expertise. However, few researchers are in a position to spend a great deal of money in gathering information, and in fact, as described in this chapter it is normally not necessary to do so!

HOW TO REACH: To locate a local consultant, you might just check your yellow pages. To find others located nationwide, check either a library copy of *Consultants and Consulting Organizations Directory* (Gale Research Company) or call a trade association of consultants by checking the *Encyclopedia of Associations* and asking for referrals.

✔ The "Hands-On" Expert

PRO: This is the person who actually performs an activity that you want to learn about—the fashion designer, master chef, computer programmer, and so on. Such people understand the subject in the intimate and detailed way that comes only from hands-on experience. You can really get a sense of the nitty-gritty by talking with them.

CON: These people's opinions will naturally be based on their own unique experiences. They are not like the journalist or industry observer who forms conclusions by gathering data from a wide variety of sources. You might receive a narrower, more limited view of the subject.

HOW TO REACH: Sometimes a professional association can refer you to a member who is a hands-on expert. Or just use your ingenuity. Ask yourself the question, Who would know? Let's say you wanted to talk to a top-notch auto mechanic. Try and figure out what type of organization would need to have a top-flight mechanic on its staff. You could call up United Parcel Service, ask for the fleet department, and then talk to the head mechanic. Or let's say you needed to learn about custodial techniques and products. Maybe you'd call Disneyland's director of grounds maintenance. Experts *are* everywhere.

TIP: Directories of experts
- Here are a few interesting sources. *The Directory of Experts, Authorities, and Spokespersons,* published by Broadcast Interview Source in Washington, D.C., is used by news shows to find experts on scores of subjects ranging from adult education to zoos. The reader looks up his or her subject of interest, and the directory provides the name of the association, company, school, or other organization that has volunteered to be contacted as an information source. For example, if you look up anti-Semitism, you find the Simon Wiesenthal Center and a person who can be contacted for information. The guide costs $47.50 and is available from Broadcast Interview Source, 2233 Wisconsin Avenue NW, Washington, DC 20007; 202-333-4904.

In bookstores, look for any of these three helpful books to find experts and information sources: *Lesko's New Tech Sourcebook* (Harper & Row), to find experts in high-technology fields; *Dial An Expert* (McGraw-Hill), for addresses and phone numbers of experts in many consumer-related areas; and *Consumers Index* (Pierian Press), to locate more than 250 toll-free "help lines"—public service organizations and institutions offering assistance and resources on topics ranging from childbirth options to impotence.

7

Making the Connection
Getting Access to an Expert

QUICK PREVIEW: MAKING THE CONNECTION

- Prepare for your talk with the expert beforehand. Do some reading on the subject, make a list of questions, and think how to best probe each particular source's specific area of expertise.

- Don't contact the leading expert first. Instead, talk to someone who is not too technical and is accustomed to explaining concepts to nonexperts. One such source could be a journalist.

- Decide if you will tape-record your conversation or take notes.

- Experts are not as hard to reach as you may think. All you need is a lot of persistence and a little luck.

- Telephoning rather than writing the experts is normally the best way to make contact. It's quicker, and you can ask questions and have a dialogue.

- Tips for reaching a hard-to-find expert: Get the secretary interested in your project. Talk to the expert's assistant. Call a related office. Be patient and keep plugging.

- If you call an organization's general phone number to try to identify an expert, figure out how to get the switchboard operator to help you.

- Don't be too quick to accept an "I can't help you" or "I don't know" response to your request to talk to an expert. If necessary, call and try again some other time.

How do you best prepare for your talk with the experts? What's the best way to track them down? What should you actually ask? Here's what you need to know:

GETTING READY BEFOREHAND

It's important that you don't contact the experts without first doing some preparation. One expert in library science who is frequently interviewed for information told me that if the inquirer has done some reading and checking around first, it makes her job a lot easier, and she can be much more helpful.

As mentioned earlier, you should first do some reading. Although it would be helpful to find and read anything the expert you're about to speak with has written, it's not absolutely necessary. It is important, though, to have done some kind of reading and research on the subject first; otherwise, you won't know what questions to ask and you may end up wasting your time and the experts'.

Before you contact an expert, also take a couple of minutes to think about how best to present what you're doing to this particular source to encourage help. What should be stressed? What should be downplayed?

TIP: You May be Helping the Expert
- Think about any ways you may be helping the expert. For example, if the information you gather is going to be published, or presented to a group of influential people, let the expert know it. If you quote or cite an expert, or include the person in a list of sources of further information, it may be an aid to his or her reputation or business. This point is especially important to get across when you interview a vendor or consultant of some kind. These people normally charge for their expertise, but will usually give you their information for free in hopes of getting customers through your information report. (This technique works equally well when you need assistance from an organization. Think of ways you will be letting others know of that firm's services.)

  So be sure to figure out in advance exactly how your work can help publicize a person. And offer to send a final copy of anything you put together so that the expert can add it to his or her professional credential file.

It's important that you spend a few minutes thinking about the best kinds of questions you could ask. These questions should reflect:

- Matters that are confusing and unclear to you after you've read information on the subject

- Areas in which you need more detailed information

- Problems or subjects unique to your needs that have not been addressed in any materials you've looked at

Also, be sure to use this opportunity to probe for a deeper analysis of your subject and to search for the significance of the information you've acquired so far. For example, if your research on the airline industry turns up the fact that "currently, corporations do not negotiate with airlines for volume discounts," you'll want to find out *the reason why not* from the experts. If in your study of the problems of the elderly, you discover that Medicare payments are planned to be reduced, you'll want to dig out *the implications of that policy* once it's instituted.

When you make up your questions, you should also consider what kinds of queries best probe a particular source's specific area of expertise. Let's say you had to find out everything you could about the subject of tents. If you are interviewing a product design expert at a leading manufacturer, a question about the characteristics of various tent materials would be very appropriate to that source's expertise. If the next expert you interviewed was a top-notch camper, then a question about efficient strategies for quickly setting up a tent would be very productive. Of course, if you value a particular source's overall knowledge, there is nothing wrong with asking questions outside his or her exact expertise. But it is important to think carefully beforehand about what a particular source's real specialties are, and then try to zero in on them.

I've found that it's helpful to actually write up a list of all your questions and have them in front of you when speaking to an expert. (If you plan to contact an expert by mail, you can write up and send the questions; see page 231 for more on phone vs. mail contacts.) The purpose of writing up your questions is to allow you to do all your planning and thinking ahead of time. This way, during the conversation, you'll have time to concentrate on what the expert is saying. You won't have to worry about what to ask next, or whether you've asked all your questions, because they will be written out on a sheet of paper in front of you. Each time you ask a question, just cross it off your list.

Once you've written up the questionnaire, you're ready for the talk.

TIP: Sound Natural
- Try to avoid making your discussion sound like you're reading a list of questions—it's better to sound natural.

SELECTING THE FIRST EXPERT TO SPEAK WITH

How do you decide which expert to talk to first? I've found that it's usually not a good idea to contact the leading expert in the field first. It's normally better to wait until after you've spoken with some other people. This way, by the time you speak with the premier expert, you'll know enough about the subject to ask the most incisive and probing questions, rather than basic questions you can get answered by other sources.

A good type of first source to contact is often a nontechnical person, for example, someone who has written a clear and concise article that provides an overview of the field or someone in an association's educational division. As you learn more and become more confident, you can speak with the more technical experts in the field.

NOTE TAKING VS. TAPE-RECORDING

Finally, the last decision to make before you actually talk to the expert is whether to take notes or tape the conversation. This decision really comes down to a personal preference. I prefer note taking; to me, it seems like a bother to set up a tape recorder and then play back the tape to hunt through the whole conversation to find significant statements. I find it easier and more efficient to quickly jot down the important points as the expert makes them. The information is then right in front of me on a piece of paper, ready to be used whenever I need it. But if you prefer taping, you can buy devices at electronics stores that attach to the phone receiver and tape the conversation. You should inform the person that you are making a tape. (That's another reason I'm not crazy about taping. Many people get nervous and withhold information.)

TIP: Tapes Plus Notes
- If you do decide to tape, you can make it easy to find specific statements by using a tape recorder with a numerical indexing counter. Whenever the expert makes an important remark, just jot down the number displayed. Later you can locate those statements simply by fast forwarding the recorder to the numbers you noted.

A couple of strategies on note taking: Try not to make your notes too cryptic. Write them as if you were penning them for another person. Otherwise you may later find yourself desperately trying to decipher your own handwriting. Also, it really does help to read over your notes immediately after the interview is over; they will make a lot more sense to you than if you read them a day or two later. Another benefit of reading notes immediately is that sometimes during an information interview you'll be writing so fast that you won't be able to write full sentences. Immediately after the conversation the details are still fresh in your mind, and you'll be able to fill in the gaps.

MAKING CONTACT

Most people think that it's very hard to reach experts. Not true. It may take a little persistence, or a bit of digging, but that's about it. As mentioned previously, most experts are not celebrities, and they can be reached easily. It's also true that people who are fairly prominent can often be reached without extraordinary effort. The trick is simply to try. Let's look at a couple of examples.

I recently needed to find information on wasteful purchasing practices going on within the U.S. Department of Defense (remember the $600 ashtray and the $400 hammer?). One day there was an article on this topic on the front page of the *New York Times*. The writer was identified with a byline at the beginning of the article, and I decided to give him a call. The *New York Times* switchboard operator asked me who I wished to speak with, and I gave her the writer's name. She rang his direct line, he picked up his phone, and our conversation began.

So what? The point is that, although this writer was of no particular fame or prominence, many of us would incorrectly assume that it's a big hassle or even impossible to talk to someone writing front-page stories for the *Times*. But it's usually simple to do so. It's easy to forget that most of these "experts" —like the rest of us—sit in an office, with a phone on their desk. When it rings, they answer it. This isn't to say that you'll get right through to a national figure—but even then, you still never know. I recently heard the story of a resident of New York who had some kind of complaint against his state government. So he decided one evening to call Governor Cuomo in Albany and air his grievance. Cuomo was working late that day, heard his phone ringing, picked it up, and spoke with the resident. Nobody likes to hear a ringing phone . . . especially one's own!

But most experts are not famous, and you won't even need extra luck to get hold of them. What you will need, however, is a little patience. Don't get too upset if you keep missing someone, or if you get transferred on the phone a few times. This is part of the process. If you can accept that, you'll be better off.

Finally, try not to be too intimidated about calling an expert. If you think about it, you really have nothing to lose.

The following are a number of strategies that will help you make contact with the experts you need.

Finding Phone Numbers and Addresses

What do you do if you read an article that cites an expert but does not tell you where he or she works or can be contacted? If you run into this problem, you'll want to contact the magazine or journal and have a little patience. For example, I recently was researching the subject of "finding free software" and found a very interesting article in *Inc.* magazine that quoted an expert on the topic. Unfortunately, the article did not say where this person worked or where he could be reached. And to top it off, there was no writer's byline accompanying the article.

I decided to call up *Inc.* magazine to try and track down the expert. I found *Inc.*'s phone number by checking the masthead and then called the magazine and asked to be connected with the editorial department. A woman answered the phone, and I gave her the issue's date, the page number of the story, and the headline. She then checked her files, found the writer of the piece, and gave me that reporter's direct phone number. I called the writer and told her what I was trying to find. She was able to look up the story in her files and inform me that the expert was a professor at the University of Texas. She gave me his phone number.

The lesson is: if you have trouble figuring out where to find an expert, don't be afraid to contact the source that cited that person to get the necessary information to track him or her down.

Phone Calls vs. Letters

Is it better to write or telephone experts? My own recommendation is to use the telephone whenever possible. It's faster, and, more important, you can have a dialogue. You can ask questions, respond to what the expert says, pick up nuances, and do so much more than can be done by mail.

Phone calls are also more demanding of experts than letters, which actually works in your favor. One frequently consulted expert in microcomputer technology who lives in Southern California told me that it's always much more difficult to say no to a person on the phone than to a letter, which may sit for some time before being answered.

TIP: When to Write
- There may be certain cases in which a letter is more appropriate. If you want to reach a superstar celebrity, for example, you're not as likely to get that person on the phone. If you do write, keep your letter simple and short, and don't ask for a lot. Make it as easy as possible for the person to respond. Enclose a stamped, self-addressed envelope. Another tip is when writing to an organization or business for information, write to the top or one of the top people. Your letter will then be funneled to the appropriate office "lower down," and will receive more attention since it came down from a higher office.

> **TIPS: Cutting Phone Costs**
> If you are concerned about running up big phone bills by telephon-
> ing experts, here are a few tips to keep costs down:
>
> - Some companies and organizations have a toll-free 800 number
> but do not publicize it well. Call 800-555-1212 to find out if there
> is a listing for the organization you want to contact.
> - If you need to call an out-of-state organization, and it is large, it
> may have a closer branch office. Check the listings for the larger
> cities closer to you.
> - You can save money by having an expert call you. Call around
> lunchtime and leave your phone number with a secretary for a
> return call. You may think it's presumptuous to leave your number
> with someone who does not know you, but the fact is, we all get
> calls at work from people we don't know, and we normally do our
> best to return them. The key is to encourage a return call. This means
> identifying yourself clearly and, if possible, leaving a message as
> to why you're calling. If you were referred by a mutual acquain-
> tance, be sure to name that person in the message. At all costs,
> avoid conveying the impression that you want to sell the person
> something.

Is there a best time of day to call? One *Fortune* 500 executive
told me that he responds better to unsolicited inquiry calls early
in the morning. He says that early in the day he's fresher, and
that no unanticipated meetings or little crises have had time to
come up and push his schedule back. Although this executive's
preference is clearly a personal one, I would agree that many
people respond best to early morning calls. As for the best day
of the week to call, the standard advice is never to call first thing
Monday morning, or on Friday afternoon. (In the summertime,
you may want to avoid calling anytime on Friday—especially
in the warmer parts of the country.)

Okay, now for a popular question—how do you "get past"
the secretary? First of all, unless you're calling a very high level
official—say, a company's chief executive or someone very near
the top—the secretary is really not so much of a barrier. In fact,
a survey done by a temporary personnel service revealed that
68 percent of top executives' incoming calls are *not* screened by
a secretary or assistant.

Persistence will eventually get you the person you want. But if you do run into secretarial problems, here is some advice:

▪ If you're returning the boss's call, be sure to say so. That should get you through automatically. Similarly, it can help if you were referred by an office or person "higher up."

▪ It can help if your call sounds pressing or dramatic. For example, if you're in New York, and the secretary is in California, be sure you say that you're calling long-distance.

▪ Politely explain to the secretary why it could be in the boss's best interest to take the call. For example, "his views on the subject may not be correctly represented," "his competitors are all included and his firm will not be represented," and so on.

▪ Try to place your call when the secretary is out of the office and the boss must pick up his or her own phone. Usually the best time is right before or right after regular working hours, when the secretary has not arrived or has just left. Lunch hours are another possibility but may not be quite as fruitful.

▪ Another, and probably better, approach is to think of the secretary as an ally and not an enemy. Try to get the secretary interested and enthused about what you're doing. Explain why you're trying to reach the boss, what you hope to get out of the conversation, and why the project is so important to you. If the secretary gets interested in what you are doing, you should find access to the boss easier. (You may also get additional background information that will help you with your upcoming conversation.)

Although one school of thought is that it's best to be gruff with secretaries, it seems much nicer to be extra pleasant instead. One researcher I know told me that when she speaks to secretaries she always refers to them as "assistants."

If you really get stuck and can't seem to get to the boss at all, the next best thing to do is to ask to speak to his or her staff associate or assistant. Often you can get much of the same information from this person. In fact, occasionally you'll find that assistants actually know more details, and if there are questions they can't answer, you'll probably be turned over to the boss.

Here are some points to remember if you're having trouble getting your expert on the phone:

▪ If the person is out of the office when you call, it is generally preferable to try phoning again rather than leaving a message —this is to avoid being called when you are unprepared. But it is certainly not unacceptable to leave your phone number for a return call. As mentioned earlier, it's fine to do this, as long as you leave an encouraging message. If the person does not get back to you, just try again.

▪ Try calling a related office. Often, someone who works nearby will know the person you're trying to reach and will be able to pass along your message.

▪ Double-check the original source where you obtained the expert's location and phone number to make sure there was no mistake.

▪ Be patient. Keep plugging. You'll find that you'll almost always get to the person you need *if* you're persistent enough.

Sometimes you know *where* you're likely to find an expert (e.g., a particular company or association) but you don't have anyone's name. Here are some strategies for finding an expert in these cases:

▪ If you know the name of the department in a company that can help you, ask to be connected with the "director" of that office. If you don't have a department in mind, ask to be connected with "public affairs" or "public relations." Although a spokesperson there will probably give you fewer details than someone who works in another department, you may still get some helpful information. Calling the public affairs or public relations department is also helpful when your inquiry relates to something that affects the company as a whole; for example, if you wanted to find out about a company's new product line or the closing of a branch office.

▪ When calling an organization's general phone number, be careful how you phrase your information request to the switchboard operator. This person is usually very busy and will not have the time to help you figure out who you want to speak with.

Let's say you need to find out about new technologies in light bulbs. An excellent information source would be a major light bulb manufacturer like General Electric. If you called up GE's main number and asked the switchboard operator, "Who can I speak with that can help me find out about new technologies in light bulbs?" you risk getting a discouraging "Sorry, I don't know" or, if you're lucky, "I can connect you with someone who can take your name and address and mail you some of our sales brochures." That's not exactly what you wanted. So, instead, try to help the switchboard operator by providing some guidance as to where to send you. For example, you might say, "I have a technical question on your incandescent light bulb products. Which department can help me?" Now the operator can feel more comfortable switching your call to a technical or engineering department. Or describe by function the "type" of person you want to reach, for example, "the person in charge of selecting new store sites" or "the manager of your computer systems." You can even try to guess the department you need— (for example, by asking for "new product development")—and you may discover that the firm actually has a department like the one you guessed! Or the operator may find a similar-sounding department (for example, "planning and development") and ask if he or she should connect you there. If it seems close, you should agree. Once connected, ask to speak with a manager or director of that division and pose your question. If that individual can't help you, he or she may be able to refer you to the appropriate division.

If you're calling a professional association, nonprofit organization, or public institution, there are certain departments common to many of these bodies that are especially fruitful information sources. For example:

The in-house library. The reference librarian is an excellent source of information and can search published resources for you.

The education department. This department is typically found in associations. Its role is to inform members and the public of the resources of the organization.

The publications department. Here you can usually get an index of what the organization publishes, and sometimes what's about to be published.

There is one final important point to keep in mind when you're trying to make contact with an expert. When you talk to the switchboard operator, an administrator, or whoever else picks up the phone, don't be so quick to take "We can't help you" or "I don't know" as an answer to your request for an expert. Often the problem is just that you've been unlucky enough to catch someone in a bad mood or someone who is not too knowledgeable about the organization's resources. Try politely rephrasing your question—a couple of times if necessary—to get some help or ask, "Is there another person in the organization I can speak with who might know?" If this does not work, then consider calling another time, when someone else may answer.

The person you speak with initially may want to turn you over to a publications department. This may not be so bad, because you may find that there indeed are some relevant publications available that will help you. But do not feel obligated to end your search at this point. You should still ask to see if there is an expert available.

8

Talking with Experts
Strategies for Getting Inside Information

QUICK PREVIEW:
TALKING WITH EXPERTS

- Never assume an expert won't talk. Most of the time the person will be happy to help you.

- Present yourself properly to the expert by identifying who you are and by asking if it's a good time to talk. Be serious, get to the point, admit any ignorance on the subject, and ask *specific* questions. Let the expert steer the conversation; put off tough questions until later.

- Think of ways you can heighten an expert's interest in what you are doing. For example, can you publicize his or her work to others or share any information that you come up with?

- During the conversation, question things that don't make sense to you, ask for definitions of technical terms, and see if the expert can help you define what it is that you really need to find out.

- Once the conversation is moving, get control and steer it to where you want it to go.

- At the end of the conversation, ask if there is anything important that hasn't been discussed, request written information, and ask for the names of other experts.

- As you learn more about the subject, update your questions. Periodically review your overall goals and strategies.

(continued)

237

- Always keep the "big picture"—your ultimate objective in the information-finding project—in mind as you proceed.

- If you encounter an expert who's suspicious of you, try gaining his or her confidence by revealing more about yourself and by offering to show a copy of anything you write up.

- If you encounter a hostile source, try to build up trust. Consider sending a written inquiry, share your findings, be as nice as possible, and let the person know how he or she is acting.

- Use the strategies outlined in this chapter to handle those experts who say, "I don't have time" and "I don't know," and who "tell no evil."

- You can try to obtain "sensitive" information by rephrasing questions, asking peripheral questions, asking for "feelings," taking a position on an issue, and keeping the conversation "off the record."

- You may confront ethical dilemmas when attempting to obtain "inside information" from knowledgeable sources. Often these dilemmas involve the issue of misrepresenting your affiliation and/or the purpose of your project. If faced with such ethical concerns, you should first make sure you've exhausted all public sources, identified easily interviewable experts, and confirmed the importance of the data you are seeking. Don't assume you need a ruse to get information—the truth usually works fine—misrepresenting yourself is not advisable.

After you've managed to make contact with the expert, the next trick is to get that person to talk to you, and share his or her knowledge. Although most people assume that experts are too busy and uninterested to spend time helping strangers find information, *usually the opposite is true.*

Whether the topic is fine china, poodle breeding, or Norwegian economics, experts have a great interest in their topic, and they enjoy discussing it. Remember, these people have devoted a great portion of their lives to learning and exploring their field. When someone approaches them needing information, they're almost always pleased to oblige.

Adding to their inclination to talk is the fact that, no matter how mundane a subject may seem, there is always some kind of controversy that excites the experts. For example, I recently discovered in the course of researching the sexy topic of water meters that an intense battle was being fought between those favoring plastic meters and those who liked bronze ones! The important point to remember is: never assume someone won't talk to you. Always try.

Although people *are* naturally inclined to help, you still need to have some strategies for approaching them to smooth the procedure and encourage their cooperation.

PRESENTING YOURSELF
TO THE EXPERT

Okay, the secretary has just told you that the boss will be on the line shortly. The expert picks up the phone and says hello. Now what?

No, don't hang up. Here's what to do to get the conversation off to a smooth start:

Identify Yourself. You've got to identify yourself—clearly and precisely—and explain why you are calling. This is very important to do to allay the natural suspicion we all have when a stranger contacts us. Don't start off your conversation by saying, "Hello. Can I ask you some questions about oil futures trading?" Infinitely better is, "My name is Karen Johnson, and I'm calling from (hometown or firm and city). I'm currently collecting information on the benefits of oil futures market trading (for a possible book or for a report for my firm or to learn about career opportunities) and I read your recent article titled 'Why Trade Oil Futures?' I wonder if I could have just a couple of minutes to ask you a few questions?"

It's also helpful to explain your goals and which sources you've already checked. The more information the expert has on why you're calling, the easier his or her job will be, and the more you'll get out of the conversation.

Ask the Expert if it's a Good Time to Talk You don't want to interview someone who's in a rush to get it over with. If it's a bad time, set up an appointment for a formal phone interview at a specific time a day or two in the future. This gives importance to your phone interview and legitimizes it. In fact, it may not be such a bad idea to make an initial call solely to set up an appointment for a future formal phone interview.

TIP: Be Sensitive
- When presenting yourself, don't make the mistake I once did of conveying the impression that you're attempting to become quickly knowledgeable in the expert's field. I had about eight weeks to write a comprehensive report on the topic of micrographics. I explained this to one of my first expert sources. He refused to help and told me that such a project couldn't be done. He was wrong, but I learned my lesson. It's kind of insulting to say to somebody who's been in a field for twenty, maybe thirty, or more years that you are going to become an "instant expert" in a matter of weeks. Instead, it's much wiser to say that you're *collecting* information and advice from experts in the field, or reporting on what the experts are saying, or anything along those lines. In essence, that is really what you are doing anyway.

Be Serious. You need to convey the impression that your project is important to you, not a lark or trifling matter.

Get to the Point. People want to know why you're calling. I find it's more relaxing and enjoyable to save friendly conversation about the weather and so forth until after the interview is completed.'

Admit Your Ignorance. If you are unsure about your subject and do not feel confident, it is *much better to simply admit that to the expert up front.* It's fine to say something like "I am just starting to learn about this subject, so please excuse me if my questions sound elementary." The worst mistake you could make is to fumble around trying to sound knowledgeable with a lot of "uh's," "well I guess so's," and so on. These only serve to arouse suspicions—the expert may think you are trying to hide something! If you are asked a question to which you don't know the answer, simply say, "I don't know," rather than trying to make believe you do know! Don't feel embarrassed or guilty that you do not know more—the whole idea of finding information is to learn! Also, once the expert knows that you are a novice, they are more likely to avoid using jargon and buzzwords and will attempt to explain concepts to you more clearly.

Be Specific. This is quite important, especially at the beginning of the conversation. Here's an example of what I mean. Suppose the topic you need to find out about is the "future of baseball in this country." If you began your conversation by posing such an overwhelmingly broad question, you'd be starting off on the wrong foot. It's too difficult and vague a question to answer and your source will feel on the spot. Instead, start off with a more specific question that can be answered easily, such as "Do you think that the drug problem in baseball has lessened during the last few years?" or "Are the followers of the baseball scene predicting that a new commissioner will have an impact on the players' rising salaries?" Even if these questions are not vital to you, they will get the ball rolling, which *is* vital to the conversation. Later, especially toward the end of the conversation, when a rapport has been established, you can throw in the "future of baseball" question. By then, the expert is warmed up and the answers given to your earlier questions make him or her more responsive.

Follow the Expert's Lead. At the beginning, let the source take the lead in directing the conversation. If the person feels comfortable talking about something that's not exactly on the right track for you, show interest anyway. Later on in the discussion you can redirect the conversation to cover the precise areas you are interested in.

Delay Tough Questions. Don't begin the conversation with questions that may stump your source. If you think you've asked such a stumper, don't press for an answer. Drop it, and go to another question. Later on in the conversation you can try bringing it back up. Similarly, if you think any of your questions could be considered offensive, save these for the end too.

TIP: Be Nice!
- Another important point is attitude. The importance of politeness should be obvious, but it's a point worth stressing. Your attitude really will make a difference: Don't ever be demanding or impatient. Try to sound confident, cheerful, and professional—present yourself as though you were interviewing for a job.

GETTING THE EXPERT INTERESTED

Everyone wants to feel important. You can help the discussion along by making the source feel good. Show some sincere appreciation, give some praise, and tell the expert how helpful the information and advice are.

TIP: Don't "Survey"
- People normally don't like to be "surveyed," but they like to give "opinions" or their "thoughts" on a matter. It's more personal.

A good way to get experts to open up is to heighten their interest in what you are doing. Here are a few strategies:

- As mentioned earlier, be sure you figure out in advance any way the expert will be helped by talking to you.
- If you work for or are on assignment for a well-known publication or company, it may help to mention it. Often people feel excited about being consulted by a prestigious organization. This doesn't mean that experts always prefer talking to someone calling from a well-known organization. Some people are actually *less* disposed, either because they prefer to do a "public service" and help out an amateur information seeker or because they do not want their remarks to be widely circulated. It's a personal preference that will vary among your sources.
- A good way to heighten the expert's enthusiasm is to let the person know of any interesting bits of information you've come up with so far in your research. Often the information you've discovered could be used by the expert for his or her own pur-

poses. Similarly, you should offer to share your final findings with the expert. Remember, you're doing a lot of in-depth digging in the expert's field; what you ultimately come up with should be of interest to that person. (Note: Again, this can be a sensitive area. Don't make it sound as though your research will be groundbreaking. Just humbly offer to send whatever information you come up with.)

▪ Finally, try to get a feel for whether your expert would be excited about being quoted or would prefer to remain anonymous.

▪ Try to interest the expert enough so that he or she really *wants* to help you. For example, if you wanted to interview an interior design consultant about some art-oriented question, you could get the person interested in talking to you by letting him or her know that talking to you will enable the viewpoint of a representative of the profession to be "heard" in your project. A different approach is to appeal a bit to ego. When you let a source know that your work is identifying the very leading experts in the field, it is very flattering—and the source will naturally want to be included in such a listing. It's also complimentary to ask for someone's ideas on a subject, especially if you mention that you'll be passing along those thoughts to others as expert opinion.

TIP: Be Persistent
▪ If your first couple of interviews don't go as smoothly as you hoped, don't despair. It's really a numbers game, and the process is such that some interviews will be great, some good, and some not so good.

GETTING THE MOST
OUT OF THE INTERVIEW

Here are some specific pointers to keep in mind during the actual conversation:

Question Things! If an expert says something that doesn't sound right, or contradicts something else you've been told, ask for more information. (For example, if an expert tells you matter-of-factly that so-and-so's theory on the link between attitude and illness is preposterous, ask the expert *why* he or she does not believe it. What are the *reasons?*) Questioning statements with a "why," instead of accepting them at face value, is one of the very best ways to deepen your understanding of any subject. Don't let questions "hang" unanswered. Politely press for reasons and explanations.

Probe for Specifics. Try not to accept general, unproven statements. If an expert on computers tells you that IBM makes the best computer on the market, ask him or her to tell you *why*. If you're then told that it's superior because the firm provides better service, ask *how* it provides better service. If the expert tells you that IBM's service is better because its response time to problems is quicker than that of its competitors, find out *how much* quicker. Again, if an expert tells you that it would be extremely unlikely for someone to get sick from eating too much of a certain vitamin, ask whether, in fact, it has *ever* happened; if so, what was the situation or condition that made it occur.

Ask for Definitions of Technical Terms. If the expert throws in any terms or buzzwords you don't understand, ask for a definition. Asking for explanations is nothing to be embarrassed about. It may be important for you to know the definitions of certain words, as they may be standard terminology in the field. Tell the expert that you want to define the term precisely—but in layman's language.

Ask for Help. Early on in your project, you'll be trying to figure out exactly what you need to know to understand your field. You can enlist the experts' assistance in better defining exactly what you need to find out. If you have a good rapport with an expert, you can ask that person to help you isolate the critical issues on which you need to become knowledgeable.

Let's say you're digging up information on dream research. Initially you probably do not know what the important issues are in that field and may not even be sure what questions to ask. But an expert will know the issues. He or she may say something like, "Well, if you want to find out about the latest in dream research, you should ask experts about some recent findings in 'lucid dreaming' and discoveries about the Senoi Indian dream techniques." What you're doing here is asking the expert to tell you which issues are important in the field, and what *questions* you should be asking other experts. In a sense, you are trying to find out the answer to the question, What should I be finding out? And there's nobody better qualified to tell you than the experts themselves.

(Because this type of question is somewhat offbeat, you should not begin your conversation with it, but work it in toward the middle or end.)

Keep in Control. You've got to keep the interview on track. Occasionally a source may think that you are interested in a subject that is actually of no concern to you. He or she will try to be helpful, but may go off on a tangent and talk a blue streak about something of no interest to you. Listen politely, but soon you'll have to rein the expert in and ask a question you *are* interested in. It's up to you to keep the conversation on course. You have a limited amount of time for each discussion, and it's important to make the most of it. Otherwise you'll be wasting your time and the expert's time. (Note: As discussed earlier, at the *very beginning* of a conversation you may want to allow the expert to talk about almost anything just to get the ball rolling. But soon you've got to move in and get the conversation on track.)

Wrap it Up. *At the very end of an information interview* there are three questions you should ask:

▪ "Is there anything important we haven't discussed?" It's possible that your source has some additional important information to discuss but hasn't mentioned it because you didn't ask. This provides the expert with the opportunity to talk about it.

▪ "Do you have any written information you can send me?" Often the expert has written articles on the subject or keeps clippings of relevant materials.

246

- "Who else do you recommend that I speak with?" This is an extremely important question that you should be sure to ask all your sources. There are many reasons why this is such an important question. One is that it is a quick way to get the name and phone number of another expert. Even more important, however, is the fact that you now have a referral person you can cite when you contact the new expert. Be sure to let that person know that you were referred by the mutual acquaintance. If you leave a message for the expert, it's worth mentioning the contact's name in the message to encourage a call back. There's almost no better way to reach someone than through a direct referral like this.

Another reason that it's so important to ask to be referred to other experts is that often the more people you are referred to, the more likely it is that you'll be speaking with someone who has the specific expertise you seek. Say that you have to find out all about new technologies in camera light meters. And say that you've decided to call a camera manufacturers association to try to find the information. Well, maybe the association's technical staffperson Tom will tell you that he keeps up only with general industry developments. But when you ask him for a contact, he refers you to his friend Pat at Nikon, who is involved more in day-to-day technological advances. You thank Tom and give Pat a call. Well, it turns out that Pat does have some good technological know-how, and you get some information from her, but she's not a real specialist in light metering components. She refers you to Bill, who heads that division, and he, in turn, refers you to the expert, Joe, on his staff.

So the process is such that when you get referrals, you often zero in on someone whose expertise is more appropriate to your inquiry. (The process can be frustrating too: it often results in your best sources coming at the very *end* of your information search, when you are trying to wrap it all up!)

TIP: Confirm Your Facts
- The end of a conversation is a good time to clear up any confusing points the expert may have made during the discussion. You can use this time to confirm important facts, state your understanding of the issues, and get them verified.

STAYING ON COURSE AND REDIRECTING FOCUS

Throughout your interviews, it's important to keep on the course you've charted. To do so means asking the right questions and directing your energies to get you where you want to go.

The questions you pose to the experts will need to be constantly revised and updated as your interviews progress. Some of your simpler questions will be answered the same way by everyone, and it won't be necessary to keep asking them. At the same time, you'll also find that you'll have to add *new* questions as you go along and experts bring up issues that you weren't aware of. You'll notice as you speak with the experts that the important issues will emerge automatically as their conversation gravitates to critical matters. You'll then be able to incorporate these issues into your questionnaire. You'll want to create questions about these new issues and ask them of future sources. So your questionnaire will be a flexible one, and it will be modified throughout your information search to reflect the major issues as you see them emerge.

If you come to a point where you start to predict the answers from the experts, it's a sign that it's time to step back a little from the information-gathering project and assess where it's going. Think about whether it's necessary to alter the direction you're heading in and, if so, in what way. Think about whether your goals have changed since you began the project and, if so, how. Are there gaps in your information that need to be filled? Are there new angles to explore? Think about any new types of sources that you haven't tried yet that should be approached. Take stock of where you are and how things are going.

For example, let's say you're digging up information on careers in journalism. After interviewing a dozen or so experts, the time is ripe to assess where you stand in the project. As you step back, maybe you realize that, although you've interviewed people in the newspaper and magazine industry, you haven't spoken with anyone in television journalism; your efforts can now be directed toward reaching those sources. Maybe you'll discover that your overall goals have changed too. When you started the project, you were interested in finding information about all types of journalism careers. Now, after a dozen interviews, you realize that you want to pursue information specifically about the career of newswriting. So you redirect your questions and choose sources to reflect that new goal.

TIP: Read Your Old Notes
- Reading over the notes you've taken during interviews up until this point will stimulate you to think of new questions and fresh angles you haven't pursued yet.

Keep the "Big Picture" in Mind. At all times during your project, keep your ultimate goal in mind as a guiding force. Try not to get sidetracked into pursuing routes that have nothing to do with why you are conducting your information search. If, for example, your goal is to find information that compares the quality of the various long-distance carriers, and you're talking to a telecommunications expert, try to avoid being led into a long discussion on, say, the legal precedent behind the breakup of AT&T. Although that topic is related to long-distance service, it really is not pertinent to your specific goals. It's fine to change your goals as you go along, but just be sure that all your activities serve that goal.

CRACKING THE TOUGH NUTS

Now, what do you do if you have a source who's really a tough nut to crack and it's important for you that this person share his or her information?

The great majority of experts *will* talk to you and give you the answers you need. But it's possible to run into someone who is not so helpful. There are a number of reasons why someone would be unhelpful. Maybe you've called at a bad time. Maybe the person is simply someone who is not the helpful type. Or maybe you've encountered someone who is protective of his or her knowledge and doesn't want to share it.

Whatever the reason, if you encounter someone like this, sometimes the easiest thing to do is to abandon the interview and move on to the next one. As mentioned earlier, not *all* of your conversations with experts are going to be perfect, so it's no big deal to drop a difficult one. But what if this one is important to you? In that case, you shouldn't give up. There are a number of strategies you can use to turn a difficult interview into a productive one.

In this section we'll examine the ways to get through the rockiest interviews. This includes strategies for dealing with reluctant sources and strategies for dealing with difficult questions and topics.

Building Up Trust

A source who is unwilling to talk to you is often suspicious. Even if you've identified yourself clearly and explained why you are seeking information, the person may still be suspicious of who you *really* are and what you're going to do with the information. From the expert's perspective, you are just an anonymous voice on the phone; you could be a competitor or someone up to no good.

One strategy you can take to help allay suspicions is to simply stay on the phone longer and keep talking. Reveal more about yourself and why you're gathering information. Slowly, the expert will get a better feeling for who you are, and you'll become less anonymous and less threatening. As you reveal more about yourself and what you're doing, the unhelpful expert often loosens up somewhat and starts to talk.

Another way you can calm the fears of a suspicious source is by offering to send a copy of anything you write before it's published or presented to anyone. A big concern for some people is being misquoted or misunderstood. Some experts feel better if they know that they can correct errors or have some control over their remarks. In fact, their review can benefit you too, because it should serve as a check on the accuracy of your information.

TIP: Handling a Hostile Source
- How do you handle a hostile source? It's very rare to encounter someone who is outright belligerent, but it can happen.

Chances are, the person is hostile because he or she is a little nervous and suspicious of you. One thing you can do to help allay suspicions is to explain as specifically as possible *who* will be receiving the information that you are gathering.

Another strategy is to offer to send a written inquiry on your letterhead or your company's letterhead. There are a couple of reasons why a letter is more reassuring to a hostile source. For one thing, an expert who sees a specific letterhead feels more certain that you are who you say you are—letters are more "solid" than phone calls. In addition, letters provide the person with time to think. One reason a source may act hostile is fear of saying something later regretted. Now a response can be made more carefully.

It's possible that your source is hostile because you're being viewed as a competitor of some kind. There are a couple of ways you can try to overcome this problem. One strategy, if your work really does compete in some way with the expert's, is to be sure to offer to share your findings. Another strategy is to downplay the competition by emphasizing those aspects of your project that differ from the expert's.

What if all these strategies fail and your source is still hostile? Be *extranice.* I've found that if you are unrelentingly nice—even if it kills you!—most of the time you will disarm the hostility. It may not be easy to do, but if a hostile source's information is very important to you, just grit your teeth and smile.

If this fails too, you have little choice but to politely let the source know how he or she is acting. You might say something like, "It sounds like this is a bad time for you. Would it be better if I call back?" Or you can be blunt. One time I was interviewing a vice president of a major tobacco company in hopes of finding out more about its innovative use of copiers. For some unknown reason, the vice president was very belligerent toward me. Finally, I just asked, "Why are you so hostile?" That question confronted the issue in a nonaggressive way and let the man realize how he was being perceived. He then became much more helpful.

Remember, hostile sources are *rare.* The great majority of people are very helpful.

Specific Problem Areas

Here are ways to handle some common tough interview spots:

The "I Don't Have Time to Talk" Expert. What do you do if your source says he or she doesn't have time to speak with you? One strategy is to ask to be given just a minute or two. This will reassure the source that the whole morning won't be used up on the phone with you. But an interesting thing you'll find is that once that expert starts talking, most of the time he or she will continue to talk for twenty, thirty, forty minutes, or more!

Another way to reassure experts is to tell them to tell *you* when they want the discussion to end. If you give them the control of stopping the conversation, they're likely to be reassured.

A different tactic is to set up a future day and time for a formal phone interview. This enables the source to budget some time to allow for a few minutes with you.

The "I Don't Know" Expert. How do you handle a source who is answering a lot of your questions with "I don't know" and you think the person really does know. Sometimes the "I don't know" syndrome occurs when an expert does not want to mislead you with an answer that's not precise. But often all you're really looking for is a general idea. If this is the case, try asking for a "rough estimate" or a "ballpark figure." This will take the pressure off your source to be exact, and it may yield the general information that you're looking for.

The Expert Who Will Tell No Evil. Sometimes in your information interviews, you'll need to find out the negative or bad side of an issue. For example, you are interviewing a trustee of a college, and you want to find out what the school's problems are. Or let's say you're interviewing a representative of the American Advertising Executives Association, and you want to find out the negative aspects of a career in advertising. In both of these cases, the sources will probably feel uncomfortable giving you this negative information. In general, people prefer

252

telling you the good, rather than the bad. It's safer, especially when one is representing a particular institution, product, or cause.

Here's a way to make it easier for the expert to reveal the negative. Ask for "the best points and the worst points," or the "strengths and weaknesses" of the matter in question. By asking experts to talk about—and indeed emphasize if they wish—the good, you allow them to dilute the bad, making it easier to divulge.

The "Too Smart" Expert. Occasionally, the very leading expert in a field may be so intimately knowledgeable of all the details of a subject and so aware of all the permutations that affect it that the person will sincerely have difficulty answering basic questions. For example, once I was writing a report on how companies can reduce their travel and entertainment expenses. One of the premier experts in the field answered many of my questions with, "That is too complicated a matter to respond to simply," or "There is no one answer to that question," or "It really depends on the situation." Although he was technically correct, he was unable to come down from his lofty plane and work a little to provide some kind of help. If you get an expert like this, don't give up. You should still be able to glean some good information out of the conversation and get a feel for what the "big picture" looks like.

Obtaining "Sensitive" Information

In many information searches, it becomes necessary at some point to ask an expert about some controversial or sensitive matter. Although you'll be surprised at how often people will freely discuss this type of information, you'll want to have some strategies for getting as much cooperation as possible.

Don't Begin with Sensitive Questions. You should not begin your conversation with a controversial or sensitive question. These are best situated in the middle of a conversation when the expert is warmed up a bit and feeling more relaxed. It's also best not to end with a very sensitive question, unless you feel it is so sensitive that it may cause the expert to terminate his or her conversation with you.

Rephrase Questions. If you've asked a controversial question that the expert is unwilling to answer, try posing it in a different form. Let's say you received a "no comment" to your question, "Will Bill Jones be next in line to be president of the National Restaurant Association?" You could then try asking something like, "Is Bill Jones a leading contender for the presidency?" or "Will Bill Jones be playing an important role in the association during the next few years?"

Go from the General to the Specific. This is one approach for getting answers to sensitive questions. For example, once I needed to find out how much money, if any, a particular company saved by implementing a "telecommuting" program— that is a system where employees can work at home via the use of a computer and a phone line hookup. Instead of asking the company how much money the program had saved, I asked a series of questions: Overall, was the program a plus for the company? Did it save the firm some money? Was it a significant amount? Roughly, about how much did it save?

Ask "Peripheral" Questions. This is a strategy to get bits and pieces of information that may shed light on your query. Again, in the Bill Jones example, you could ask questions about the vice presidency, previous association voting patterns, and so forth to try to piece together a picture.

Ask for Ballpark Figures. When you need to find out some sensitive numerical fact, you may find that it's easier for experts to provide rough estimates or a "range" rather than precise numbers. Another strategy for getting sensitive figures is to suggest a few numbers yourself to get a reaction. Often an expert won't volunteer the information, but will respond to your estimates.

Ask for "Feelings." You may find it easier to get an answer if you try to elicit an emotional response. Ask the person how he or she *personally feels* about a controversial topic.

Take a Position. This is an old news reporter's trick. Suppose you're trying to find out from an oil company executive whether there's any truth to the rumor that the firm is lowering its imports by 2 percent next year. If you bluntly ask the question, you're likely to get a "no comment." Instead, try taking a position on the question—state it as a fact—and continue the conversation. You might say, "Since your company will be reducing imports by 2 percent next year, will there be a corresponding increase in domestic production?" Your source may have to bite his tongue to let your assumption go unanswered—especially because he may fear that you will later think you got the information from him! You may not get a definite answer on the subject through this ploy, but you may get more than if you just asked the question bluntly.

Keep Your Conversation "Off the Record." Sometimes an expert source won't mind talking about controversial topics, but doesn't want to be identified as the source or see remarks in print. If you think this is the case, be certain you assure the expert that his or her remarks will be off the record if so desired. Most of the time, it doesn't matter a bit to you if a source speaks off the record—you just want to have the information for your own knowledge.

If you decide that under no circumstances will your source divulge the sensitive information you want, you should consider contacting other people who may have access to the same information.

TIP: Negotiate an Agreement
- If you do need to quote a source or write up certain sensitive information, you can often negotiate with the expert how much or what type of information you may use. For example, although an expert may want remarks to be off the record, you might ask to use only one particular statement made during the conversation. Many times you'll discover that the expert will agree. Similarly, you can negotiate exactly how you will identify the source. For example, the expert may not let you use his or her name, but may not mind being identified as "an employee of Jax Manufacturing in Boston," or something similar. The more choices you can give the expert, the more in control the person will feel, and the more comfortable he or she will be about agreeing to some type of attribution. But remember, most of the time it's not necessary to work out attribution arrangements. All you need to do is to get the source to share expertise with you.

Offensive Questions

What do you do if you have a question or remark that you think may offend the source? You should always try to phrase your questions diplomatically to avoid insulting the expert. For example, if someone tells you, "It's a scientific fact that wearing wool hats causes baldness," you can express your skepticism politely. You might say, "Do you think your opinion on this is in the minority? Why don't you think there is more support for this view?"

Here are two other strategies to keep in mind. First, if you think the question is offensive enough to cut off the interview, save it for near the end to prevent the conversation from ending early on. Second, use another reporter's trick—pose the question in the third person. Don't, for example, ask, "Since you have never been invited to present your research results to the scientific community, isn't your information of dubious value?" Instead say, "Some people have said that since you have never been invited. . . ."

ETHICAL ISSUES IN OBTAINING SENSITIVE INFORMATION

What do you do if you need to interview someone for information, but do not want to tell the person who you are or why you need it? Sometimes this happens when you want "insider" information on a specific firm or competitor company—and the only place to find that information is by talking to individuals who work at the company itself!

This is an issue that professional researchers who conduct "competitive intelligence" have recently been grappling with. (There is even a trade association of competitive intelligence professionals!) It's a tricky issue because it revolves around the definition of what is and is not misrepresentation. There may be gray areas where the researcher does not out-and-out lie, but is tempted to withhold the "whole" truth out of fear that such disclosure would discourage the source from sharing his or her knowledge.

What should you do if faced with this type of situation? There are a number of questions worth asking yourself:

▪ Have I truly exhausted all public, published sources? As outlined in this book, there are scores of government documents, computer database records, trade magazine articles, and other public information sources available just for the asking. Make sure you have thoroughly researched the existence of all these potential sources.

▪ If you are sure no published information exists that can answer your question, try to identify persons you can interview where you feel more comfortable revealing who you are and the purpose of your project. For example, if you need to find out facts about a company's future strategic plans, you can obtain insights by interviewing Wall Street analysts, trade magazine editors, and other types of experts.

▪ If those persons still do not have the information you need, ask yourself how vital it really is that you find that specific piece of information. Are there related data that could be helpful? Is there peripheral information from which you can piece together a picture?

- If you are sure that you still need that precise information, you may be convinced that the only way to get it is to misrepresent yourself. But this is not always so. Say, for example, you need information on a competitive company. You just might find that if you call the knowledgeable source, are upfront, polite, and gracious, you may get unexpected cooperation! The source may help you for any number of reasons: he or she might have questions to ask you, the person may just enjoy talking, or he or she doesn't think what you are asking is particularly sensitive—who knows! The point is don't assume you need to make up some ruse—as Mark Twain said, "When in doubt . . . tell the truth." You may be pleasantly surprised at the results!

If, finally, you are certain that the only way to obtain the information you need is by hiding who you are or making up a story, you should ask yourself whether you really want to take that approach. Here are my arguments as to why misrepresenting yourself or even withholding relevant information (e.g., the nature of your research project) is *not* advisable:

Self-interest

- An unethical research activity may eventually be revealed to others. How will this affect you or your organization's reputation?
- Unethical data-gathering activities will eventually cause organizations to become so suspicious of researchers—with good reason—that sources of information will dry up. The job of the researcher will become much more difficult.
- With no standards set in this area, you and/or your own organization becomes a target for unethical information gathering.

Personal Ethics

- Take a hard look to see if any research activity you are considering will violate your own personal code of ethics. For example, most of us would not consider telephoning someone and misleading them into sending a check for $500. But today, information is as valuable a commodity as money. We would all like an extra $500, but recognize legitimate boundaries in how to obtain it. Don't the same standards

258

hold true for precious information? You should put yourself in the other person's shoes and ask yourself how *you* would feel if you were the recipient of what you are considering. Would you feel that you were dealt with fairly?

Finally, it is important to remember that just because there are ethical guidelines to follow, excellent research can still be performed by legitimate methods and by intelligent and thoughtful analysis of data.

9

Information Quality

Evaluating Sources and Determining Accuracy

QUICK PREVIEW: INFORMATION QUALITY

- As more information has been created and disseminated, it has become more difficult to distinguish good from bad information.
- When evaluating published documents, consider the *type* of document—whether it is a primary or secondary one—and the purpose of the publication—why is it being published?
- You should also scrutinize what you read to determine whether you are getting all sides of the story and whether the author of the piece is attempting to influence you with loaded words and other techniques.
- Other important considerations when evaluating published information is determining how the information was collected, if the data are presented in a logical and organized manner, and the manner in which the report is marketed.
- Polls and surveys are fraught with hazards. You should be sure to check whether the sponsoring organization is nonpartisan, what type of selection criteria was employed for selecting the sample, if any questions are "loaded," and the placement of questions.

(continued)

Also ascertain if memories or recollections are asked for and if any of the questions are complex, vague or ask persons to reveal any sensitive information (all of these can elicit unreliable answers).

- In addition to evaluating published data, you can also evaluate the experts that you interview. Look out for biased sources. Be aware of an expert's affiliations and loyalties. Try to supplement potentially biased sources with more objective ones.

- Beware of those who have a very narrow scope of expertise or who are out of date, too far removed from the subject, unaccountable, or confusing.

- Evaluate your sources by noting whose names are cited frequently in leading trade publications. Ask experts for their opinions of others' work, use certain sources as "yardsticks" and probe for facts behind general statements.

- Evaluating the quality of your information means being a critical thinker. Critical thinking means not just believing something because everyone says it's so, or because something is repeated often or it is the first opinion you hear. Critical thinking also means questioning, probing, and looking for connections between data until you yourself are convinced of the truth of the matters under investigation.

- In cases where evidence is nonexistent or unconvincing, you can still examine related information to make a rational determination on the validity of the subject under investigation.

INSURING THE QUALITY
OF YOUR INFORMATION

Ironically, as more and more information is created and disseminated, it has become even more difficult to be able to discern the good information from the bad. One of the most critical issues of the information age is information *quality*. Today, the researcher's problem is not simply *where* to find information, but how to *evaluate* the accuracy and reliability of the facts and data collected. In a sense, information has become another "commodity," and users need to become "informed consumers"!

The issue of data quality has grown more important with the increase in information available from computer databases. Data viewed on a computer screen may *appear* more "official" and reliable but, of course, is not—in fact, in certain instances there is room for an increased number of errors. (For more information on reliability of computer databases, see pages 192–194.)

Information accuracy is an important and complex subject,

and a full treatment deserves an in-depth and extensive discussion. Although such a treatment is beyond the scope of this book, some basic advice is provided in the following two sections, "Evaluating Published Sources" (this includes information "published" electronically on-line) and "Evaluating Experts."

Evaluating Published Sources

The following are some key considerations to note when determining the accuracy of published data:

What Is the Type of Document? There is a critical distinction between a *primary* and *secondary* data source. A primary source is the originator of the data, and a secondary source secures the data from the original source. A researcher should never terminate a search with the secondary source. Secondary sources often delete the methods employed in collecting data and sometimes fail to reproduce significant footnotes or comments which may qualify the data in some way.*

What Is the Purpose of the Publication? A source is suspect if published to promote the sales, to advance the interests of an industrial or commercial or other group, to present the cause of a political party, or to carry on any sort of propaganda. Also suspect is data published anonymously or by an organization on the defensive, or under conditions which suggest a controversy, or in a form which reveals a strained attempt at "frankness."†

Are You Getting All Sides of the Story? Try to determine whether the article, report, or book is presenting only one side of an issue when there is clearly more than one point of view.

---

* Nemmers and Meyers, quoted in Churchill, Gilbert A. Jr., *Marketing Research: Methodological Foundations* (Hinsdale, Ill.: Dryden Press, 1987).
† Ibid.

For example, an article that cites *only* the problems associated with, say, national health insurance, without at least referring to potential benefits could not be viewed as a balanced presentation. That piece may still be useful, however, for example, to learn of the claims of those opposed to such a program, for finding out about other studies cited, and to obtain leads for further research. The point is, it should not be used as a single source of information.

Note that this issue of "balanced coverage" is tricky, however, and it's not always easy to determine what constitutes balanced coverage. In fact, one can even make the case that presenting both sides of an issue is not always legitimate. For example, if one is writing about a clearly outrageous case of child abuse, does the best coverage give equal time to the abuser to give his or her side of the story? These kinds of questions are thorny journalistic and sociological issues beyond the scope of this book. Suffice it to say: *be aware* as to whether or not you are getting all *reasonably legitimate* points of view on an issue, and if it is clear you are not, do not use that source as a definitive one.

Is the Author Trying to Subtly Influence You? It's not enough to determine simply whether coverage of a topic is "balanced"; it's also critical to be able to detect the more subtle ways that an author may be trying to insert his or her views into a piece. Choice of words, placement of names, and other techniques can be employed consciously or unconsciously by the writer to influence the reader.

For example, see how the choice of the following words that mean the same thing can connote totally different feelings and elicit different reactions.

Free enterprise	Capitalism
Persons incarcerated	Criminals
Mixed drinks	Hard liquor
Spiritually renewed	Born again
Stronger defense	More money for missiles
Increased revenues	Higher taxes

264

Even something as simple as the insertion of quotation marks, or the use of a different word, can subtly change connotations. For example, compare these two sentences:

- John Doe, director of public affairs, said that he was instituting the clean-up committee to make headway in cleaning up the environment.

- John Doe, director of public affairs, claimed that "helping the environment" was the reason he was instituting the clean-up committee.

By setting Doe's words within quotation marks, the writer seems to imply that his remark should not be read as a fact; it almost seems like the writer is winking at the reader. The word *claim* is another way to cast doubt on the speaker's trustworthiness. The writer could have also shown his or her skepticism by beginning the sentence with the innocuous words *according to*, which again would add a subjective element to the sentence, decreasing Doe's credibility.

Keep your antenna up and be attuned to these subtleties— again, if you detect that information is being presented in a slanted manner, it does not mean you have to disregard the material; keep an open mind and just try not to let yourself be influenced by the *manner* in which a piece is written. You will need to make up your own mind after consulting a variety of different sources.

Is the Information Presented Logically and Is It Well Organized? Are the data internally consistent? Are conclusions supported by the data and evidence presented? Look for data presented in a well-organized manner, tables clearly labeled, and lucid accompanying explanatory material. Typically (although by no means always), these elements reflect a well-thought-out study.

Is the Information Based on a Poll or Survey? The quality of individual polls and surveys vary enormously. There is a science to accurate data collection that involves technical considerations such as sample size, rate of response, sampling and nonsampling errors, and more. It's important to find out how the information was collected (e.g., mail questionnaire or phone), who was interviewed, and the other details behind the study.

Polls and surveys that purport to measure people's views and behaviors are so fraught with hazards, in fact, that some observers believe that even the finest and most well-known survey organizations cannot overcome the great number of barriers that exist in accurate reporting. For these reasons, polls, surveys, forecasts, and the like should be utilized by researchers only with a great deal of caution.

Dr. Jared Jobe, director of the Collaborative Research Program at the U.S. National Center for Health Statistics, notes that there are a number of areas where polls and surveys can be misleading or inaccurate. The following are some of the most common problems:

- *Partisan sponsoring organizations.* Organizations that have a motive to manipulate surveys to achieve a desired result are obviously suspect.

- *Selection criteria.* By what mechanism and approach was the group selected? Was it a random sampling? The key point is whether the respondents were a *representative* sample of the particular population of interest. Jobe advises researchers to watch out for mail surveys, magazine subscriber surveys and telephone call-in polls, because these are often biased by the fact that only persons with a particular reason for responding will answer the questions (those with extreme positions on an issue may be overrepresented).

- *Loaded questions.* Jobe's research has shown that people's opinions are greatly affected by the tone, manner, and choice of words of the interviewer. Other studies have shown that people will provide totally different opinions depending on whether the words the interviewer uses contain positive or negative connotations. For example, according to one study, public opinion shifts if asked about favoring more spending "to aid the *poor*" compared to spending more for *welfare*. Sometimes, responses differ even when alternative words are used that do not seem to be loaded. For example, people were found to be less willing to approve speeches against democracy when asked whether the

United States should "*allow* public speeches against democracy" than when asked whether the United States should "*forbid* public speeches against democracy."*

- *Placement of questions.* Question placement can affect the way people respond. For example, say a subject was asked whether defense spending should be increased by 10 percent. If he or she replied no, the subject might then be more inclined to say yes to a follow-up question as to whether the United States should increase defense spending by 5 percent. Had the respondent *only* been asked whether defense spending should be increased by 5 percent, he or she may have been more likely to have replied in the negative.

- *Asking for memories and recollections.* Jobe says that people are notoriously poor at remembering their past actions and activities.

- *Complex questions.* People often will answer questions they do not understand.

- *Vague questions.* Questions that are open to more than one interpretation obviously make for poor research results.

- *Sensitive questions.* Queries that ask people to admit to socially unacceptable behavior are less reliable. For example, today people often do not like to admit that they smoke.

- *Misleading conclusions.* Sometimes the survey process is fine, but the conclusions are misleading. For example, Jobe cites the commercial that says "no toothpaste gets your teeth whiter." Such a claim can simply mean that the brand is no worse than all the rest.

The best way to guard against these problems is to get a copy of the actual questionnaire utilized and study it to try to detect any of these pitfalls. Jobe advises researchers to look at many surveys, conducted by more than one organization at different times. If these surveys reveal generally the same findings, then you can feel fairly confident about the results.

---

* For further discussion and examples, see Rich Jaroslovsky, "What's on Your Mind America," *Psychology Today*, July/Aug. 1988, 54–59.

EVALUATING EXPERTS

When you interview a "live" expert, how do you evaluate that person's credibility and knowledge? Here are some strategies.

Signs of a Good Source

Here are a few helpful indicators of a good source:

Peer Recognition. Has the source had anything published in trade journals or spoken at industry conferences? If so, it's an excellent sign because it signifies recognition by peers. Peer recognition is one of the very best indicators of an authoritative source. If you don't know whether a source has written or spoken on the topic, there is nothing wrong with politely asking. Use your judgment when applying this rule. If an expert has made a brand-new discovery or just finished a research project, it may take time to be recognized.

Referrals. How did you find the source? If you were referred by a recognized expert in the field, or someone you felt was a worthy source, it is a good sign. Good experts typically refer you to other good experts.

Repetition. Does the source repeat things you've heard before that you know to be true? If so, it's another good sign.

Attentiveness. Does the source pay careful attention to your questions and respond sensitively? I've found this to be a sign of a good source.

Sources to Beware Of

The Biased Source. Bias is a tricky matter. The critical thing to be aware of is where a particular source is "coming from." For example, is he or she a salesperson for a product, a political appointee, or a representative of a special cause? Take this into account when evaluating the information. This doesn't mean that people with certain viewpoints or leanings are not going to be truthful or accurate. It simply means that each person's perspective must be uncovered so that you know how to evaluate his or her information.

For example, once I was digging up information on how certain cities cut their energy costs by forming fuel-buying cooperatives. One of the people I talked to was the president of a regional association of fuel dealers. He told me co-ops were a very bad idea; he said that although the participants might cut their purchasing costs, they suffer in the quality of their service. I noted his objection seriously, but at the same time realized that because he represented a group of fuel dealers, his constituency would have the most to lose if this co-op idea really caught on. I decided to call the individual co-op members directly to find out if they had indeed encountered service problems. It turned out that none had.

You must also stay on guard against organizations that do not easily telegraph their biases. These organizations often have impartial-sounding names but actually promote a very specific stand on an issue. For example, you locate an association innocently called "Citizens for Energy Awareness." The name suggests merely that the committee wants to help spread information. But it's possible that the committee's sole raison d'être is to advance the cause of nuclear energy—or to ban it. To check for such biases, find out what kind of people the association is composed of. Are most of the officers of the "Citizens for Energy Awareness" executives at nuclear power plants? If so, you can guess why that organization has been created! Take a look at some of the organization's brochures and research reports. Do its studies and findings unfailingly reach the same conclusion and support the same side of a controversial issue? You might still get some good information from this special-interest group, but be aware that you will not get a balanced picture.

Another type of biased source that you need to be on guard against is the "overly enthusiastic" source. This kind of person is typically involved in implementing a new project of some sort. You're sure to get rave reviews from this person when you ask how the project is going. Nobody wants to express doubts about the success of his or her new ventures, so you have to be careful not to take glowing reports as gospel. In the above case of the fuel cooperatives, for example, the co-op members themselves may want to paint an overly rosy picture of their project. Probe for as many hard facts as you can.

When you run into cases in which you feel your sources have too many personal interests to be totally unbiased, try to supplement those sources with more disinterested experts. Again, in the case of the fuel-buying cooperatives, I would probably get the most objective information not from the fuel dealers or the co-op members, but from a government expert in the Department of Energy or another more unbiased authority on fuel.

The Overly Narrow Source. Let's say you are trying to find information on crime trends in the United States, and you find an expert on supermarket shoplifting. You'll have to ask yourself whether that person's opinions go beyond his or her area of expertise and extend to overall U.S. crime trends.

The Out-Of-Date Source. Are you looking into a field that is constantly changing? If so, you want to be sure your sources have kept up with the changes. Try to find out the last time the person was actually involved in the subject. In certain fields —microcomputer technology, for example—information from only six months ago is quite dated.

The Too-Far-Removed Source. High-level sources with very broad administrative duties are often too far removed to provide you with the nitty-gritty details you need. For example, if you are digging up information on upcoming design trends in small automobiles, the head of the public affairs department of General Motors would be able to give you only the sketchiest and most basic information. You'd be much better off talking to design engineers to get more specific details. (Calling the public affairs office can still be worthwhile, if only to ask to be referred to a technical expert.)

The Unaccountable Source. The opposite of talking to a high-level official, like a public affairs executive, is the problem of talking to someone lower down on the company ladder who is not as accountable for what he or she says. While the public affairs person may not give you the nitty-gritty that you want, the person is careful about what he or she says, and the information you get should at least be accurate. The shop foreman may not feel so restrained and cautious and will give you the details you want. But try to get those "facts" confirmed by other sources before relying on them as indisputable.

The Secondary Source. Is your source a true expert or just someone who is reporting on the experts' work or reorganizing existing information? Secondary sources *can* be helpful, but they are not ordinarily as intimately knowledgeable about the subject as primary sources.

The Confusing Source. If the person talks only in technical jargon and is unable to communicate his or her expertise to you, you're not going to get much out of the conversation. Move on to the next one.

Evaluation Strategies

Here are a few methods you can use to help evaluate your sources:

- Note the names of people who keep appearing in the articles that you read. When you see somebody quoted often, and in a variety of periodicals, it's usually a sign that the person is a leader in the field and has something valuable to say.
- It's fine to ask experts for their opinion of other sources. Just be diplomatic about how you ask. One way is to ask if they "agree" with so-and-so's conclusions about the subject in question.
- Think about using certain sources as yardsticks. If you've spoken with someone you feel is a top-notch authority, you can measure other sources' responses against that person's.

- If a source makes a statement you're skeptical of, politely ask where the information comes from. His or her research? Hands-on experience? Something read somewhere?
- If you doubt someone's expertise, you can test the person by asking a question to which you already know the answer.
- Does the expert say something definitively that you already know is absolutely incorrect? If so, that is obviously not a good sign!
- Have you had a chance to read anything the expert has written? I have found that the most useful experts to speak with are those that can write a clear, well-organized article or report.
- Does the expert simply repeat what everyone else says or does he or she have some fresh perspective on the issue? I've found that the truly superior experts can take an issue and not just describe the current situation, but see implications and add some new angles.
- I've found that one intuitive way to evaluate an expert is simply to ask yourself after you've had your interview whether you feel satisfied.

CRITICAL THINKING

Much of the advice given in this chapter could fall under the heading of "critical thinking." Being a critical thinker is vital for a researcher. But what does critical thinking really mean?

Critical thinking means a number of things. It means:

- Not just believing something because everyone says it's so
- Not just believing something because you have heard it repeated so often
- Not just accepting the first opinion you hear

Critical thinking means constantly asking questions, probing, and digging deeply into a subject to learn more and more until *you yourself* are satisfied of the truth of the matter.

Critical thinking also means looking at bits of data, pieces of information, and bodies of knowledge and searching for connections—and differences. It means sitting down and simply thinking hard about all that you've uncovered and trying to figure out what it all has in common. What are the threads that link the data? How do they differ?

What about the concept of trust or faith? Can a critical thinker ever decide simply to believe what someone says just because he or she trusts a person's judgment? I think yes. However, the trust will be an *intelligently placed one*. The experienced researcher sometimes intuitively feels when to trust a source and when not to. But this is a very difficult task, and it may not always be possible to make a decision on whom to trust. But you can ask yourself certain questions to help you explore your "gut" feelings:

- Has the person proven himself or herself to be reliable and accurate in this subject in the past?
- Does the rest of his or her work show integrity?
- Does the person have an axe to grind in this case or does he or she seem unbiased?

When Evidence Is Not There

What does the researcher do when he or she does not find any hard evidence to support a claim or position? Must the researcher dismiss any conclusions or findings as simply unproven and therefore not worth accepting? Let's look at a scenario where such a situation might be faced.

Let's say I came across a scientist who claimed that his work and analysis showed that there was a strong link between levels of air pollution and the onset of heart disease. Say that currently the medical establishment had not proven any link between the two and, in fact, there was no evidence at all linking the two phenomena together. How would one evaluate the scientist's claims?

Obviously, few researchers are in a position to definitively determine whether or not this person's claim is valid. There are scientific methods of discovery that are performed extremely carefully under intense scrutiny to determine whether or not a reported phenomenon is indeed a reliable finding. However, you may find yourself in a position where you must make some kind of unscientific judgment on such a matter.

Although the judgment will be unscientific, it can still be of great importance, because it is these types of informal, unscientific—but rational—judgment that can provide enough interest in a subject to get the gears in motion for the scientists to set out and create their rigorous tests to discover truths. There is a lag time between the discovery of a phenomenon and its proof (or disproof), and the researcher can be a vital link in the process for assisting in facilitating the movement from the stage of initial theory or discovery to the stage of proof.

Let's look at an example. Say you start reading a researcher's claims about the link between air pollution and heart disease. The researcher's conclusions are unproven and unaccepted by the scientific community but you need to determine for yourself the likelihood of the theory being correct. What would you need to do? There are a number of paths you could pursue. First, you could find out the answers to these types of question:

- What is the manner in which the person is presenting his or her findings? Is it in a sensational way, making claims like "revolutionary . . . fantastic . . . unbelievable," or are the claims presented in a more reasonable and rational way? Does the researcher provide advice on how to best interpret his or her work or just run down a list of amazing benefits?
- Are there backup records available to document claims? If the research is very new, is there at least an attempt to carefully collect records and document findings for the future?
- What types of outlet is the researcher choosing to publicize his or her findings? For example, does he or she advertise in the classifieds of *National Enquirer* and ask people to send in $10 to get his or her secrets or does the researcher approach the mainstream media and/or scientific community? What kind of audience is he or she trying to reach—a gullible one or one that will provide intense levels of scrutiny?
- Does this person make all of his or her records and findings open for anyone to inspect or is much of it "secret formula" claims that will not be released?
- What else has this person worked on? Does the researcher

show evidence of achievement in related fields? Is he or she respected by peers?

As you can see, most of these questions do not ask you to analyze the actual claim itself, but to look at relevant peripheral information that can be an aid in making the judgment. And, of course, it is possible that even someone who fits all the "right" answers will ultimately be proven incorrect (or vice versa, but less likely). But you may need to make a judgment call. Finally, your role as a researcher cannot be to comment on whether or not the claims are correct, but whether or not a phenomenon does or does not deserve serious scrutiny and attention from the larger community. And this is no insignificant job.

10

Wrapping It Up

Organizing and Writing Up Your Results, with the Benefit of the Expert Review

---

**QUICK PREVIEW:
WRAPPING IT UP**

- You'll know it's time to conclude your talks with the experts when you can predict the answers to your questions and when you're putting out a lot of energy but not receiving much new information.

- Before you consider your project complete, have one or more of the best experts you've spoken with review your work for accuracy. This is a *critical* step in the process.

- Organize the information you've collected by subject rather than by source. This will make it easy to arrange your final work.

- When deciding what is worth including in your final report, select information that's relevant and reliable.

- Make conclusions whenever appropriate.

- Always remember to be fair—search for opposing views, be complete and honest.

Eventually you'll come to the point in your interviews when it is time to start winding down your information search. But there are a number of critical steps that still need to be attended to at this late point. Here are the things you need to know.

KNOWING WHEN TO CALL IT QUITS

How do you know when you've done enough work? Here's a guideline you can use: be aware of when you can predict how the experts are going to answer your questions. As discussed earlier, when this first occurs, it's a good time to step back and redirect your focus. But if you've redirected once or twice already, and you can't think of any new paths to pursue, it's usually a sign that you've covered your subject well, and you don't have to go any further.

Another guideline you can use to decide when it's time to quit is when you discover that you are putting in a lot of work but not getting much new information. When you reach this point of diminishing returns, it's also probably time to wrap it all up.

One other rule you may decide to use: if you are approaching a deadline and you're out of time, you may have no choice but to quit! I've found that you need to budget something along the lines of 80 to 85 percent of your total allotted time for research and 15 to 20 percent for writing up the results.

MAKING SURE YOUR FINAL INFORMATION IS ACCURATE

After you decide to end your talks with the experts, the next critical step is to make sure you've covered your subject effectively and that the information you've gathered is accurate and complete.

The first thing you should do is to think back to your early expert contacts. Were there top-notch sources you spoke with, but did not know at that early stage what kinds of questions to ask? Now that your knowledge of the subject is deeper and clearer, it might be worth going back to those people to talk to them again. Write an outline of your findings. Where do gaps still remain? Think of which sources you could consult to fill them.

Another step you might take at this point is to confirm the accuracy of certain discussions. Say, for example, that you spoke with an expert but you're not quite sure you understood the person completely. Jot down your interpretation of that source's points and send it off for confirmation.

The next step is very critical to complete this whole talking-to-the-experts process and make it really work. This is the "expert review" procedure and it works as follows.

If you are writing up your results, write a draft. If you are not writing up your results, write a rough draft anyway. Now go back and review all the different experts you've spoken with during the course of your information interviews. Select one or two that were especially knowledgeable and helpful—your very best sources. Get in touch with these people again and ask them to review your work for accuracy. Tell them that all their comments, suggestions, and criticisms are welcome. Be sure to tell the reviewers that they have indeed been specially selected. Ninety-five percent of the time these people will be flattered that you've singled them out, and they will be more than happy to take a few minutes and read your draft. You can even type in questions at locations in your draft where you are unsure of certain points.

If you are going to be writing up your results, you should acknowledge the expert reviewers' assistance somewhere in the work, and tell them that you plan to do this.

Your reviewers will almost never ask for a fee to do this job for you. A big reason for this is that you have been very selective in your choice of reviewers. You'll find that in any information-finding project you will always "hit it off" with at least a couple of experts along the way. The process is such that about 10 to 15 percent of the people you talk to will not be too helpful or knowledgeable, 60 to 70 percent will be quite helpful and provide you with very good information, and 10 to 15 percent will be of superb assistance. There is always that percentage of extranice experts who go out of their way to help you in any way they can. *These are the people you get in touch with again* to ask for this review.

I usually prefer two or three reviewers, each with a different perspective. For example, after I wrote a report on the topic of microcomputers, I sent one draft to a computer programmer, another to a consultant, and a third to a vendor. If you know of an expert who specializes only in one aspect of your study, you can send just that particular section of your work to that person.

There are two ways you can actually carry out this review procedure. One way is to mail your draft to your reviewers and ask them to mark it up and send it back to you. This is okay, but I prefer another approach. I would recommend that you send the draft and ask them to read it and mark it with comments. Then you should get on the telephone with each reviewer, have a copy of your draft in front of you, and go over the draft page by page with the expert. This way, you can ask the reviewers questions about any of their points you don't understand, and you can explain yourself on any points in your report that weren't clear to the reviewers.

In essence, this expert review is completing the circle—the experts are now reviewing the expert information that you've gathered. At this point, if you've done a thorough job, you should feel like an expert yourself.

NOTE TAKING AND ORGANIZATION

As mentioned previously, whenever you consult a written source of information, or talk to an expert, you'll want to take notes and keep your information organized.

There are naturally many different approaches you could take to organizing information. I've found that one particular method seems to work quite well for the purpose of organizing a lot of unfamiliar information gathered from a multitude of sources.

The way it works is as follows. Get a pad of paper, and for the first batch of written information sources you consult (say, five to eight) take your notes on a pad, clearly marking at the top the name of the source, where it can be found, and the pages consulted. After you've finished with this first batch, you should be knowledgeable enough to be able to define the key subtopic categories within your subject and fit all future information you collect (from both written sources and talks with experts) into those categories you've established.

For example, let's say I was trying to find out everything about the sport of ballooning. After reading and taking notes on a number of articles on the topic, maybe I'd determine that there were fifteen critical subtopics within the subject. These might be purchasing a balloon, setting one up, safety considerations, fuel, and so on. My next step would be to get a stack of index cards and write each subtopic on top of a different card. Then I'd go back to my pad and copy the notes onto the appropriate index card. So if one sheet of the pad contained notes about a number of subtopics (fuel, safety, etc.) but were drawn from one source, I'd break up those notes into those categories and copy them onto the appropriate index cards. This would eventually result in my having a stack of cards, each containing information about only one subtopic, but gathered from a number of different information sources. In theory, all my future notes should be able to fit into one of those categories.

As you continue to uncover information, however, and become knowledgeable about your subject, you may find that you'll need to modify the categories you originally created.

Some subtopics may prove to be very minor and can be incorporated into a larger category. Or there may be additional categories to add as new topics arise that you hadn't considered.

This method of arranging information by subject, rather than by source, will make the final organizational steps simple. You can just shuffle the index cards until you're satisfied that the subtopics are arranged in a logical and smooth order. Then, if you are going to be writing up your results or making an oral presentation, you have an outline already created.

You may find it convenient to continue to take notes on large pads of paper even after you've created your index card categories. That's fine. Just be sure to copy the notes on the appropriate cards.

WRITING UP YOUR RESULTS

Here are some pointers to keep in mind if you plan to formally write up the results of your information search.

Sort the Gems from the Junk. As you read through all the notes you've taken—notes from magazine articles, government reports, talks with experts, and all other sources you've consulted—you'll need to decide which pieces of information should be included in your report. How do you discern the valuable from the not so valuable? How do you decide which fact is important and which is useless?

Although this is a common concern among first-time information seekers, if you've done a thorough job in your search, you will understand the subject well enough at this point to know which information is important and which is not. But here are two guidelines that can help you make a decision:

- The most important question you need to ask about any piece of information is whether it is *relevant* to your investigation. Does it add information, shed new light, suggest a trend, or provide background for your subject? If a piece of information, no matter how interesting, does not advance the specific goals or fall within the scope of your project, it should not be included.

▪ When evaluating your information, think about who provided it. Was it from a source you considered reliable or did it come from a biased or otherwise suspect source?

Be Complete. When you write up your results, don't tease with a remark that leaves the reader hanging. It's very important to fully explain your points clearly, and preferably with a concrete example. A statement like "The Model W skis are the best because they meet all important criteria" would only be helpful if you explained what the important criteria actually are. Anticipate the questions your statements will elicit from a reader, and then do your best to answer them.

Make Conclusions. Another common question among beginning information gatherers is whether it is appropriate to state one's opinion or make conclusions on a controversial issue. Let's say you've just spent three months learning all about the racquetball industry. You've spoken to club owners, association executives, sports columnists, and equipment manufacturers. You've read articles in leading trade publications and in the general press. As you read over your information, you begin to come to the conclusion that indicators are pointing to an imminent drop in the popularity of the sport. Are you qualified to state that conclusion?

In most cases, I would definitely say *yes*—with a couple of small cautions. If you've done a thorough job digging out information on your subject, you are certainly justified in drawing conclusions and stating them. If you realize that the facts point to certain trends, or add up to certain conclusions, you should state them. In fact, findings like these are one of the most important things that can come out of these information-finding projects.

Now, although you can draw broad conclusions, it's best to quote the experts themselves on factual data and opinions. Let's say you are doing a study on the fight against some rare disease. A statement in your report like "This disease is not at all contagious" should be attributed to a particular expert, or at least preceded by words like "according to experts I spoke with. . . ."

282

But in any information-finding project you are certainly permitted to step back, look at the big picture, and give your opinion. You should then indicate in some manner, however, that this is *your* conclusion. In the racquetball case, you could phrase your statement along these lines: "After investigating the industry and talking to numerous experts in the field, this author feels that the game will soon be decreasing in popularity. The major reasons for this, I believe, are. . . ."

What do you do when there are arguments and evidence on both sides of an issue, and you're not sure who is correct? I recently worked on a project that required finding information on potential health hazards of video display terminals (VDTs). There were two distinctly opposing viewpoints: government and industry tests all showed that radiation levels fell well within safety standards; but unions and certain workers organizations claimed that there was little information on the long-term effects of the VDTs' low-level radiation, and they cited cases of higher-than-expected health problems among certain VDT workers.

It was not totally clear—to me at least—what the "answer" was regarding the safety of this equipment. So I decided to present the arguments of both sides as clearly as possible and leave it up to readers to draw their own conclusions.

In many information searches you'll run into these gray areas; you'll want a simple answer, but there won't be one. That's okay. Just present the facts as you see them.

Also be sure to ask yourself whenever you write about a controversial or sensitive issue whether you are being *fair*. Fairness is pretty tough to judge, but I think the *Washington Post Deskbook on Style* defines it well. According to the editor of that book, being fair includes the following guidelines:

- *Search for opposing views.* In other words, don't be lazy and accept the first opinion you hear. Get both sides of the story.

- *Be complete.* Don't omit facts of major importance. Otherwise, your reader will be misled.

- *Be relevant.* Unnecessary information will cloud an issue.

- *Be honest.*

To Quote or Not to Quote

People often wonder when it's necessary to attribute information to an expert or a written source, and when it's acceptable to use the information without attribution. Although one wit claimed that "to steal ideas from one person is plagiarism; to steal from many is research,"[1] the general rule is that when you use somebody's own idea or work, you must attribute it to that source. But if somebody provides facts or general information that can be obtained from many sources (e.g., Death Valley, California, has the highest recorded temperature in the United States), it is not necessary to do so.

What about obtaining permission to quote the experts that you've interviewed? If you are writing a very sensitive piece you can play it safe and specifically ask each expert for their permission, but normally it's not necessary. As long as you've identified yourself to the expert, explained that you are writing an article or a report, and made no off-the-record agreements, the expert should realize that you are using his or her remarks for publication.

Another common question regards obtaining permission to excerpt or quote published information. Here the general rule is that you may make what is called "fair use" of published materials without seeking permission. In general, "fair use" allows you to quote a few lines of a short article or a couple of paragraphs of a longer piece or book *with attribution* but without getting permission from the publisher. If you want to use more than this, you should send a letter to the publisher explaining exactly what information you want to use, exactly where it is located, and why you want to use it. The great majority of the time, the publisher will *not* charge you for the use of the material, but will require that you print a specific credit line. The publisher may also want you to send it a copy of the final work.

These general rules are exactly that—general. Each case is different. The best rule is to use your common sense and, if there

[1] Arthur Bloch, *Murphy's Law Book 3* (Los Angeles: Price Stern, 1982), p. 50.

is any doubt at all about attributing information or obtaining permission, to err on the safe side.

If for some reason a publisher is unwilling to grant permission, try to track down the author of the piece yourself. Then you can interview that person for information, and the expertise will be available to you without a hassle.

Libel is a much more complicated matter, and a full discussion of the topic is beyond the scope of this book. It's worth noting, however, a concise definition that was published in the *Washington Post Deskbook on Style:* "Basically, a libelous statement is a published statement that injures a person (or organization or corporation) in his trade, profession or community standing." Although traditional defenses against a libel charge have included "truth" (i.e., the information published was accurate) and "reasonable care" (on the part of the writer), it is impossible to generalize about this topic. The *Post* advises writers to again consider simply whether they are being fair. Did you give the party a chance to respond?

Finally, don't forget about the grammar hot lines mentioned on pages 68–73. Using these can make your writing job a little bit easier.

One last point. Be sure to show your appreciation to the experts you speak with. If you can think of any way that you can help them, or return the favor, offer it. And if someone ever comes to you with an information request, remember how much you appreciated the experts who helped you and try to do likewise.

11

Trouble Shooting

Typical Questions
Information Seekers Ask

Here are some of the most typical questions I am asked by researchers who are undertaking an information-finding project.

Q. How do I know where to begin my information search?
A. There is rarely any single *perfect* place to begin your research. The "Information Seeker's Map" on page xxii should help you get started. The key is to get started on your research and begin learning about your subject. As you begin to gather information and understand your topic, the question will become irrelevant.

Q. How do I know whether to use print or electronic databases when starting my research?
A. This can be confusing, especially since many periodical indexes and publications today can be found both in print and electronically. The basic rule of research stays the same though: start off with basic sources and build up your knowledge gradually. So whether you choose print or electronic, your initial sources should be non-technical and geared for the popular user. Keep in mind, too, that print sources still retain certain advantages over electronic: there's still *more* information in

print, especially on more obscure topics; they go back further in time and provide historical perspective; they are usually cheaper to use; they are *always* fulltext; they are generally more pleasant to read from; and you don't need a computer!

Q. I know that there must be some information on the topic— but I can't find anything!

A. It's extremely doubtful that *no* information whatsoever exists. One possible cause for not finding anything is that you might be unaware of any standard terminology that your subject would be categorized under. For example, say you were researching the topic "static electricity"—you would need to know that "electrostatics" is the standard scientific term for that phenomenon and that all indexes and materials will categorize that topic under that heading. Also, make sure you check as many sources as possible before you conclude there is nothing available on your subject. If you still cannot find anything, look up related or broader subjects. In the rare instance where there is truly absolutely nothing written on your subject, it could mean you are onto something interesting—and the results of your research could add to the body of knowledge!

Q. I've found some articles on the subject, but I can't understand them.

A. Don't worry. Keep on researching the topic and look for articles written for a more general audience. If you can't find any at all try finding a description in an introductory textbook or encyclopedia. Then call some experts, explain that you are a layman on the topic and have some very basic questions to ask.

Q. I'd like to call some experts, but to tell you the truth I'm afraid.

A. You are certainly not alone! Just about everyone who gets into this field gets very nervous about calling strangers and asking for information. But think about it—you've got nothing to lose. Chances are the person is going to help you out, and if worse comes to worse and the phone conversation doesn't work out you can always say, "Thanks for your time," and hang up.

It took me almost two years' of talking to experts before I felt really relaxed before making these kinds of calls—so don't be too hard on yourself!

Q. I can never get hold of these experts—either they are out or they don't return my calls!
A. It's not that you can't get hold of them, it's just that you haven't made enough calls! The process of reaching experts is, to a great extent, a numbers game—call enough people and you will always reach at least a certain percentage. It's a time-consuming process, but it works!

Q. I got the expert on the phone, but he talked so fast I don't think I wrote it all down.
A. Don't worry. Note taking is a skill that improves with practice. After you speak with a number of people, you'll intuitively know how to capture the key points. And it really does help to read over your notes *immediately* after the conversation so you can fill in gaps while the conversation is still fresh in your mind. If it looks like you missed something critical, just call the person back to go over those issues again.

Q. How do I know when to stop doing research?
A. There is no perfect time, but as mentioned earlier in the book, when you feel you can predict the experts' answers, have reassessed the direction of your project, and are expending a lot of research time but getting little new information, it's probably time to wrap up. You can try writing a draft of your findings to see if there are gaps still remaining that require additional research.

Q. Help! I think I may have collected too much information! I'm swamped with articles, notes, and other data!
A. Your problem is probably not too much information, but not enough organization. Start going through your notes and begin categorizing each statement of fact under a topic subheading and transcribe all related facts under each heading. This will make your big stack of information more manageable. Get rid

of information that, although interesting, does not directly relate to the scope of your project or advance its mission.

Q. Uh-oh, I've got conflicting information in my notes—how do I know who to believe?
A. This is common—often there is more than one opinion on a subject. See chapter 9 on evaluating information sources. Sometimes you may simply have to present both points of view and allow the reader to decide the merits.

Q. I really enjoy doing this kind of research. How can I find out about careers in this field?
A. That is a very interesting question, and it is one I have been asked many times. There are a number of different careers that involve digging up and analyzing information. The most obvious and well-known field involving finding information is library science—however, many researchers do not wish to work in a traditional library environment. Some ex-librarians have started "information broker" businesses (see pages 206–207) and sell their research skills to businesses and organizations for a fee. Other careers that involve heavy amounts of research include certain types of journalism, private investigator services, new business or product development, and market research.

Q. One area you haven't really given any advice on is how to find information on getting a job. Any thoughts here?
A. Yes. Although the question of how to find a job goes beyond the scope of this book, I think the question is important and relevant enough to merit a few pointers. The main point I'd like to stress is that you can use the sources described in this book to first learn about organizations that appeal to you as a place to work and then utilize the phone-interview techniques to track down department heads, managers, directors, vice presidents, owners, and others who have the power to hire. Ask to speak with them about thoughts you have on how your background and skills might be of value to their organization—and then send them a written letter outlining your ideas, along with a

statement of your qualifications. Try to approach the process as one professional seeking to establish a relationship with another.*

After reading this book, you may find that all of the sources and strategies described are a bit overwhelming, like there is just *too much* out there. But don't worry about trying to memorize the whole book. Just take a look at the Information Seeker's Map on page xxii to get a feel for the entire process, start some research at one of the "easy start" sources identified in chapter 1, then go with the flow and consult the book for help if you run into problems; and remember the basics:

- The information you seek is almost certainly available for the asking
- There are experts around who will talk to you and answer your questions

---

* For much more information on how to go about finding information on jobs and careers, I highly recommend *What Color Is Your Parachute* by Richard N. Bolles (Berkeley, CA: 10 Speed Press, 1993). Also, you can learn much about different careers and jobs by consulting two reference books published by the U.S. government: *Occupational Outlook Handbook* (U.S. Bureau of Labor Statistics, Washington, D.C.) and *U.S. Industrial Outlook* (Department of Commerce, International Trade Administration, Washington, D.C.); most libraries carry both of these volumes.

PART III

Two Sample Searches

—————————————————

The strategies I've recommended to unlock the information storehouses sound fine in the abstract, but how will they work when applied to actual information-finding problems, such as the ones you may have? To demonstrate how these strategies can be applied in specific situations, I decided to investigate two topics about which I knew very little: *starting a new business—specifically a health and fitness center—and finding career opportunities in the field of computers.*

In these chapters, I'll show you step by step how I used the strategies outlined in this book to quickly unearth valuable information on both of these topics. Although the subjects *you* will be researching are undoubtedly different, these two case studies can serve as handy blueprints for approaching any information quest. The phrase "Case Point" will alert you to a specific discovery I made that could help you in your own investigations.

12

Opening a Health and Fitness Club

If you were thinking of starting up a new business like a health and fitness club, you would want to get as much information as possible before investing time and money. Using the strategies outlined in this book, I began searching for information on opening a fitness center. Although I initially encountered some dead ends, I soon uncovered enough free or low-cost information to give anyone thinking of starting such a club a clear idea of what he or she is about to get into. Here's what I found, and the steps I took to find it.

STEP 1. DEFINE GOALS

As mentioned earlier, the first step to take in any information-finding project is to define as specifically as possible what questions you want answered. Normally, the more specific you are, the easier the information search will be.

After a little reflection, I decided that the following would be the chief questions on my mind if I were thinking of opening a health and fitness club:

- What is the current state of the industry?
- How well are the clubs doing financially?

- What problems do clubs face?
- How do clubs attract members?
- What types of exercise facility should be offered?
- How does one determine the best location?

I would probably also want information on the subject of fitness itself, as well as basic advice on how to start a business —any business.

STEP 2. CHECK LIBRARY RESOURCES

Because the subject I was investigating was business oriented, I consulted a nearby library that had good *business* resources.

A. Easy Starts

New York Times Index. There were a few citations that sounded somewhat useful, but none were right on target. Here are some examples of articles found:

Jane Fonda to close downtown fitness center because vibrations caused by exercising have disturbed neighbors

Vertical Club, a glamorous celebrity-studded health club on Manhattan's Upper East Side, replacing singles bars

Judging from the description in the index, these articles seemed too "light" and oriented toward the general public to offer the business information I sought. Therefore, although I noted the citations, I did not obtain the original sources.

Case Point:
- When checking the *New York Times Index,* I had to look under "Health," "Fitness," "Physical Fitness," and "Spas" before I could identify under which term the *New York Times* prefers to index health clubs. Be sure to think of as many synonyms as possible for your subject when using an index for the first time.

Readers' Guide to Periodical Literature. Here I found mainly consumer-oriented articles. As was the case with the *New York Times* citations, they seemed interesting, but not exactly what I wanted. For example:

A shopper's guide to spas *(Health)*

Joining a health spa? *(Changing Times)*

Business Periodicals Index. Not unexpectedly, this turned up the leads that sounded most promising. Most of the articles sounded business oriented. For example:

Design human factors into a fitness facility *(National Safety News)*

Spas for men *(Venture)*

Pumping iron in executive suites *(Venture)*

Les clubs grands *(Venture)*

Case Point:
▪ One of the most important discoveries in checking the *Business Periodicals Index* was that *Venture* magazine had more relevant-sounding articles than any other publication listed. When a particular periodical stands out like this, it's a good idea to get hold of the publication's most recent issues to check for articles that have not yet been indexed.

Subject Guide to Books in Print. There was nothing listed under "Health Clubs" or "Fitness Clubs," but there were scores of entries under "fitness." This indicates that any decent-size bookstore should have shelves of fitness books.

B. Special Periodical Indexes

The most appropriate Wilson index for this case study was the *Business Periodicals Index,* which had already been consulted.

C. Magazines and Newsletters

A periodical targeting the health club industry could be a source of much valuable information. A check of the largest listing of periodicals, *Ulrich's International Periodicals Directory*, turned up a number of titles that were related to our subject, but none seemed right on the money:

Aerobic Times Magazine

American Health Consultants Magazine

Executive Fitness Newsletter

Spa and Sauna

D. People Information

This category is not relevant here, because there were no *people* about which I needed to find information.

E. Business and Industry Information

The two sources that looked best to try were the *Funk & Scott Index* and the *Wall Street Journal Index*.

Funk & Scott. These two citations sounded promising:

"Living Well" plans two-year $100 million acquisition drive to become the "IBM of Fitness Clubs" *(Inc.)*

"Gymboree"—Franchised firms offer popular parent and child 'infant aerobics' classes *(Wall Street Journal)*

Wall Street Journal Index. Surprisingly, there was little recent information published on health and fitness clubs, except for the above citation found in *Funk & Scott*.

I obtained and read the original articles found through *Funk & Scott*, but it turned out that they were mainly case studies of the particular companies' business operations, and they provided little general information or advice of use to prospective owners and operators.

F. "Insider" Directories

Managers and owners of health and fitness clubs could prove to be valuable experts to interview. For this reason, I consulted *Directory in Print* in hopes of finding a listing of such clubs. The *Directory* listed two directories that looked somewhat helpful:

New Age Directory. Covers more than 1,200 "New Age" Centers, including health resorts. Price is $3.

Spiritual Community Guide. Lists 3,000 yoga, health, growth, and meditation centers. The entries include name, address, phone, activities, and a contact person's name. Price is $7.95.

Before we leave the library, let's sift through what we found to see if anything of value was uncovered and whether any experts were identified.

As it turned out, the most promising item found through the library proved to be one of the *Venture* magazine articles, "Les Clubs Grands," which was identified by searching the *Business Periodicals Index*. The article covered exactly what was being sought—the state of the health and fitness club industry, problems owners face, how to get started, and more. Here are some quotes from the piece:

The field is notorious for failures . . . most failures are small clubs that were too narrowly specialized or offered the wrong activities.

Growth of clubs, both small and large, is impressive. In 1975, there were about 2,000 fitness centers in the United States. Today, it's close to 5,000.

What makes the field especially attractive to entrepreneurs and investors is ease of entry. . . . All you need is 5,000 square feet, a little money for advertising, and maybe a smattering of knowledge on fitness.

Fitness entrepreneurs have found several keys to success, the most important being getting the most bucks out of their square footage.

Centers' fixed costs don't change with the addition of new members. The trick is substantial (and often costly) advertising early on.

This little gem of an article was also a key source for identifying experts, which we'll focus on later. It quoted a director of the National Association of Fitness Centers numerous times.

Another helpful source was buried in the *Changing Times* article that was located through the *Reader's Guide*. The piece mentioned that the Federal Trade Commission was investigating deceptive practices by health club owners in advertising and member recruitment. The mention of the FTC proved to be a valuable lead, as we'll see later.

STEP 3. THE "SUPERSOURCES"

Some "supersources" that seemed worth checking for this project included associations, conventions, the U.S. Government Printing Office, and the U.S. Bureau of the Census.

Associations. As we've discovered, almost every industry or occupation has an association, and these associations usually offer a storehouse of information about the business their members are engaged in. The *Encyclopedia of Associations* turned up a number of associations that sounded potentially useful:

Association of Physical Fitness Centers

International Racquet Sports Association

International Physical Fitness Association

National Fitness Association

I contacted each of these associations, and—somewhat surprisingly—it turned out that the International Racquet Sports Association was best geared to helping would-be owners of fitness facilities, whether or not the facilities would include racquet sports.

The *Encyclopedia of Associations* also contained the names of some organizations that might be useful to contact to learn more about the subject of fitness in general. These were the

American Physical Fitness Research Institute, which deals with a wide spectrum of "total wellness" activities, and the Institute for Aerobics Research, whose goals are to promote understanding of the relationship between living habits and health and to promote participation in aerobics.

Conventions. The International Racquet Sports Association holds an annual convention and sponsors various seminars. This could be an excellent source for locating club owners and other experts in the field.

U.S. Government Printing Office. Although the GPO's subject index did not have a heading for health and fitness clubs, it did list the subject of "physical fitness."

U.S. Bureau of the Census. Here I found a source that could help a new fitness-center owner decide where to build. The bureau publishes a report called "The Census of Service Industries," which contains a section providing various statistical data on "reducing salons and health clubs." The report is broken down by state, large counties, and large cities; within these categories, it states the total number of establishments, their receipts in thousands of dollars, payroll figures, and the number of paid employees. The document is available for a low price from the Superintendent of Documents.

Of the information located through the supersources, the single best find was the International Racquet Sports Association, which turned out to be a gold mine of information. Here are some of the reports the association produces—all of which seem tailor-made for someone considering opening a club.

- *Industry Data Survey.* Statistics on hundreds of operating clubs, including their financial structure, personnel, and profit-and-loss figures.
- *Club Location: A Site Analysis Study.* Defines the market characteristics associated with profitable racquet sports and fitness clubs. Profiles typical members according to income, age, and so forth.
- *The IRSA Directory.* A directory supplying names, ad-

dresses, and phone numbers of club operators in the United States and Canada.

- *Why People Join.* Gives information on what people like and don't like about fitness facilities, and what makes them join.

In addition, IRSA publishes (for members) a monthly periodical called *Club Business Magazine* that focuses on issues that concern club management.

Clearly, this association is a superb information source for anyone looking into the subject of health and fitness clubs. Although many of its resources are restricted to its membership, other information and experts are available to anyone on request.

STEP 4. GOVERNMENT DEPARTMENTS AND AGENCIES

By scanning the specialties of the federal departments and agencies described in chapter 3, I noted that there aren't any that specifically cover health and fitness clubs. However, there were two Washington agencies worth contacting:

The FTC. As I mentioned, an article in *Changing Times* magazine noted that the FTC was looking into deceptive practices in the health and fitness field. I contacted the agency and was informed that no report had actually been issued on the subject. However, I was given the name and phone number of a person working on the case.

Department of Health and Human Services. Since this department's scope includes physical fitness, it could be a source of help and published materials in the field.

STEP 5. BUSINESS INFORMATION

I checked two seemingly relevant sources: The International Trade Administration and the Small Business Administration.

The ITA did not have an industry expert in the area of health and fitness clubs. The SBA, not surprisingly, proved to be a wealth of information and advice on starting up a new business. Here are some of the services the SBA offers that would be of use in this type of project:

Venture Capital. The SBA has a program to help new businesses find venture capital through guaranteed loans. It can assist with two types of loan: those made by private lenders, usually banks, and guaranteed by SBA and those made directly by the agency. In general, these loans carry interest rates slightly lower than those in the private financial markets. In addition, the SBA's Small Business Investment Corporation has a free directory listing small business investment corporations that may be contacted to apply for venture capital.

Expert Advice. The SBA also sponsors SCORE—the Service Corps of Retired Executives. This program offers new entrepreneurs *free* business counseling from men and women who have had successful business careers as company executives or owners of their own businesses. These counselors define and analyze business problems and help the new entrepreneur find solutions. SCORE counselors can be found in all fifty states, and many specialize in particular industries—from ladies' ready-to-wear retailing to food services to construction.

Inexpensive Publications. The SBA publishes a brochure listing various publications that range in price from 25 cents to $5. The following sounded particularly applicable to our case study: "The ABC's of Borrowing," "A Venture Capital Primer for Small Business," "Budgeting in a Small Business Firm," "Locating or Relocating Your Business," "Planning and Goal Setting for Small Business," "Plan Your Advertising Budget," and "Learning About Your Market."

Description of Services. A publication called "Your Business and the SBA" explains how the agency's programs can help the businessperson.

STEP 6. TALKING TO THE EXPERTS

With the wealth of printed material available to the information seeker, it's easy to forget that people can be an equally valuable resource. There will likely be a number of questions still remaining that can be answered only by an expert in the field you are investigating. For example, I might have an idea about where to build a health club and want to discuss the idea with an expert. I might also want feedback on some thoughts about how the club will be run, the services and facilities I'd offer, the rates I'd charge, and the policies I'd set. Or I may simply want to talk to some health club owners to get a feel for what it's like to operate such a facility on a day-to-day basis.

In our research thus far, we've uncovered a number of sources that might yield experts on the subject of fitness centers. Where should we begin?

Probably the best place to start is the International Racquet Sports Association, because one of the association's reasons for being is to help would-be club owners obtain information. Not only is it likely that knowledgeable people work at the association, but the association's contacts with club owners and managers could prove invaluable as well. The only drawback to using the association as an information source is that it charges for some of its information. But I can get free assistance by using the expert-interviewing techniques described earlier in this book. Locating the right expert at this association should be simple enough: all I need to do is call the association's phone number (listed in the *Encyclopedia of Associations*) and explain the kind of information I am seeking.

Here are some other experts worth contacting:

- *Convention experts.* As noted earlier, the International Racquet Sports Association holds conventions. I could write away for a preliminary program that would provide names of experts who will be presenting sessions.
- *SCORE volunteers.* These retired executives, available through the SBA program mentioned earlier, are a source for obtaining expert opinion on starting and running a business.

Again, the SBA's very reason for being is to help people who need business advice. And in this case, the advice is guaranteed to be absolutely free. I would contact the SBA to get the ball rolling.

▪ *Magazine writer.* The best magazine article uncovered was the *Venture* piece, "Les Clubs Grands." The article was thorough, well organized, and comprehensive, and it's a good bet that the writer would be equally clear and enlightening. Although the writer may not be sufficiently familiar with the health club industry to offer advice on how to start a club, many of his sources are probably experts in the field, and there is a good chance he could direct us to them. To talk to the writer or to find how to reach him, I'd contact the publication directly.

▪ *Association executive.* The *Venture* article repeatedly quoted the director of the National Association of Fitness Centers on the subject of opening and operating a health club. The fact that *Venture* magazine singled this person out suggests that the director is a leading, if not *the* leading, expert in the field.

Case Point:
▪ You may want to make a leading expert like this one of your last interviews. This way, your basic questions will be answered by other sources, allowing you to maximize your time with this type of expert by asking the most probing and sophisticated questions. To find the director, look up the organization in the *Encyclopedia of Associations.*

▪ *Federal Trade Commission.* Another expert identified was the FTC contact investigating unfair practices among health club owners. It's possible that this person has amassed a variety of industry data that could be of use.

13

Careers in Computers

If you were considering a career in computers, where would you go to find out more about the profession? Using the information-gathering steps outlined in previous chapters, I set out to see what could be found on this subject in a short amount of time. The information that was ultimately uncovered would give anyone considering employment in this field a good head start. Some of the sources that proved fertile were different from those discovered in the previous case study on opening a fitness club, but the steps taken to find the information remain the same.

STEP 1. DEFINE GOALS

Again, our search will be greatly aided if we begin by identifying the specific questions we want to find answers to. Here are some questions that would probably be on the mind of anyone thinking of embarking on a computer career:

- What is the job outlook? (Statistics, projections, and so forth)
- What kinds of jobs are available? Which jobs are hottest right now?
- What level of training or education is needed for different jobs?

- What about working conditions? Are the hours long? Is the work performed in comfortable surroundings?
- What are the salaries? (Statistics, chances for increases)
- Where are the jobs? What part of the country?
- What kinds of firms are hiring? Who are potential employers?
- What are the job requirements?
- What are the best strategies for finding a job?

STEP 2. CHECK LIBRARY RESOURCES

"Computer careers" is hardly an obscure subject, so any good-size library should be of help. Here are the highlights from the library sources I checked:

A. Easy Starts

New York Times Index. A number of useful-sounding articles were found through this index; three are summarized below:

- A "careers" column on job opportunities in the computer field noted that industry experts are not as optimistic about the job outlook as they were a few years ago. What used to be a growth area for jobs has probably reached maturity, the experts say.
- An article reported that advances in database technology have revolutionized the way data are collected, packaged, and distributed. This has created job opportunities in database management and a greater demand for specialists in this area.
- A second "careers" column explored the expanding role of the "Manager of Electronic Data Processing."

Case Point:
- Note the existence of the "careers" column. It would be worth finding out how often and when this useful column is published in order to review relevant articles not yet indexed.

All of the above articles sounded promising enough to warrant locating the original source and reading the full story. Often, you'll be surprised at the wealth of material that can be gained from just one source. Let's take a look at what was found when the original article on job opportunities in database management was consulted.

The article first provided some background on the growth of this new job: "As companies place greater value on information processing, the position of 'database administrator' is growing. The job is to decide what information should go into the company 'database,' and how to store and circulate it for easy availability."

Various experts were quoted throughout, including:

- The Dean of the School of Information at Syracuse University

- The editor of an industry association newsletter, who claimed that "database administration" is one of the fastest-growing areas of data processing

- The vice president of a personnel consulting firm, who said that the best opportunities are in corporations with large main-frame computers. He also mentioned that jobs are available in the on-line database industry, as well as in other institutions that generate information, such as museums and libraries

- A consultant who said that the most important job qualification is "experience"

- An industry expert who remarked that excellent job opportunities exist at insurance companies and banks

- *Datamation* magazine, which reported that the average salary for the position of database administrator is $29,000 per year and can go as high as $55,000

This one article was so chock-full of experts and advice that I could almost end my library search with it. But let's see what else is out there.

Readers' Guide to Periodical Literature. This yielded a few interesting citations:

- A career profile of computer professionals *(Popular Computing)*
- Pay in data-processing services by occupation and urban area *(Monthly Labor Review)*
- Even high-tech workers can get pink slips *(U.S. News and World Report)*

Business Periodicals Index. This index also turned up a number of relevant citations, including:

- Computer professionals pleased with jobs *(Infosystems)*
- A boring career *(Datamation)*
- Job fairs can offer career advancements to data-processing professionals *(Data Management)*

Case Point:
- The *Business Periodicals Index* cited numerous relevant articles from *Infosystems* and *Datamation* magazines. These publications would be worth looking at in more depth.

B. Subject Guide to Books in Print

Scores of general how-to-get-a-job books are listed under headings like "Occupations" and "Vocational Education" (e.g., *Change Your Job, Change Your Life*, and *How to Do What You Love for a Living*). One book sounded particularly useful:

- Wright, John W. *The American Almanac of Jobs and Salaries* (Avon, New York)

Books specifically related to computer careers were found under the heading "Computer Industry—Vocational Guidance." Two that sounded interesting were:

- Carron, L. Peter, Jr. *Computers: How to Break into the Field* (Liberty Publishers, Cockeysville, Maryland)
- Grundfest, Sandra, ed. *Engineering, Science, and Computer Jobs* (Peterson's Guides, Princeton, New Jersey)

C. Forthcoming Books

Because computers are a fast-moving technology, I'd want to locate the latest books published or those soon to be published. A check with this subject guide turned up one book particularly worth watching for:

- Herrup, Steven. *Exploring Careers in Research and Information Retrieval* (Rosen Group, New York)

This index also alerted me to the fact that a new edition of the book published by Peterson's Guides, found above through the *Subject Guide to Books in Print,* would be published in the coming year.

Let's take a look at what just one of the above books—*The American Almanac of Jobs and Salaries*—could tell us. The book included a section titled "Computer Technologies and Professionals" that gave the following information:

- A few paragraphs of introduction to the field.
- Descriptions of forty different kinds of jobs in the computer field. (The book noted that the job descriptions were provided by *Datamation* magazine.) Examples:

Manager of Systems Analysis: Analyzes how data processing is applied to user problems, designs effective and efficient solutions.

Senior Systems Analyst: Confers with users to define data-processing projects, formulates problems, designs solutions.

Applications Programmer Trainee: Is learning to program. Usually works under direct supervision.

Also in this section was a *New York Times* article about the high demand for computer programmers. The writer's name was included.

- Salary data, broken down by title and by industry (e.g., banking, education, federal government, heavy manufacturing). For example, you could find out that the average salary of a manager of database administration in the banking industry is $31,000.

Another salary survey was cited, this one from the U.S. Office of Personnel Management.

Case Point:
- The *Almanac* contributed more evidence that *Datamation* magazine is a leading source on computer careers and warrants closer examination.

D. Special Periodical Indexes

One appropriate Wilson index, the *Business Periodicals Index,* had already been consulted.

Another Wilson index worth checking was the *General Science Index,* because the science-oriented periodicals scanned by this index cover the world of computers. Relevant citations identified here include:

Telecommunication firms monopolize software engineers *(New Scientist)*

Help wanted: canny computer scientists *(Science Digest)*

Case Point:
- Note that the citations found in the *General Science Index* are a bit more technical than those found in the *Business Periodicals Index.* Be aware that some indexes will naturally be more technical than others, because of their subject matter and the publications they scan.

E. Magazines and Newsletters

Gale Directory of Publications. Quite a few computer magazines were identified in this directory—some general, others geared to a specific market (such as users of Apple computers). However, none of the titles specifically addressed the topic of careers in computers.

Ulrich's International Periodicals Directory. One periodical was found under the heading "Computers, Computer Industry —Vocational Guidance":

New Computer Careers, Middlesex, England

F. People Information

Not relevant here, because I was not trying to find information about any specific individual.

G. Business and Industry Information

Wall Street Journal Index. One citation located looked helpful:

A special report: technology in the workplace. Without question, women and minorities are vastly under-represented in the growing high-technology job categories. The Labor Department says that in the category of computer systems analyst—the fastest growing and highest paid computer related job—women have only 30% of the jobs, blacks 5.3% and Hispanics 1.8%, all well below their overall representation in the work force.

H. "Insider" Directories

Directory in Print. Under the heading "Data Processing Industry—Employment Services and Opportunities," two potentially useful directories were identified:

Information Industry Marketplace (R. R. Bowker). This directory provides information on about 2,500 firms and individuals who produce information products or supply or service the information industry. It could be helpful in identifying potential employers.

Engineering, Science, and Computer Jobs (Peterson's Guides). I had already located this source in the *Subject Guide to Books in Print,* but the *Directory of Directories* provided more details. It informed me that the guide covers over 1,000 research, consulting, manufacturing, government, and technical service organizations. Entries include the organization's name, address, name of contact person, type of organization, number of employees, education required, starting locations, and salaries.

Abstracting and Indexing Services Directory. Here, two listed bibliographies seemed certain to index published materials unavailable through other sources:

Science and Engineering Careers: A Bibliography (Scientific Manpower Commission, Washington, D.C.). This is a listing of career-guidance booklets in science and engineering, as well as sources of financial aid.

Chronicle Career Index (Chronicle Guidance Publications Inc., Moravia, New York). This is an annual annotated bibliography of English-language vocational and educational guidance materials published in the United States. A typical entry includes the publisher's name and address and title citations.

STEP 3: THE "SUPERSOURCES"

Associations. Although the *Encyclopedia of Associations* did not list an association that seemed specifically geared to computer careers, there was no shortage of general computer-oriented associations. Among them, the following were contacted, and they sent a variety of useful information.

American Federation of Information Processing Societies, Reston, Virginia. This organization sent a helpful pamphlet titled "A Look into Computer Careers" that examined what computer workers do, educational requirements for the jobs, desirable personal characteristics, and salary statistics. It also provided a step-by-step planning guide for exploring computer careers.

Data Processing Management Association, Park Ridge, Illinois. This association sent a variety of helpful information:

"Computer Careers," a pamphlet describing types of careers and their education and training requirements

"Comp-U-Fax," a newsletter covering issues of interest to people who work with computers

Your Computer Career, a quarterly publication containing employment advertisements, as well as articles about job-hunting tips (e.g., how to handle a job interview), employment forecasts, and case studies of computer curricula available at colleges and universities

Data_Management magazine, with articles on career planning (working your way to the top of the field, how job hopping can pay off, and so forth).

Two other associations identified that might be worth getting in touch with are:

Association of Information System Professionals, Willow Grove, Pennsylvania.

Association for Computing Machinery, New York, New York.

New York Public Library. Officials at the library's Job Information Center informed me that it maintains a great deal of information on computer careers. The officials said that they try to refer people with questions to the appropriate books, journals, and other sources.

Colleges and Universities. Because so many schools offer courses in computers, it would be worth contacting one to consult with a faculty member for advice or for names of other experts.

Library of Congress. The library ran a computer search on the topic computer careers for me and subsequently sent a package containing a number of useful sources, including:

A *fact sheet* describing resources available from the U.S. Department of Labor's Bureau of Labor Statistics. The sheet included a list of the bureau's publications (*Monthly Labor Review*, "Employment and Earnings," "Current Wage Developments," and so on) and a description of other services available from the bureau. Its Division of Information Service, for example, will respond to inquiries, make referrals, and provide advisory services.

A photocopy of the section of the *Occupational Outlook Handbook* that covers computer-oriented careers. A contact person and phone number were included for those who need further information.

Descriptions of relevant books:

Careers in Computers (Messner, New York) discusses career opportunities in computer science and the preparation needed for each.

Careers in the Computer Industry (Watts, New York) examines a number of computer-related careers, including systems analysis, programming, data processing, and computer service.

Exploring Careers in Computer Software (Rosen Group, New York).

The Library of Congress identified one magazine that would be of high interest to anyone investigating this subject:

Computer Careers (McGraw-Hill). This quarterly publication is filled with helpful articles. Readers can learn where the best job opportunities exist (e.g., the defense, aerospace, and automotive industries) and can also get *regional* outlooks for computer jobs, including the names of specific firms and what kinds of help they are looking for.

Case Point:

▪ *Computer Careers* magazine was filled with advertisements placed by firms wanting to fill computer-related positions. Magazines in many fields have a "marketplace" section where readers can locate such ads and announcements.

All the sources provided by the Library of Congress were no more than two years old. In a fast-moving field like computers, information much older than that would not be too helpful.

U.S. Government Printing Office *Subject Bibliography Index.*

Three subject headings seemed related to our topic, and I ordered these bibliographies:

Computers and Data Processing. The bibliography I received listed a number of technical reports available (a guide for software documentation, local area networking, and so on). A document costing only $1 sounded interesting: "Computer and Mathematical Related Occupations," which provides occupational outlooks for computer operators, service technicians, programmers, and systems analysts.

Vocational and Career Education. This bibliography listed a couple of potentially helpful booklets, but most seemed out of date.

Occupational Outlook Handbook. This handbook, described in the material sent by the Library of Congress, proved to be a valuable discovery. It gave a concise overview of careers in computers. For instance, the job of "Computer Systems Analyst" was listed under the larger category "Mathematical Scientists and Systems Analysts." The handbook provided a cogent definition of the job, identified the kinds of firms that are most likely to offer such positions, and described typical job duties. Here is the handbook's description of the typical duties of a systems analyst:

Analysts begin an assignment by discussing the data processing problem with managers or specialists to determine the exact nature of the problem and to break it down into its component parts. If a retail chain wished to computerize its inventory system, for example, system analysts would determine what information must be collected, how it would be processed, and the type and frequency of reports to be produced.

The handbook also described working conditions, training and advancement opportunities, job outlook, earnings, related occupations, and sources for more information. Reprints of specific pages in the handbook describing the outlook for a particular occupation are also available for $1 to $2.

Also available is *Occupational Outlook Quarterly*, a periodical that keeps readers abreast of developments between editions of the *Occupational Outlook Handbook*. The quarterly contains articles on new occupations, training opportunities, salary trends, career counseling programs, and the results of new studies conducted by the Bureau of Labor Statistics.

STEP 4. GOVERNMENT DEPARTMENTS AND AGENCIES

For a subject like the one at hand, the principal agency to contact in Washington would most likely be the Bureau of Labor Statistics, whose relevant information I already obtained through other sources.

Step 4. Government Departments and Agencies

Other agencies or departments contacted did not turn out to be helpful on this particular subject. Three were tried:

U.S. Department of Commerce's Institute for Computer and Science Technology. The institute had no information on computer careers. A staff person there suggested contacting the U.S. Office of Personnel Management or the Department of Education.

U.S. Office of Personnel Management. I found this office impossible to reach during the two weeks that I tried. The phone was either busy or not answered.

U.S. Department of Education. The department's Office of Vocational Education did some searching for me but didn't come up with much on computer careers.

Case Point:
- Note the difficulties encountered in finding a helpful Washington office in this case. That's sometimes the nature of any information-finding project. There will always be paths that come to a dead end, while others will lead you to what you seek.

STEP 5. BUSINESS INFORMATION

One source consulted was the Department of Commerce's *U.S. Industrial Outlook*. Although the source yielded much valuable industry data—such as which data-processing companies are the largest, the long-term prospects for the industry, foreign competition, and so on—it gave little in the way of concrete career information.

STEP 6. TALKING TO THE EXPERTS

In our search for information on computer careers, we've uncovered a significant body of material. We've found detailed, up-to-date material on the employment outlook, specific job descriptions, working conditions, salaries, opportunities in various industries, and job-hunting strategies, among other things. But our information-finding job is not necessarily complete. We could dig deeper by talking to some of the experts.

How would talking directly to knowledgeable people help us

gather more information on computer careers? We might want more details about a particular type of computer job. We may need more facts about computer jobs in the banking industry or another specific industry that interests us. We might have some expertise in a particular field such as political science, and we would want to know how to combine that background with a computer career. It could well be that the answers to these and other questions are available only from authorities in the field.

In this case study, we've identified a number of experts or places where experts can undoubtedly be found. As mentioned earlier, the best type of expert to start with is someone who you are pretty sure will be forthcoming and who won't be talking on an overly technical level. A good choice in our case would be an expert at one of the *computer associations* we found, since these organizations are accustomed to providing information to the nonspecialist. The Data Processing Management Association seems an especially promising group to start with because it publishes many reports about computer careers. To contact this or any other association, just call the phone number listed in a library copy of the *Encyclopedia of Associations* and ask to speak to someone who can help answer your questions.

There are other experts uncovered in this case study that would be worth talking to:

- *Magazine editors.* In addition to being good information sources themselves on the industry, trade magazine editors can often put you in touch with their field contacts, who can prove equally valuable. These contacts may include experts who have written articles for the publication. In our case study, *Computer Careers* and *Datamation* were two magazines identified as excellent information sources. You could locate the editors' names on the magazines' mastheads.

- *Writers.* Another expert worth talking to could be the author of the *New York Times* article on declining job opportunities in computers. The author could probably provide you with more information on his subject and refer you to the experts he spoke with in researching the article. However, he will not necessarily be an expert on computer-career topics other than the one he wrote about. (To contact the author, you would just call the *New York Times*.)

• *Personnel agencies.* Personnel agency officials were cited as an interesting source in several published articles. A computer-careers expert at a personnel agency should be a particularly good source of up-to-the-minute information on questions about salaries, the most sought-after jobs, which firms are currently doing the most recruiting, and the best regions of the country to go job hunting. You can locate such officials through a personnel agency association (check the *Encyclopedia of Associations*). Ask the association for the names of agencies that specialize in placing people in the computer field.

• *Consultants.* Also cited in a number of articles I found, consultants can be excellent information sources. One caution in using consultants is that their level of expertise varies. Try to get an idea of the credentials and background of the consultant with whom you are speaking. (A consultant quoted in the *New York Times* is a good bet to have solid qualifications, since the *Times* normally seeks out an authority in the field.)

• *Authors.* Authors of relevant books that you've found during your investigations are also possible resources. But you should make sure an author has been keeping abreast of developments in the field since his or her book was published.

CASE STUDIES REVIEW

In both these case studies, a number of lessons about the information-finding process emerged.

First, note that in both cases only a handful of sources among those tried turned out to be fruitful. In the health club case study, the best sources were a magazine article, an association, and a couple of government sources—notably the Small Business Administration. In the computer-careers investigation, some of the same kinds of sources were helpful, along with some additional ones like the Library of Congress and the *Occupational Outlook Handbook*. Each information-gathering project is different, and for each, different sources will be useful. Sometimes you'll find your best information in newspapers and magazines, sometimes from the federal government, other times from conventions and so on. It's important to note, however, that in both case studies we discovered that associations provided top-notch information. In my experience, this is the case with most information-finding projects. There usually exists a professional association that will prove to be of great assistance.

In both case studies, we also encountered some minor hurdles that had to be overcome. In the health club project, we had to find out how our subject was classified in the various indexes we were consulting. Key terms could be *health* or *fitness* or *spa* or *physical fitness*, depending on the index. Another small obstacle was learning to distinguish which materials were geared to the consumer and which were better suited to the businessperson. We also had to do some calling to find out which of the associations we located was most closely related to our subject. In the computer-careers case study, one challenge was checking the currentness of information uncovered. Another was to avoid discouragement when faced with the lack of relevant information available from federal departments.

Recap: The Six Steps of an Information-finding Project

Now that you've read this book, here's a quick review of the process of finding information. This recap will help you organize your project and put the sources and strategies you've learned to use in a coherent and logical manner.

Although every information-finding project is different, in most cases the *process* of learning about a new subject follows a similar path. Generally, the trick is to build your knowledge of the subject by first using nontechnical sources and gradually proceeding to more advanced and technical ones. Any information-finding project I undertake generally goes through *six steps*, outlined below. Although in practice these steps will overlap, I've found it useful to keep them in mind separately when planning my investigations.

Define your goals		Locate basic sources		Obtain technical sources		Talk to experts		Redirect your focus		Get expert review
1	→	2	→	3	→	4	→	5	→	6

- **Define your goals.** The first step is to analyze your information-finding project. Break it down into its component parts. Determine *why* you need this information and *what* you plan to do with it. This will make your information search clearer to you and easier to conduct.

- **Locate basic sources.** Because you probably know very little about the topic at this stage, you'll first want to obtain definitions and understand basic concepts. The best information sources to consult at this early step are nontechnical ones that explain unusual concepts and terms clearly and without jargon. Such sources can include newspapers and magazines geared to a general audience, reports published by the government for the public, and literature for consumers from manufacturers of products.

- **Obtain technical sources.** Now you're ready to seek out more specialized information. After you've grasped the basic terms and concepts of your subject, you're ready to dig into more technical material. Sources to check at this point could include trade publications, research center reports, and transcripts of convention presentations.

- **Talk to the experts.** When you've gotten all you can from published material, you should feel confident enough to begin contacting some experts to get answers to the questions you still have on the subject.

- **Redirect your focus.** This is the time to step back and review your progress. Compare what you've learned with what you decided you wanted to learn in step 1. Make adjustments or redirect your focus, if necessary. Go back to earlier steps to fill in gaps, if needed.

- **Get expert review.** Get one or more experts to review your work for accuracy. Don't neglect this very important step.

Now, congratulate yourself for having completed your information-finding project and succeeded in becoming an "instant" expert!

You may wonder if it is possible to know *which* of the many information sources uncovered in this book will be best for *your* project. Unfortunately, it is almost impossible to know for certain which sources will turn out to be the most fruitful for a specific information-finding project. In one case you may find that your best sources turned out to be research centers and museums; in another, a specialized bookstore and a trade magazine, and in other projects different sources. The only way to know whether a particular source is going to pay off for a particular search is to try it. Dig up as many relevant library resources, "supersources," federal government sources, business information sources (if appropriate), and finally, the experts themselves, until you feel you've found what you were looking for.

This is not to say that you cannot make some educated guesses and choose sources that seem *more likely* to pay off. For example, if you need information on some very timely matter, it would likely be covered in a newspaper or magazine; a more obscure scientific matter, at a laboratory or research center. Similarly, a public-policy or consumer-oriented issue is likely to be covered somewhere in the federal government, an art-related issue at a museum or maybe a university, and so on. So you don't really have to fly blind. Read the descriptions of the sources in this book, and use your best judgment to try to zero in on the ones that will most likely cover your subject.

The "Quick Search" Alternative

If you are very short on time, and you don't know where to begin, here is an alternative "emergency" plan to try. I've found the following sources to be the most fruitful and easiest to use for finding information on almost any topic. Here is where to go and what to do if you have time only to check out a few sources.

- *Find an association.* As mentioned earlier, for nearly any subject, there is an association that exists to promote its cause. *If I had time to consult only one type of source, this would be the one I'd choose.*

- *Check the federal government.* So much good and free information is available from the government. To find what you need, look down the list on pages 77–79 and try to identify a department or agency that covers your subject. Then contact a "rich resource" or the public affairs department and find out if there are free reports or government experts to talk to. In addition, look up your subject in the very helpful *Washington Information Directory* or the *Federal Executive Directory* and try to zero in on a government office or other Washington organization that can help you. If you don't have luck with these paths, see if the Library of Congress or the Federal Information Center can help you.

- *Dig up a few newspaper, magazine, and journal articles.* This is a fast way to get information. Just go to the library, and look up your subject in the *New York Times Index*. Also check a subject index like the *Readers' Guide to Periodical Literature*, the *Business Periodicals Index*, or a more specialized one (e.g., *General Science Index*). Be sure to note down the names of experts you find when reading the articles and reports you uncover. You can quickly find journal articles by spending just 15 minutes or so on a library's CD-ROM. Just be sure you choose the most appropriate disc, and know how to do a basic search. You're likely to at least get abstracts, and if you use a fulltext CD-ROM, you won't even have to track down the original articles!

▪ *Get help from a special library.* Find out if there is a special library on your subject. Then write to the library with your inquiry to find answers and/or referrals to other sources.

▪ *Add to the list.* Use any sources mentioned in this book that are geared to providing a specific type of information that is critical to your project (e.g., company, people, or geographic information).

▪ *Talk to at least three to five experts.* No matter what your subject is, it always pays to talk to at least a couple of experts. Clearly, this is a very general and broad approach, but if you are really stuck, it's a way to begin. And you'll be surprised at how much information you'll end up with, and how much knowledge you'll obtain, just by following this shortened plan!

APPENDIX

Sources of Further Information

The following is a selected listing of books, magazines and associations that can assist you in learning more about research and information finding. Most of these sources are inexpensive or free. However, the magazines and journals are geared more to the professional researcher and will cost more.

BOOKS

BARZUN, JACQUES AND GRAFF, HENRY F. *The Modern Researcher*, 5th ed. (Harcourt Brace Jovanovich, 1992; $21.50). A classic book on the art of conducting research. Provides great food for thought on the problems, dilemmas, and challenges in the researcher's quest for truth.

BERKMAN, ROBERT I. *Find it Online* (Windcrest/McGraw-Hill, 1994: $19.95). This is a book I've written that is specifically devoted to finding information via electronic databases. It covers and evaluates the major on-line systems in detail, and offers advice on using and searching CD-ROMs. A special "Finder" directory section at the back of the book identifies and describes hundreds of consumer-oriented on-line and CD-ROM databases.

BRADY, JOHN. *The Craft of Interviewing* (Random House, 1977; $12). Another classic; this one on how to conduct an interview. Aimed especially at journalists, this book provides strategies, tips, and advice on how to reach a subject and then get them to cooperate with you.

FULD, LEONARD. *Competitor Intelligence* (John Wiley, 1985; $39.95). Leonard Fuld is one of the country's leading experts on the topic of competitive intelligence—finding facts on competitor companies. This book lists basic reference sources, provides creative information-finding strategies, and discusses the reasons for a competitive intelligence activity in today's business world.

GARVIN, ANDREW. *The Art of Being Well-Informed* (Avery Publishing Group, 1993; $12.95). Written by the President of the worldwide research and consulting group Find/SVP (and co-authored by me), this 193-page paperback is geared to "raising the information consciousness" of businesspersons. It offers advice and case studies as to why research and information gathering systems are critical to businesses today, and provides a listing of a number of sources.

GLOSSBRENNER, ALFRED. *How to Look it Up Online* (St. Martin's Press, 1987; $15.95). Glossbrenner is the guru of finding popular information via computer databases. His book is easy to read and an enjoyable discussion of the joys and frustrations of finding information on-line.

HOROWITZ, LOIS. *Knowing Where to Look* (Writers Digest Books, 1988; $19.95). An extremely comprehensive identification and analysis of library and other important reference sources. Some readers may find the exhaustive listing a bit tough going, but it is a valuable tool for researchers.

LAQUEY, TRACY. *The Internet Companion* (Addison-Wesley, 1993; $10.95). A slim, easy to read and understand introduction to the Internet. An excellent resource for beginners on how to get started on this fast-growing global network. (Note: There are scores of new books being published today on searching the Internet. Other popular books include *The Whole Internet Catalog* (O'Reilly), *The Internet Yellow Pages* (Random House), and *Zen and the Art of the Internet*. Just browse the "Computers" section of any bookstore to find others you may find of interest.)

LESKO, MATTHEW. *Lesko's Info-Power Sourcebook* (Info USA, 1990; $33.95). Lesko is nationally known for his expertise in finding information sources from the U.S. government. The book identifies thousands of sources of information and assistance from U.S. federal agencies and departments.

For some different and thought-provoking perspectives on the information age, you may also want to check out Alvin Toffler's **PowerShift**, Bill McKibbon's **The Age of Missing Information**, and Neil Postman's **Technopoly**.

MAGAZINES, JOURNALS, NEWSLETTERS

Business Information Alert (Alert Publications, 401 West Fullerton Parkway, Chicago, IL 60614; 312-525-7594; $115 per year). Useful reviews of new reference sources and tips on locating business information.

CD-ROM World (Pemberton Press, 462 Danbury Road, Wilton, CT 06883; 203-761-1466). This publication is devoted specifically to the use of CD-ROM databases. While many of the articles are geared to more of a technical and specialist audience than a consumer one, it's the only magazine covering only CD-ROMs that can be found at a newsstand.

Database and *Online* (Online Inc., 462 Danbury Road, Wilton, CT 06897; 203-761-1466; $99 per year). Both of these magazines, put out by the same publisher, cover similar material. They are geared to a sophisticated and professional audience of librarians and on-line researchers. The publications review new databases, provide industry news, offer search hints, and so on.

The Data Informer (Information U.S.A., P.O. Box 15700, Chevy Chase, MD 20815; 301-657-1200; $128 per year). This is Matthew Lesko's monthly newsletter that alerts readers to new federal and state information sources. It's a compilation of listings plus advice on how to get the most out of the government.

The Information Advisor (FIND/SVP, 625 Avenue of the Americas, New York, NY 10011; 212-645-4500; $130 per year). This is the newsletter I started up in the fall of 1988. It's devoted to locating the most useful business information sources, comparing features of competing information sources, and providing advice on how to evaluate the quality and reliability of the information you find.

The Information Report (Washington Researchers, 2612 P Street NW, Washington, DC 20007; 202-333-3533; $160 per year). This monthly newsletter keeps businesses up to date on a variety of new information sources available from the government, professional associations, universities, publishers, and more. It takes a competitive intelligence angle in the selection of its sources.

Online Access (Chicago Fine Print, 920 North Franklin Street, Suite 203, Chicago, IL 60610; 312-573-1700). The only completely consumer-oriented on-line magazine, *Online Access* covers the basics of database searching in easy to read and understand articles. You can find this publication in the computer section of many large newsstands.

Wired (Wired, 544 2nd Street, 3rd Floor, San Francisco, CA 94107; 415-904-0660). An avant-garde, alternative-type publication probing the sociological and technological meaning of living in the digital age. Hip, unique, designed to the hilt, and not to everyone's tastes. A different "'zine" altogether: kind of like *Rolling Stone* magazine in virtual reality.

PROFESSIONAL ASSOCIATIONS

If you really are interested in learning more about research and information gathering, you should contact one or more of the following organizations. In addition to their regular services, all publish various newsletters or magazines and hold regular conferences.

▪ *Special Libraries Association* (1700 18th Street NW, Washington, DC 20009; 202-234-4700). A leading and highly respected organization of librarians that work in corporations, technical organizations, and various institutions outside the traditional public library.

- *American Society for Information Science* (8720 Georgia Avenue, Suite 501, Silver Spring, MD 20910; 301-495-0900). This group attracts a somewhat similar membership to the Special Libraries Association's, but its members tend to be concerned more with the theory and science of information and are somewhat more technically oriented.
- *Association of Independent Information Professionals* (170 Lexington Drive, Ithaca, NY 14850; 607-257-0937 or 713-537-9051). This is a relatively new organization, whose membership includes independent information professionals involved in computer and manual organization, retrieval, and dissemination of information. Many information brokers belong to this group.
- *Information Industry Association* (555 New Jersey Avenue NW, Suite 800, Washington, DC 20001; 202-639-8262). This is a trade organization that consists of many of the largest information-providing corporations (e.g., AT&T, McGraw-Hill, and Dun's Marketing) as well as smaller firms. It is concerned with many "macro" issues affecting the industry of providing information, for example, future trends, competition, and so forth.
- *Society of Competitive Intelligence Professionals* (c/o Washington Researchers, Ltd., 2612 P Street NW, Washington, DC 20007; 202-333-3499). SCIP consists of professionals who evaluate competitors and competitive conditions and wish to improve skills.

Index